WILD LIFE

WILD LIFE

AMAZING ANIMALS, EXTRAORDINARY PEOPLE, ASTONISHING PLACES

SIMON KING

HODDER &
STOUGHTON

First published in Great Britain in 2009 by Hodder & Stoughton
An imprint of Hodder & Stoughton
An Hachette UK company

1

A CIP catalogue record for this title is available from the British Library

HB ISBN 978 0 340 98105 4
TPB ISBN 978 0 340 98106 1

Typeset in Monotype Sabon by Ellipsis Books Limited, Glasgow

Printed and bound in the UK by CPI Mackays, Chatham ME5 8TD

Hodder & Stoughton policy is to use papers that are natural, renewable
and recyclable products and made from wood grown in sustainable forests.
The logging and manufacturing processes are expected to conform
to the environmental regulations of the country of origin.

Hodder & Stoughton Ltd
338 Euston Road
London NW1 3BH

www.hodder.co.uk

To my mother and father

Contents

Chapter 1

I Want to Be an Elephant When I Grow Up

'SIIIIIMOOOON . . .! What on *EARTH* is that dreadful SMELL?!!'

The aroma had, by now, crept into every corner of the house, including my mother's bedroom, where she was trying to take a well-earned break. I had left the badger's head to simmer on a low flame, whilst I returned to my own bedroom to get on with the more pressing task of skinning a common shrew carcass that I had found that morning during my walk through the local woods. Maybe I'd been neglecting the boiling head a little, but I'd felt that the longer it bubbled away, the easier it would be to peel away the flesh and so expose the skull beneath, which was the point of the exercise in the first place. I hadn't really noticed the appalling stench until my mother's raised tones drew my attention to it. Perhaps the equally pungent shrew carcass was helping to mask it.

I shot downstairs to the kitchen, to find that the lid of the pan was bouncing happily on a ring of green-tinged foam, some of which had dribbled down the side and into the flame. At eleven years old, I was not the most adept of cooks. I was soon joined by my mother, who, holding her nose, moved to the cooker, turned off the gas and simply said, 'I don't know what you've got in there, Simon.

I don't really want to know, but would you please take it out to the garden? It's rather smelly. Oh, and Simon,' she added, with touching concern, given the circumstances, 'be *very* careful with the hot water. I don't want you to burn yourself.'

My long-suffering mother, Eve, was by now well used to my habits. I spent my weekend mornings, from first light, stalking through my local woodland on the edge of Bristol, looking for signs of life. Any fresh – or not so fresh – carcass was a potential addition to my 'museum': a drawer in my bedroom that housed plaster casts of wild animal footprints, broken birds' eggs (I never collected viable eggs from nests, even at a time when many still did) and a host of other 'exhibits'. Among my favourites were the birds' wings, which I would separate from roadkills and then pin to cardboard. Drying these natural works of art once again meant I had to commandeer my mother's cooking facilities – something the size of a jay took roughly forty-five minutes on a very low flame in the oven. Once cooled, I would mount the wings on a wooden plinth and then hang them on my wall. They would last a good year before beginning to fall apart.

Though I treasured these trophies, they were merely trinkets, souvenirs of sorts, to remind me of my adventures watching the local wildlife. My overwhelming ambition during those early morning walks was not to find dead animals, but live ones. Just when my obsession with watching wildlife started is hard to say. I simply can't remember a time when I was not captivated by the wild world around me.

*

I was born in Nairobi, Kenya, on 27 December 1962. At the time, my father, John, was working for BFBS, the British Forces Broadcasting Service, as a DJ. My parents already had a daughter, my sister Debbie, who'd been born in London on 12 January 1959. Much of what I know about our time in Kenya comes from the stories my parents told me in later life; for example, I had apparently survived sleeping next to a six-inch-long, venomous centipede, which had somehow found its way into my bedclothes. Meanwhile, my sister had been rescued from near certain death by our janitor, George, who skilfully threw his machete to decapitate a spitting cobra before it could strike her. My father told of the evening he felt sure we were being robbed; brandishing a baseball bat, he crept on all fours to the front door, ready to beat any intruder over the head. To add further to the sense of high drama, our little dog was barking maniacally and jumping up at the door. My father decided against opening the door to challenge the intruders – which was fortunate, because in the morning, large leopard footprints were found running up to the threshold.

I was, of course, too young to recall any of these adventures first hand, since we left Kenya when I was not quite two years old, but I listened to the tales later with saucer eyes. Far from putting me off the idea of experiencing similar encounters, instead it gave me a desperate yearning to get really close to wildlife.

It's true that many of these tales could well have been embellished a little, given the nature of my father's chosen career – that of thespian. He had trained at the Royal

Acadamy of Dramatic Art with a burning ambition to join the likes of John Gielgud and Richard Burton, the great actors of his day. The trouble was, he was a bit of a ham. He had tremendous presence – he was a big man in every way, with Sean Connery-type good looks – but his acting career never really took off, and with a young family to support he decided he needed other work to fill in the gaps whilst he 'rested'. My mother was no stranger to the performing arts either – her father was a professional jazz musician and she had begun appearing on stage whilst still in school. She had moved with her parents and two brothers away from her birthplace – Glasgow – to live in southern England when she was twelve, and there started to sing in bars and clubs. After leaving grammar school, she later earned a five-night-a-week residency to sing with a band in Portsmouth.

So, between them, my parents could make any story of everyday life turn into the most colourful adventure, and with it send a young boy's imagination flying.

One image that I retained from the brief time I spent as a child in Kenya is not incredibly exciting, but it is at least my own. I clearly remember sitting on my mother's lap, in the front passenger seat of a vehicle driving along a dusty road. A little way ahead, running with a body-shaking, loose-legged gait, was an adult male ostrich. I heard my mother saying, 'Bloody ostrich, BLOODY OSTRICH!' It's not unusual to see ostriches in the national parks or reserves in Kenya. But the heady mix of incongruous spectacle and my mum's response somehow combined to make an impact on my childish mind; I was suddenly aware of there being other living things, besides ourselves, sharing our world, and was captivated by them.

Our time in Kenya was cut short abruptly when my father was offered the opportunity to start work with the BBC in Bristol as a reporter for the regional news programme, *Points West*. It was to be the last time I would see my birthplace for twenty-two years, but I continued to carry a sense of being Kenyan when we moved to the UK in 1964. We brought back as mementos some carved wooden animals and a Masai shield and spearheads, though my mother was careful to ensure that I didn't become impaled by the curved horn of the mahogany rhino, nor get my hands on the spears, which stayed out of reach, crossed behind the shield on the wall.

If the seeds of a passion for the natural world had been sown on African soil, they now found themselves a little starved of nourishment in a flat on the edge of Cotham, just north of Bristol city centre. Even if I had left behind more spectacular species in Kenya, back in the UK I did not lose my fascination with animals. Here, my most vivid memory is of the scent coming from caged guinea pigs – pets of my sister's. I remember little or nothing else of the flat, bar the smell of musty sawdust – of animal – drawing me to the chicken wire to stare at the bundles of fur within.

In 1965, we moved to Sea Mills, an area of northwest Bristol bordering Portway and the River Avon. And here, at last, I reconnected with the earth. Or, to be more accurate, the mud. Because there we had a garden: not a big or grand one, but a garden nonetheless. For me it was the most wonderful playground. Safe within the privet-hedge boundary I was free to roam my turf jungle, crawling on all fours and growling at passers-by.

It was at about this time that my first burning ambition began to take shape. I reasoned that, with hard work and a great deal of luck, I might grow up to become an elephant. I could think of nothing I'd rather do with my time than patrol the African plains at a royal, sedate pace, together with the rest of my herd, pushing down trees and trumpeting as we reached the water hole. I knew my human mother would understand and support me in my goal, once she realised how important this life was to me, and, though I'd miss her, I knew she could visit the herd any time she fancied.

Being told, gently, that I would never be able to realise this ambition – that it was in fact a physical impossibility – was my first taste of real disappointment. I really couldn't see why I shouldn't be any species I wanted to be in later life, and the knowledge that I wasn't going to be able to join the ranks of the wild was certainly a blow.

I soon found release by concentrating on my plastic animal figurine collection instead. I can't express too strongly how important these plastic animals were to me. Indeed, the thought of visiting Dawson's Toyshop (sadly no longer trading) on Whiteladies Road in Bristol with my father, and staring into the glass display case at the ranks of hippos, elephants, lions and buffalo that marched within, still makes my chest tighten slightly with longing. I would check my carefully saved pocket money to see if I was able to afford the new crocodile, which had a moving jaw, or if I would have to settle on the cheaper option by adding another lion to my pride. I might, grudgingly, settle on a zebra, so that my lions had something suitable to chase.

Once home, I would dash to my bedroom, and pull from my toy cupboard the biscuit tin that housed my precious menagerie. The bedroom floor became the African savannah, and the new recruit to the pride would dash and cavort around with the well-established members (some of which, rather irritatingly, had slightly gnawed tails as a result of my careless chewing). I had plastic elephants, too, which I grudgingly loved, despite the fact that I now knew they would never allow me to enter the inner circle of pachyderm society.

I find it hard to express the pure joy I got from these simple games of make-believe. To this day, I can still remember the thrill and escape this parallel world offered. On many occasions, I would not hear my mother's call to the dining table until she had made her way to the bedroom to catch my attention, so engrossed was I in a battle royal between my plastic lions and a herd of zebra. If friends came to play, and the 'animal tin' came out, they would have to play by my rules: I would pedantically insist, for instance, that they could not use the tigers to attack the zebra, since they lived on different continents. Usually, they would suggest we skip the animals and move on to toy cars, so as to avoid being lectured by this precocious five year old.

Though I was indeed obsessive (and still am) about my passions, these were not restricted to an interest in animals. At about this time, my mother's brothers had formed a successful pop band called Simon Dupree and the Big Sound, and for a while my father managed them. My mother contributed to their success by helping to compose some of their songs; though she didn't write their most successful single, called 'Kites', which made it to the top ten in the charts in 1967.

As a very young boy, I was often taken along to 'gigs', which soon, in the glow of success, became 'concerts'. I would sit in the wings of the stage, as my uncles Derek, Ray and Phil (Shulman) strutted and pranced, dressed in elaborate flowing shirts, to the screaming adulation of girls in the crowd. I don't recall ever watching them play from in front of the stage with the audience; instead I always had this privileged side perspective, through the narrow gap in the curtains that shrouded stage right. I do recall being treated very sweetly by a number of pretty women, different at each show, who were also invited to share this side view from time to time. I was delighted to be cooed over and told what a cute little boy I was, and, occasionally, to be taken onto their knees to be bounced along to the music.

On one occasion, my uncles' band was playing support to Gene Pitney, who was very popular at the time. I was in the dressing room backstage before the gig, as usual, when Mr Pitney appeared and spoke to me. 'What a cute little boy,' he said in his American drawl. 'What's your name, kid?'

'Simon,' I answered curtly, for whilst I didn't know him from Adam, and had no reason to dislike him, I had picked up an atmosphere of competition amongst my relatives and instinctively knew that this man was the cause of it.

After Gene Pitney's visit, Simon Dupree went out and gave a sterling performance, to the screams of a thrilled crowd, and to the delight of a six-year-old boy on the side of the stage. The main act – Mr Pitney – probably performed an equally wonderful show to an equally rapturous audience, but I had lost interest the moment my uncles had left the stage.

Soon after the applause had died down, Mr Pitney came back to my uncles' dressing room to thank them for their support and for playing a wonderful set. Still charged by the adrenalin of his performance, he noticed me, now sitting with my mother, and asked me, 'Hi kid, did you enjoy the show?' Thinking I should be loyal to my relatives, I answered, 'No, I didn't!'

'What a revolting little boy!' spat Mr Pitney, and stormed from the room.

I could sense an air of disbelief amongst my uncles and mother, and for a moment thought I might be in for what would have been a well-deserved dressing down. But instead, there were sotto voce murmurs and giggles and my mother suggesting I ought not to have spoken to him like that. The mix of embarrassment and misplaced pride at having defended my family's honour ensured the moment would stick in my psyche.

The stage and theatre was as much a part of my childhood as grazed knees and Vicks VapoRub. The latter played a major part in my life due to the seemingly endless stream of colds and flu I suffered from as a child. I'm not sure if I was more susceptible than my peers (I had, apparently, been a sickly kid in Africa, giving my mother and father a couple of scares, having suffered raging temperatures and even comas), but it felt as though I lurched from one bout of fever to the next between the ages of five and seven. I would reach astonishing levels of boredom during these play embargoes, and once again it was my plastic animals that came to the rescue, taking me away from the smell of eucalyptus and Lucozade and into their world of endless horizons and high drama.

When I was not nursing a cold, it was back to the garden for me, and into one of my favourite role-play games. With the prospect of swapping species sadly scrubbed from my wish list, I now decided to focus on the next best thing. I wanted to be Tarzan. Here again I faced a few physical barriers. I was quite short for a six year old, very skinny, and had a mop of curly hair. Not exactly your archetypal Tarzan physique. On the plus side, I did get to grips with the yodel, as created by the master himself, Johnny Weissmuller. I would sit captivated by the 1950s movies, as Johnny – still the best movie Tarzan in my opinion – yelled 'Ungawa' at his elephant helpers, wrestled lions and immense crocodiles with his bare hands, and rescued Jane from the clutches of the bad guys. I was terribly proud of my falsetto yodel – and, truth be known, still am. I can still just about squeeze it out, though now with rather more mature sub-tones! Years later I worked in Rainbow Springs, Florida, filming a diving bird called an anhinga, and discovered that these crystal waters were where Johnny was filmed wrestling the immense (plastic) crocodiles in the films. It was the closest I ever got to the great man.

To further add to the realism of my Tarzan fiction, my mother sewed some chamois leather to the front and back of my tiny leopard-print swimming trunks to emulate the Tarzan loincloth. This, naturally, became my preferred attire for all but the coldest December days, when I hankered after a zebra-skin wrap, but had to make do with a woolly jumper. The blue metal climbing frame in our back garden was transformed, with the help of my sister and some sneakily commandeered balls of wool and bed sheets, into a complex jungle of liana vines and forest canopy. The privet hedge and lilac bushes were the outer reaches of an unexplored wilderness.

It was about now that my lifelong love of tree climbing was firmly established. We had no forest giants in the garden on which to hone my skills, but the lilac was sufficiently towering for a vertically challenged six year old, and I learnt to live with a succession of scuffed knees, whilst my mother learned to live with my clothing (most often my loincloth) being permanently coated in green smudges from the lichen on branches. I never felt more alive or in touch with my world than when scaling a tree. Even now, when I'm a little low, or struggling to cope with a social situation, I find there's nothing like a good spell of tree climbing to make me feel better. I have been known to slip away from very elegant parties and find the nearest tree for a quick fix of my reality.

Tree climbing can be dangerous, of course. But I hate to think that 'health and safety' concerns might stop youngsters gaining independence and getting close to nature in this way. As a nipper, my father gave me clear instructions on the rudiments of safety in the branches. 'Always have three points of contact on the tree, keep your weight as close to the trunk as possible, and always think about how you might get down before you go up.' All advice that has stood me in good stead, with nothing more than the occasional and proudly earned cut and bruise to show for the odd mishap.

As I grew, the back garden jungle began to shrink. It never ceases to amaze me how the concept of scale shifts with time and maturity, shrinking one's surroundings. Perhaps this is one of the driving forces in my constant search for wide horizons, both literal and metaphorical.

The back garden did still hold its mystique and wonder, though. Blackbirds nested in the privet hedge and song thrush in the lilac. Sparrows fussed with grass moustaches as they built nests under the roof tiles, and from time to time I would discover a common toad striding purposefully through the flower borders at dusk. But the most impressive wild visitor to our postage stamp of green was undoubtedly the local fox family.

My mother and father separated when I was nine years old. Though my father remained very present in my life, and we spent many weekends enjoying outings together, the fact that he no longer lived 'at home' meant that many of the more subtle adventures and discoveries I would encounter from that point on were coloured by my mother's guidance. She suffered my absorbing passion for all things animal with remarkably good grace, given that she had (and still has) a crippling phobia of mice and rats, and only a grudging tolerance for most other animal life forms. That I never detected her intolerance was testament to her capacity to nurture my enthusiasm for the natural world rather than stifle it.

For all that, it was my mother who first started attracting the foxes to the garden at night. Perhaps seeking distraction from what must have been difficult personal circumstances, she would, unbeknownst to me, put food scraps onto our modest, concrete-slab patio and wait in the small hours for the first ruddy ghost to dash from the shadows and into the light that spilled from the kitchen window. Only when the visitors' habits were well established did she let on that she had been nurturing this new nocturnal relationship. One Friday evening, bathed and ready for bed, I was told that I could stay up to watch the wild spirits that came to visit the garden by night.

I can still feel the ache of expectation and physical discomfort as I lay with my nose pressed to the lowest pane of glass on the patio door, hoping to come face to face with a wild fox for the first time. After what felt like an age but what was I'm sure no more than ten minutes, a darkening in the shadows at the base of the hedge caught my eye. From the gloom, a pointed muzzle stitched a course across the lawn to the edge of the patio; after hesitating momentarily, the fox darted forwards, grabbed a string of bacon rind in its mouth and slipped back into the darkness. By now my pulse was thumping in my ears, my fingertips tingled with adrenalin and my view had been all but obscured by my condensing breath on the glass. And the smile on my face was verging on painful. This was quite probably the first time I had experienced the thrill of waiting for a brush with the wild (forgive the vulpine pun) and it was intoxicating. No discovery of a bird's nest, no encounter with a toad had ever given me this feeling of energised compulsion to sit and wait for wild things to show themselves, and I loved it. I love it still.

Our nocturnal encounters were to continue through the summer of my ninth year. In time I was able to lie flat on my belly on the patio, and have the local foxes take food from no more than a metre or so away from my face. I positioned my black Anglepoise lamp at my open bedroom window to cast a clearer light on this mini-theatre, and would only leave and go to bed once my mother had implored me to do so for the fiftieth time.

My ambitions had, by now, veered away from a life spent dressed in a loincloth wrestling oversized crocodiles to the more achievable goal of being a zoo keeper. This, I'm certain, had a great deal to do with Johnny Morris, whose wonderful television series, *Animal Magic*, was a ritual 'must-see' for me, as for many thousands of children. His gift for mimicry allowed him to have comic dialogues with anthropomorphised creatures, including Dottie the ring-tailed lemur. It was partly filmed at my local zoological gardens, Bristol Zoo in Clifton.

Looking back, I can of course think of a hundred reasonable criticisms of the way in which animals were housed and managed back then. Polar bears would repetitively pace tiny concrete pits, and gorillas looked sullenly at the crowds through a chunky lattice of steel. Public attitudes to such collections – and indeed the management policies of them – are barely recognisable today. But despite the discomfort of a knowledge blessed with hindsight, I still look back very fondly on my visits to the zoo.

I would dash first to the big cats and stand on tiptoe to peer over the guardrails at the Asiatic lions or leopards. They were, of course, anything but content, but for my young, hungry mind, simply witnessing the true scale of these magical creatures was inexhaustible manna. And unlike any photograph, film or TV show, seeing them at the zoo would enable me to soak up the heady musk of the animals, to hear their breath. I would return home after each visit with my head full of roars and dreams of adventure and discovery.

Until I was able to revisit Kenya, fifteen years later, these encounters with captive, charismatic megafauna, augmented by the occasional visit to Longleat Safari Park, were the closest I would get to being on the African plains or in the jungles of Asia. I maintain that, even today, well-run and -managed zoos serve an invaluable purpose in enthusing and nurturing a sense of wonder and humility in people. However many times you see a lion on TV, you never really *see* a lion until faced with one in the flesh. It would of course be glorious if part of every school syllabus included a mandatory visit to the African savannah or the Antarctic (paid for by the state, of course!). But in the absence of this ideal, well-run zoos and safari parks are the only contact that many millions of people will ever have with some of the planet's most wondrous creatures.

If one visitor in a thousand is touched to the point of caring, of being motivated enough to do something to help care for the natural world, whether it be a simple donation, or committing their lives to a conservation cause, then the ambassadorial role played by the captive creatures has perhaps been justified.

I explored my new ambition of being a zoo keeper with my own modest collection of creatures at home. There was the family dog, Wiggy. He'd originally been named Stallion, after a TV drama that my father was producing on Dartmoor. Unfortunately, as a cross between a King Charles Cavalier and a sheepdog, he would never quite grow into his name, and so Wiggy became the moniker of choice, largely to avoid embarrassment when calling him from across the public playing field. Yelling 'Stallion!' at the top of your voice builds up a certain expectation in onlookers as to what might appear from the bushes. Other conventional pets included a cat named Socks, and a gerbil. My sister went through a series of hamsters that mysteriously died each autumn and were given solemn burials in biscuit tins. I would later discover that hamsters are prone to going into torpor as the days shorten, their bodies stiffening, their breath reducing to a few shallow gasps per minute. It is very likely that my sister's hamsters, and millions more besides, were simply trying to hibernate. I only hope they never woke to discover their predicament.

But in addition to these family friends, I began to keep more exotic creatures. These were the days before the current strict (and proper) controls over the keeping of wild animals were in place, and my bedroom housed a ring of aquaria and vivaria. Inside the tanks were toads, frogs and newts. From time to time I would be guardian of a common lizard or a grass snake, until either they escaped (much to my mother's horror) and were discovered with fluff on their nose behind a bookshelf, or else I let them go back in the pool or crumbling wall in which I'd originally found them. I started sketching my charges, and recording their antics. My first taste of the delights of the close study of animal behaviour came as I watched palmate newts display and lay eggs in a thirty-centimetre aquarium in my room. I felt I was breaking new ground as I solemnly sketched the male and female engaged in a face-to-face aquatic dance. My interpretation of what was going on was broadly correct, but significantly lacking in detail. Nonetheless, and unwittingly perhaps, this marked the beginning of a lifelong desire to understand the things I was watching, and to do so by spending enormous amounts of time watching them.

Just as foxes visiting our suburban garden in Bristol were my first real taste of a close encounter with a wild spirit, so too were they central to my first professional engagement. At the age of ten.

Chapter 2

The Fox and his Boy

'I could do that, Dad. No, really, I could look after them and then help with the filming.'

My father had been planning to produce and direct a new drama for television. *The Fox* was to be set on Dartmoor in the Victorian period. It was a simple tale of a young boy who finds a fox caught in a gin trap, rescues it and tends it back to good health. My father was auditioning a number of young actors for the role, and had settled on a shortlist of three or four lads between the ages of twelve and fourteen. But, though the young actors might have been able and willing, their families were less keen to welcome a fox into their household, a prerequisite of the job to ensure the relationship between the main protagonists was convincing.

And that's where my incessant nagging came in.

The idea that I might be able to look after a fox was thrilling. The idea of acting in the film was not. It wasn't that I had an aversion to acting, which is anyway rather too grandiose a word to describe a ten year old playing make-believe. Indeed, I had been chosen to play a number of almost-leading roles in the annual school plays, from Huckleberry Finn in *Tom Sawyer*, to chief weasel in *The Wind in the Willows*. I enjoyed the challenge and discipline of learning lines and singing on stage. I can admit to enjoying the ego-inflating flattery that sometimes followed too; including – after one play depicting the Bristol Riots – being approached by an unknown and very pretty girl backstage, who declared herself to be a fan. My ego inflated to bursting point, until it was neatly and properly popped by some words of levelling wisdom from my family.

No, I did not want to get involved for the fame or glory, but just for the chance to nurture a wild spirit. Since those nose-to-nose encounters with foxes in the back garden, their swift, restless energy and enigmatic nature had captivated me. I was desperate to spend more time with them.

Though my parents had recently separated, they never allowed their differences to colour my relationship with either one of them, an act of strength and character for which I am eternally grateful, especially with the benefit of more mature and experienced hindsight. Behind closed doors, my parents discussed together the idea that I might help look after a fox and, furthermore, play the part of the boy in the drama. Finally, a joint parental proposition was put to me.

I could help with the husbandry of the fox, and it would also make sense if I played the part of the boy in the film, since I would have established a relationship with the animal. This could only happen if several criteria were met. I would not miss any schooling and so the drama would be filmed during my summer holidays. The foxes would go to a wildlife park after the project and not live in the house forever. And any attention – positive or negative – that I received from other kids in school once the film had been screened had to be accepted with good grace.

These were big issues for a ten year old to grasp, but all had to be settled before we were to go any further. Some would be very hard to adhere to, I knew, particularly saying goodbye to the fox once the project was complete. Others were much easier to agree to, particularly my response to other kids' reactions. If the film provoked some teasing and bullying, then I could deal with it. As a slightly built kid, I had often been picked on by the more robust boys in school and, though unable to tackle them physically, had always stood up to them anyway. A stubborn streak in me found it impossible to acquiesce to demands for sweets or orders that I walk on a different path. I suffered bruises and cuts as a result, but my spirit wasn't dented. Teasing I could handle. Especially if it meant I could look after a fox.

That my mother was prepared to have a fox in the house was another example of her capacity to give. I have no doubt that the prospect filled her with some dread, particularly as foxes have a reputation for being somewhat pungent, and it was likely to cause some havoc, peeing under the sofa and chewing at the furniture. But she could see how important the idea of this close encounter was to me and so gave the impression she was all for it.

In the event, we took charge of two foxes. I would be responsible for an orphaned cub, Nipper 1, that had been received by a wildlife rescue centre, and the second, Nipper

2, was an adult female who had suffered from rickets from an early age and was to be cared for by my sister Debbie.

I adored the challenge and responsibility of looking after the fox cub, but looking back I feel guilty that we dealt with their upbringing in quite such a naive fashion. Taking care of a wild animal is, of course, a huge responsibility. It is not simply something one does for fun or for a project. Attitudes in 1972 regarding captive wild creatures were of course different; nowadays we are better informed and can be morally more responsible. For all that, our foxes enjoyed a good life in and around the family home. Each had a large enclosure – which took up the whole back garden, in fact – and each would have plenty of time outside the cage every day, including walks around the block on a lead and lots of play in the living room – which inevitably did result in lots of pee under the sofa! Our little dog, Wiggy, adored wrestling with Nipper 1, and the fox cub shared the enthusiasm. The pair would endlessly chase around the house in games of tag and come together in a writhing knot of russet and shaggy black fur.

As Nipper 1 grew through the early summer, he became more and more independent spirited – which I now know is a well-established facet of fox behaviour. In contrast, Nipper 2, the older fox, remained calm and indifferent to the changes she saw about her. I learned to suffer the occasional bite to the hand or finger without objection, and still rather proudly bear the scars, though you might need a magnifying glass to spot them.

As the date approached when we were all going to head

down to Dartmoor for the summer, it became clear that the character of Nipper 2, the fox my sister was caring for, was far better suited to the role of vulpine thespian. My much-loved fox cub had failed his audition. It was with a very heavy heart, shortly before the start of the school summer holidays, that I went with him to Westbury Wildlife Park in Bristol, where he would be cared for in a vast enclosure together with a couple of other orphaned fox cubs from the year.

Just plain Nipper, as she was now known, since there could be no confusion, accompanied us on the three-hour drive to a rented cottage in the heart of the moor with no complaint. I have no doubt that my sister's nose must have been put out of joint somewhat. After all, she had cared for this lovely creature for several months and now her younger brother was muscling in on all her hard work to take over the care of and contact with her fox. But if she was miffed, she never showed it; in fact she helped look after the fox again when I was unable to, without a word of complaint.

Filming was to start in July and take the best part of four weeks. I was dressed in costume to suit the period: knickerbockers and, to my embarrassment, little canvas shoes that had rather effeminate high heels. A puff-sleeved shirt finished the look, and away we went. My on-screen parents were played by Adrienne Corrie and Peter Arne. Adrienne had a rather scary, stern manner, which was perhaps not meant to be intimidating to me, but nonetheless had the same effect on me that a feared maths teacher might. As a true method actor, perhaps she nurtured this aura in order to encourage the air of deference and respect that children would have shown to their parents in the Victorian era. Peter, by contrast, was warm, friendly and fun, and always very patient with his young cast member. He was a total gentleman throughout the filming and a very great and understated actor.

On set over the coming weeks, I survived being crushed by a runaway horse and cart, which reversed uncontrollably and almost rammed my dangling legs against a dry-stone wall, and retinal burning leading to temporary blindness, which was caused by an ultraviolet light missing a filter. For me, though, the main focus of the exercise was not the film itself, but Nipper the fox and a life on the moor. I would search for frogs in the marsh, swim in an icy pool known romantically as Breaky Firs, and watch the buzzards circling over the hills. Together with the son of the landowner, Anthony Coker, I would secretly fish for trout in the cold, clear rivers and streams. Our technique to avoid detection by the water bailiff was to casually enter the bar of the Forest Inn in Hexworthy at lunchtime, where he was a regular, and eavesdrop on his conversation.

'Paant of the usual please, George,' he would utter in broad Devonshire tones, a preamble that would bring Anto and me closer to the bar, eager to gather vital intelligence.

'Ahd'reckon Ah'll patrol the West Dart tonight. See if any of them young scallywags are out aafter mah trout.'

It wasn't until years later that I realised that his loud declaration of intent was meant entirely for our young ears. If we paid attention, he could ensure he had no reason to catch or chastise us. This was policing done the proper way: allowing the inoffensive adventure of youth to run its course.

With nothing more than a rod, line, hook and a small bait-tub of worms extracted from the stable dung heap, we would creep out at dusk to hide beneath the arched stone bridge below the farm. From there we would allow our bait to drift downstream in the rapid current, bouncing past the glossy-dusk forms of granite boulders, to slow in one of the eddying pools. Fingers poised on line, we waited for the telltale tug of a bite and the thrill of catching a bronzed bar of wild trout. I would then proudly, and very naively, return to the Forest Inn and ask someone in the kitchen to prepare my catch for supper. If the bailiff was still present at the bar, he would – to his eternal credit – simply congratulate me on my catch. I, of course, thought I was getting away with murder, which, I suppose, I was.

The summer of the production of *The Fox* was halcyonic. I got to play make-believe by day with my fox companion, and my little dog (whose pseudonym was Rats, more suitable for a Victorian canine sidekick) throughout the day, and discovered the joy of listening to plays on Radio 4 with my mother during the evening. I learned to ride horses (poorly) and how to whittle a whistle from an ash branch. By default, I absorbed the language of storytelling and television film-making. Terms such as 'wide-angle', 'close-up' and 'cutaway' became part of my vocabulary, though I never imagined at the time that I would be putting these phrases to practical use throughout the whole of my professional life.

Once the shooting was over, I accompanied my father in the dubbing theatre, sitting quietly in the darkness as he and the technicians painted the sound effects onto the canvas of the film. Much of the time I doodled; drawing dinosaurs, horses and eagles as my father uttered requests and directions to the dubbing editor. And of course, once again, I absorbed the technical terminology being used around me. 'Dissolve', 'fade to black', 'atmosphere' and 'spot effects' all found a home in my vocabulary. By the end of the summer, I had a fairly firm grip on the basics of film structure, storytelling and terminology. What a superb and select film school I had the good fortune to attend!

Shortly before *The Fox* went on air I had my first taste of the publicity machine that lurches into gear to bring the imminent release of a film to the public's attention. Kindly journalists asked me all manner of questions, and subsequently published copy that bore little resemblance to my answers. I was to learn quickly that the old adage 'the truth should never get in the way of a good story' was, and still is, the axiom behind a great deal of media-related journalism.

The film was aired. If I'd secretly been hoping for some adulation or admiration from my peers, then I was to be disappointed. As my parents had probably predicted, I was duly teased in school. But to my frustration, even amid the barrage of jibes, I never earned a credible nickname amongst my peers. The best anyone had ever come up with up to this point was 'Kingy'. Now, for a very brief period, I was known as 'Foxy', until my schoolmates realised that far from being embarrassed by the new identity, I loved it, so it was quietly dropped.

In the wake of *The Fox* I had the thrill of being asked to appear on *Animal Magic*, the BBC's natural history programme for children, and to chat to its host, Johnny Morris. I was very impressed at meeting the doyen of vocal anthropomorphism, and presented him with a ten-centimetre-long diplodocus I had fashioned from modelling clay. Johnny very sweetly gave the impression of being thrilled with the gift, though goodness knows what he could have done with my creation: an ugly, marbled beast with a sagging head and thumb-printed torso.

It was at about this time too that I first met David Attenborough. I have to confess to being largely unimpressed by fame itself, but being presented with the embodiment of natural history knowledge, adventure and humility all rolled into one was quite another thing.

We met by chance, during a visit my father had arranged to the Natural History Museum in London. Diplodocus played a part in this encounter, too, though this time it was the full-scale skeleton of the immense dinosaur that greets you as you enter the great hall of the museum. My father and I had just walked beneath its towering frame, and were about to ascend the stairs at the end of the hall when, coming down the stairs towards us, was David, chatting to another man.

As we neared, David greeted my father with a smile. 'Hello, John, how are you? And who might this be?' he asked, glancing at me.

I had completely lost my tongue, and could only stare

in awe at this man who had already touched and inspired so many with his knowledge and enthusiasm.

'This is my son, Simon,' answered my father, after slightly too long a pause during which he realised I had been struck dumb.

'A pleasure to meet you, Simon. I do hope you have a marvellous day,' he said to us both as he headed off, down the stairs and into the throng.

I tried to play it very cool, but it was clear to my father I was enormously impressed, not least because David knew my dad's name. I discovered later that in his role as controller of BBC Two, David had an extraordinary memory for those people working within the corporation at the time, and particularly those who might show an interest, as did my father, in natural history.

When I look back now at all the avenues leading towards my becoming involved in wildlife film-making full time, it seems an inevitable outcome, but my own interests and ambitions were yet to firmly gel. I wanted, above all, to spend more and more time in the wilds, but was increasingly fascinated by the detail of zoology and began to devour any literature on the subject that I could get my hands on. Since I was only eleven years old, the texts I went for were not highly advanced, but nonetheless the local library in Sea Mills became my regular weekly haunt in my search for information on my favourite subject.

Despite my relative lack of interest in the world of television and film, it was at this stage that I unwittingly, and very briefly, courted the interest of Hollywood.

My mother and father had received several enquiries after the transmission of *The Fox* as to my availability to 'act' in other productions, the most significant of which was a modern version of *The Prince and the Pauper*. The producer was Alexander Salkind, who would go on to enjoy great success with the new generation of *Superman* movies starring Christopher Reeve. Oliver Reed was to play Miles Hendon in the swashbuckling melodrama, and Alexander was searching for the right young man to play the lead as the prince – and pauper, of course. Somehow Mr Salkind had received a copy of *The Fox*, and his wife had watched the film. She clearly had influence with her husband, since it was she who had requested a meeting.

All this detail was kept from me; the only sign that something was afoot was that I was introduced to the wonderful Maggie Parker, who would be my agent. I had no idea what this meant, but I was enormously impressed by her floral enamel lavatory bowl and the fact that she lived in an apartment on Park Lane in London, which I assumed had been named in her honour. Maggie was wonderfully flamboyant but not in the least pushy, and I thought her an exciting mix of grandmotherly indulgence and matronly efficiency. At Christmas I received spectac-ular gifts from her, including a box kite that was taller than me, and which I promptly lost on its inaugural flight on Durdham Downs in Bristol on Boxing Day.

Early in the New Year, I was treated to a day in Regent's Park Zoo as my birthday outing, and it was there I met Alexander Salkind's wife. The meeting had been orches-trated by my parents and Maggie, but my mother especially was keen that I not be 'put on the spot' by any formal interview, and so it was that this charismatic raven-haired lady first greeted my father at the penguin exhibit, then crouched down to say hello to me. I thought it odd that she was so thrilled to meet me, and that she studied my face and curly hair (which I had a mop of at the time), as though I too were an exhibit. She joined us for the rest of the tour of the zoo, and chatted with me very casually about my interests, likes and dislikes.

After lunch at the zoo, we all took a cab back to an office in town, where I was introduced to her husband, Alexander, who sat behind an immense mahogany desk with nothing but a telephone on it. I remember him looking much older than his wife and significantly less enthusiastic about meeting my father and me than she had been. Only when he came from behind his desk to share tea and biscuits did he become animated and smiling.

After half an hour or so, my father and I left the office with much hand-shaking and promises of seeing each other again soon, and it was in the taxi to the station that my father revealed what all this had been about. I felt a short rush of excitement when the idea that I might be involved in a feature film sank in, a feeling that was quickly replaced by a dread. I had many pets at the time, including a green iguana, called Iggy, and these were the centre of my world. The filming, if it went ahead, would take place outside the UK, and my overriding concern was how my pets might accompany me. I need not have been worried. The second phase of the selection process soon weeded me out of the running, especially when I made it perfectly clear that I could not travel without my menagerie. The actor Mark Lester got the role, and rumour had it that for his eighteenth birthday, on set, Oliver Reed hired a gaggle of working ladies to delight him. Hindsight is a very precise science, but I can look back with amused relief that the path to Tinseltown had ended in a natural cul-de-sac.

My father had by now been appointed head of what was then known as the 'General Programmes Unit' in the BBC in Bristol, and as such was to pioneer new strands of subject matter from looking at antiques on television (he created *Going for a Song*, which was to evolve into the *Antiques Roadshow*) to light entertainment strands. The Natural History Unit (NHU) was already well established and producing marvellous programmes, through the work of luminaries such as David Attenborough and Peter Scott. Quite what the politics involved were of my father launching a natural-history-based series from another branch of the BBC, I shall never quite know, but I am guessing that his suggestion of a new approach to the genre probably met with stern disapproval from certain more traditional and influential members of the NHU.

Whatever the reason, *Man and Boy* was to use the model of a series of books that my father used to love as a child called *Out With Romany*, where a wise old woodsman, George Bramwell Evans, passed on his knowledge of the wilds to a young boy. These were based on the weekly broadcasts he made on BBC *Children's Hour* from 1932 to 1943, which reached audiences of more than 13 million people, including a young David Attenborough.

My father already knew I had the hunger and aptitude to appear as the student, and set about seeking someone to be the tutor. Many people who remember this series often mistakenly assume the grown man on screen was my father, but it wasn't: not only did my father feel it inappropriate to take the role; he also, frankly, did not have the knowledge. His interest in being in the wilds was largely limited to coarse fishing, for which he had a passion. When it came to telling apart a blue tit from a great tit, he floundered.

The BBC in Bristol was a fertile ground to search for expertise, and my father found it in a man who had been in charge of the NHU film library for many years, Michael Kendall. Mike, as well as having a great knowledge of wildlife film-making, was also a naturalist of the highest order. Added to this, I was to discover he was the most gentle and patient of men, with a genuine desire to share his knowledge and thrill at the detail of the wild world around him. One of our earliest meetings involved a rendezvous in a patch of woodland near Cheddar, where a skeleton film crew had been assembled to test the 'screen chemistry' of both of us.

I cannot remember being filmed. But burning as brightly in my mind's eye today as on the day itself was the magic Mike spun as he unpicked the secrets of the forest around me. Whereas, before then, I had struggled with vinyl discs of bird song, trying to remember the differences between the silver fluting of a blackcap and a garden warbler, here was a man who could help me listen through the twittering blanket of sound in the wood and find the quirks that made each bird's voice its own. He could point at a tiny, bounding silhouette of a finch, high in the sky, and tell me confidently whether it was a chaffinch or a greenfinch, without having to study it through binoculars, simply because he was so familiar with their chirping flight calls.

Perhaps most impressive of all, though, was Mike's ability to talk to the animals. As dusk began its premature creep between the towering oaks of the wood, Mike suggested we try to see a tawny owl. I had of course heard owls in the past. I had been lucky enough too to find them roosting up against ivy-clad trees by day. But seeing them in their fully flighted nocturnal glory had been the stuff of my imagination only.

Mike prepared by pursing his lips and cupping his hands to his cheeks, and then he hooted. A full, woody, tawny owl call came from this gentle man. We waited, Mike hooted again, another wait, and then, from deep in the wood, the first murmurings of an answer. I was hugely impressed, and excited by the notion that we human beings might be able to bridge the gap between species. But this was just the opening of the show. Patiently, Mike slowly coaxed the owl from its diurnal roosting place and into the shadows of the coming night. The bird's answers came closer, then closer still, until suddenly and with a whispered exclamation of 'There!' Mike pointed to a gap in the trees overhead. I looked up to see the broad-winged, moon-faced bird glide silently over our heads no more than ten metres away. It might be the fancy of a young boy's embellished memory, but I can still see the eyes of the owl, staring down and looking into my own. It was a breathless, timeless epiphany for me, the confluence of my hunger for knowledge, my passion for the wild world and my desire to be a part of it.

Mike and I were to work together on two series of *Man and Boy* over the coming two years. Our friendship was cemented during this time, and Mike would often call to tell me of a rare bird in the Cheddar area and take me to see it, or perhaps just to visit the local reservoirs, Chew Valley or Blagdon, for a spot of birding. He unlocked further secrets of communication with the wild world too, from tapping a tree with a stone to excite the interest of the local great spotted woodpecker, to hooting in broad daylight to bring a little owl into full view. I would stay with Mike, and his wife Val, in their house near Cheddar, and take walks on the Somerset Levels, lifting jacksnipe before us from the meadows or waiting for a barn owl to stitch the evening light with its buoyant, almost luminous form.

Back at Mike's house, I would pore over his collection of old Christmas cards, almost all of which were adorned with bird or other wildlife art. I came to be able to discern a Robert Gillmor from a Raymond Harris Ching – both magnificent bird artists of differing styles – and also became more and more familiar with the variety and form of our avian neighbours. Standard reading, at almost any hour, was the *Collins Pocket Guide to British Birds* by Fitter and Richardson. I studied the silhouettes on the inside jacket until I could name them all without hesitation, worked hard to memorise the Latin names of birds (Mike had pointed out how important this was if I was to be able to talk about a species internationally) and learned to view all things with a selective eye, as the guide suggested, looking for the detail and difference in an eye-stripe or a tail feather.

Our adventures around the British Isles during the making of the two series took us from the Highlands of Scotland, in search of golden eagles and red deer, to central Wales to see some of the very few breeding red kites that still clung to this remote corner of the nation at the time. We would stay in hotels, together with the crew, and venture out for a week or so on our rambles. Our constant companion throughout these travels was Mike's dog, a rough collie called Tia.

On one occasion, on the edge of Exmoor, we arrived at a hotel to a very tepid reception. It was clear that the policy regarding dogs at the establishment was less than welcoming, and unfortunately Tia was to be banished to an outhouse for the duration of our stay. Soon after our arrival, I noticed my father having a quiet word with the manager, who nodded sagely, then looked over my father's shoulder at Tia, who was waiting patiently by Mike's side. Another few whispered exchanges and then an astonishing turnaround of attitude: Tia was more than welcome to accompany Mike to his room. Furthermore, she could come into the lounge area with us, and she was even served a bowl of water before any of us was offered tea. The owner of the hotel patted her head gently and whispered, 'Hello Tia', then looked up to me and winked with a confiding nod.

Only later, when my dad revealed to me what he had

said to the manager, did I understand. He had told him that Tia was the dog's pseudonym, and that she was in fact Lassie, star of the silver screen. The story was that we had to be careful not to reveal her true identity for fear of dog-nappers, but that she was the focus of the show and the filming was to centre around her.

I found it very difficult to perpetuate this story without breaking into giggles, but for the duration of our stay, and perhaps to this day, the owner of the hotel was convinced he was playing host to the most famous dog on earth.

Between the two series of *Man and Boy*, I also played a part in another television drama written and directed by my father. This time, the story was set in southern England during the Second World War. It was loosely based on my own father's experiences during the early 1940s, particularly his relationship with his grandfather, whom he knew as Bumper, and whose passion for fishing gave rise to my father's inherited adage, 'If fishing gets in the way of work, give up work!'

The Secret Place was the tale of a young refugee summering in a rural paradise whilst the unseen horrors of war rage all around. Shot on a very limited budget, the drama of the conflict was alluded to, rather than illustrated, in all but one scene, when dog-fighting aircraft were to rip into the idyllic peace of the woods and lakes that were the playground of the central characters. The vast majority of my role involved catching grass snakes, fishing for carp and befriending a girl – the latter was of least interest to me at the time – but the script demanded that when the battling aircraft burst onto the scene, I was to be in the thick of it, and that included being inadvertently caught by a strafe of gunfire as the planes flew low over the ground. This, naturally, thrilled me beyond words. As well as being obsessively passionate about wildlife, I also spent hundreds of hours building plastic model kits of Spitfires, Messerschmitts and Hurricanes. The thought of having two of the genuine articles flying low overhead was a dream come true.

To achieve the effect of gunfire, a pyrotechnic expert was employed to plant explosive charges in the track down which I was to run as the Messerschmitt flew overhead in pursuit of his foe. The whole event had to be carefully choreographed to ensure the plane, the explosive charges and I all came towards the camera at the same time. My sense of excitement turned to trepidation as I heard the low growl of the approaching aircraft and prepared to sprint down the track. The growl turned to a roar, and my father yelled the command, 'Action!'

I was off, trying to stick to the line I'd been told to take to ensure I didn't run into the explosives. But it is very tricky indeed not to look back when you hear the thunderous scream of an approaching fighter plane about to bear down on you no more than twenty metres or so off the ground. The plumes of soil and grit were already rising on each side of the track as the explosives went off, imitating the action of the bullets hitting the ground. As I looked back, my gangly-legged path wavered, and I strayed onto an explosive charge just as it detonated.

I suddenly found my right foot being blasted off the ground in a shower of pebbles and dust, and it was all I could do to maintain my balance and keep running. But run I did, despite feeling horribly ashamed that I had probably ruined the one and only chance we had at getting the shot.

Once I passed the camera, my father called 'Cut!' Then, having checked to see that I was unhurt, he exclaimed, 'That was absolutely stunning! Well done, well done!' I was confused, sure that I'd ruined the whole expensive exercise. But my father had immediately seen that this was an opportunity to add further spice to the plot; since it now looked as though I had been grazed by a bullet, a whole new scene was hastily written, and later filmed, to accommodate my mistake.

But the adventure of the fighter planes was not yet over. For all of the meticulous planning, one small detail had been omitted. How were we going to let the pilots know that the shoot had been a success and they could fly home? No ground-to-air radio was available, so the only mode of communication was by visual signal. Our first attempt involved the whole crew waving madly in the direction of the nearest airstrip, but this was understandably taken to mean, 'Please go around again for another shot' by the pilot. At our next attempt, we all joined hands to form an arrow, pointing in the same direction. The pilot flew low over our signal, and once again assumed we needed him to conduct another fly-past. Finally, we arranged ourselves once more to form the vulgar but emphatic letters F.O. The pilot flew by, did a magnificent wing-wobble and barrel-roll, and disappeared over the horizon.

Whilst filming *The Secret Place*, I was taught a salutary life lesson by one of my father's close colleagues, an eccentric and compelling man called Dixie. He was employed as a mix of general helper and field assistant, and he brought to this role a font of country knowledge and know-how, together with solid mechanical and practical skills. I had known Dixie since the making of *The Fox* on Dartmoor and considered him a hero. He was extraordinary in many ways, not least for his habit of referring to himself in the third person. For example, he might start the day by saying; 'Dixie is going to show Simon how to catch minnows,' and proceed to illustrate how to cut a hole in the base of a wine bottle, add a canvas stop to the neck and bait the simple trap. He would then show me where best to place the contraption and, twelve hours later, retrieve it, complete with its fishy occupants.

Whilst we worked on *The Fox*, I felt Dixie enjoyed my sense of wonder and my hunger to learn all that he had to show me. He took on the role of favourite uncle and mentor, treating me with an equal, unpatronising manner that encouraged me to behave in as adult and responsible a way as possible. When, a year or so later, we worked together on *The Secret Place*, I felt we had a bond, a friendship.

It was during the shooting of a scene, where I was sitting on a five-bar gate and delivering a line to my on-screen friend, that this sense of solidarity was abruptly shattered. I can't even remember what I said or did, but I probably thought at the time that it was amusing, a further step towards my integration in the adult world. In reality, though, from the mouth of a twelve-year-old boy, it obviously sounded grotesquely rude and precocious, since the response from Dixie was understated yet crushing.

'Dixie used to know a nice boy, a boy who had respect,' he observed. 'Now Dixie doesn't know that boy any more.'

I tried to brush the comment off, but in truth I was devastated. This man whose skills and knowledge were almost holy to me had, with a few words, made me face myself and realise how unpleasant I had been. The same comment from a parent, relative or sibling would not have had the same impact. It was precisely because I respected Dixie so greatly, but had no right to assume unconditional love from him, that these words of criticism hit their mark so profoundly and accurately. I shall be eternally grateful to him for his timely and honest reaction. I had obviously got puffed up with self-importance, and his words were a timely reminder – not only of how critical it is to maintain an honest sense of humility, but also that real friends will let you know when they think you are in the wrong.

Seeing at first hand the mechanics of film-making on projects like *The Secret Place*, I began to develop a greater interest in the discipline of the cameraman. I would ask how the film was loaded, how the exposure was set, and took every opportunity to look through the eyepiece and to experiment with the lenses. Whenever a telephoto lens was deployed, I would hover by the camera and wait to be invited to use it to study a subject in the distance, especially if it happened to be a living thing. This interest blossomed into a desire to try my own hand with a camera.

I had, for some time, experimented a little with photography, but in a very superficial and directionless fashion. My equipment had been basic: an old Kodak box camera and a Zenit E 35-mm film camera with a 50-mm lens. Neither was likely to yield magnificent results in terms of wildlife photography, or at least that was my excuse for a series of images of soft-focus, distant blobs that I assured my parents were either water voles or foxes, though I couldn't be sure which from the cryptic image. These early disappointments in my development as a stills photographer established very shaky foundations for my ambition to move into cinematography. Nonetheless, I dropped endless and unsubtle hints to my folks that I should very much like to try my hand at filming animals, and they eventually succumbed to the attrition by presenting me on the Christmas Day just before my fourteenth birthday with a Super 8-mm film camera. I was thrilled to the core with the gift, despite it being made clear that it was for Christmas and my birthday combined (a common handicap for those of us with birthdays close to 25 December). I promptly deployed all my saved-up pocket money in getting some simple editing equipment: now I was ready to start my epic documentary of the wildlife around our home in Bristol.

Chapter 3

Talking to Trees

My first attempt at wildlife camerawork was to take place in the woods whose border was a few hundred metres from our home. At thirteen years old I was lucky enough to have a loving mother who trusted me, but also to be living in an era when there was not the same fear for children's safety as there seems to be today. So I was at liberty to run wild, enjoying the freedom to roam from the earliest hours of the day until I had to make my way to school, and then again on the way back home, a daily adventure that was only curtailed by my hunger, the need to do homework or the onset of night.

I attended Henbury Comprehensive in Bristol, which involved a walk of about thirty minutes through Blaise Woods from our house, and though there were many facets of school life I enjoyed, nothing there could compete with the draw of my woodland explorations.

During the spring and summer months I would rise early, often before first light, dress in my school uniform, and head for the forest. Walking alone among the looming silhouettes of great beech trees and oaks that bordered the path would, from time to time, play on my imagination, but I learned to banish any fears by memorising the forms of key forest giants by day (they were giants to me at the time), so that I could recognise them easily in the darkness. To further stave off any rogue thoughts of monsters in the shadows, I began talking directly to the trees, and so came to feel I was surrounded by friends rather than demons.

'Morning, Mr Beech, I hope you had a good night. Any owls visit you recently? How is Mrs Nuthatch? Finished putting mud round her nest hole yet?'

From time to time, I would bump into a fellow early riser walking their dog, most of whom I'm sure were unnerved by this boy walking in the half-light, in full school uniform, talking to the trees.

Often I would climb one of the larger oaks, whose branches overhung the footpaths, and watch the handful of other humans who ventured out at this early hour pass below. I had a sense of ownership, a misplaced but profound feeling of territorial right to the forest that was being infringed by these trespassers; but by going unseen I was still able to consider my place amongst the branches as privileged.

I would arrive at the school gates dishevelled, my trousers spotted with green lichen and my shirt hanging below my blazer, and hastily tuck and brush myself into some form of respectability before heading to class. Most of the teachers and form tutors in the school were well aware of my obsession and considered me a lost cause. But by and large, I did just enough to avoid being singled out and no more. Once, during a double period of chemistry, which happened to be the last lesson of the school day, I fell asleep, head on desk, hidden only by a Bunsen burner and the two rows of pupils in front of me. Rather than wake and punish me, the teacher chose the far more effective course of leaving me in peaceful slumber, making sure all the other kids kept quiet as they left the class and headed for home. I awoke with a start at the sound of the janitor's bucket slamming onto the floor beside me, a good hour after the school bell had rung.

During my explorations of Blaise Woods, I discovered birds' nests, foxes' earths and bats' roosts, and at the weekend would head out with my camera to try and capture all this on film. I soon realised that the task was far from simple. The 8 x optical zoom lens on the camera was desperately inadequate for all but the most confiding creatures, and the challenge of securing even moderately good images of wild animals required a great deal more than simply knowing where they lived. In order to begin to film these wild spirits properly, I would have to learn their habits and how to predict their movements, yet remain unseen.

I discovered – for instance – that by placing a prominent perch over the River Hazel that flowed through the valley basin, I could encourage the local kingfishers to take a pause in their bullet-like flight along the watercourse. Then, hidden in the bushes, I would wait for the shrill piping call of the birds as they smeared their cobalt blue against the shadows of the stream, before arriving with startling and electric splendour on the perch I had provided, giving me a chance to snatch a shot or two before they headed off once more between the high banks.

Sparrowhawks, kestrels, grass snakes and water voles

all featured in this epic production, along with a cameo appearance from fallow deer. Even though the deer were actually filmed in a park in West Sussex, they added a little colour and drama to the plot, I thought.

Then, long hours were spent cutting and splicing together the images, resulting in a fifteen-minute spectacular of colour and life. That's what I'd envisaged, anyway. In reality the results were, of course, dreadful. Birds of prey appeared as dots in the centre of screen. Out-of-focus and wobbly views of creatures that were so distant or underexposed even I could not remember what they were and why they warranted inclusion, gave way to achingly long pans across countryside, or a hesitant zoom into a silhouetted cluster of sticks that I assured my audience (direct family only) was in fact a sparrowhawk's nest. Both my father and mother viewed the film and congratulated me on my achievement, but I knew that I had a very long way to go before I could consider my work worthy of a broader public exposure.

I was to fall squarely on my feet when it came to a serious introduction to the world of the specialist wildlife cameraman. My father had recently left the BBC to start an independent production company. He kept close links with his former employer, however, and many of the projects his new company produced were commissioned by the Beeb. One such was for the already well-established strand, *The World About Us* (later to become *Natural World*), and was to feature the New Forest in Hampshire. The film, entitled 'The Royal Forest', was to look at the rich mixture of human and natural history in the area, and the principal cameraman was Hugh Miles.

Hugh had justly carved a reputation as one of the leading wildlife cameramen in the world, and had won several awards with his pioneering and stunningly beautiful camerawork in films whose subjects ranged from ospreys to lions. I had seen and marvelled at his definitive portrait of Scottish ospreys, created whilst he was a senior cameraman working for the RSPB, and was thrilled at the thought that I might meet him.

During the spring half-term break, I accompanied my father to the New Forest on one of the shoots and there was introduced to Hugh, who was living in a tiny cottage on the Beaulieu Estate for the duration of his stay. I was immediately struck by the apparent contradiction between his obvious physical strength, as he effortlessly heaved camera and tripod onto his shoulder, and the soft and gentle synergy he displayed with his natural surroundings.

Hugh and I chatted a while about the wildlife of the forest, and swapped notes about birds we had seen over the past few days. Then, and without warning, the gateway to my professional future was unlatched.

'Right then, Simon, fancy giving me a hand with filming a sparrowhawk nest? I've put the tower in place and the hide has been up a few days, but I could really do with a "walk-away". The chicks hatched a couple of days ago, and I want to try and film the female feeding her new family.'

I tried to play it cool, but already my pulse-rate had

doubled. I was about to help one of the greatest wildlife cameramen of all time with his work. Sure, the skills involved in being a 'walk-away' were limited (the job entails seeing the cameraman into the hide, then walking away so that the birds being filmed believe the coast is clear and return to their nest quickly and calmly), but it was something even I might be able to pull off. On top of that, for the first time I would see the infrastructure and ingenuity used by such specialists to reveal the hidden details of the natural world.

We arrived at the location at first light the next day. Hugh loaded me up with gear from the back of his estate car, and then threw three times more kit into his own rucksack, which he swung onto his back. I followed him silently into the larch forest, barely able to see where I was putting my feet, but determined not to stumble or make a sound. After a few hundred metres, Hugh's pace slowed and then he knelt in front of me and pointed. 'There it is. I think she's still sitting,' he whispered, pointing into the trees ahead.

At first I could not make out a thing, but gradually I separated the well-hidden scaffold tower from the silhouettes of tangled tree trunks. On top of the tower was the dark mass of the canvas hide, and a few metres to the right, at the same level as the foot of the hide and some ten metres off the ground, was the much smaller but equally dark mass that was the sparrowhawk's nest. I missed a breath. I was looking at the occupied nest of one of the most mercurial of woodland hunters.

'How do you know she's there?' I hissed.

'Look at the edge nearest us: you can just see the tip of her tail. The male will be nearby; I'm surprised he hasn't spotted us and warned her yet.'

Almost as the words left Hugh's mouth, a tiny bullet of a bird flashed through the trees to our right, and released a shrill chatter. Duly warned of an approaching threat, a larger dark form rose from the nest and silently dropped from its edge. The female sparrowhawk spread her wings and was swallowed by the gloom and the trees.

'Quick, let's go,' urged Hugh as he rose and half trotted towards the base of the metal tower. I followed as closely as I was able, only just managing to keep up with my burden of camera equipment. By the time I reached the base of the scaffold I was puffing, but Hugh was already two-thirds of the way up and pulling the weighty ruck-sack from his back to push it onto the hide platform. Once done, he was back down in a flash, with one of a pair of walkie-talkies in his hand.

'I'll take those bits now, Simon, thanks for carrying them. Wait until I get settled in the hide, please, then make your way back to the car and wait for me. I'll call you on the radio when I'm ready to come out.'

Hugh lifted himself deftly into the hide with one hand, the other carrying the remaining kit, and then called down that he was ready and that I should go.

The light was lifting as I made the two-hundred-metre walk back to the car, my head full of images of what it was that Hugh might be seeing. How long would it be before the female came back to the nest? Would she bring food? What did the chicks look like?

I took my job seriously, regularly checking the radio was on (why I thought it might switch off spontaneously, I have no idea), and keeping an eye on the forest edge in case I might catch a glimpse of the raptors' arrival or departure. I saw nothing of them, but amused myself by watching passing flocks of finches, which included crossbills, and fallow deer that nosed out of the forest four hundred metres away to graze on the edge of a glade.

After three hours or so, the radio crackled and Hugh's voice checked to see if I was listening.

'I'm here Hugh. Are you ready to come out? Over,' I answered in as efficient and cool a manner as I could muster.

'Yup, all done here for a bit. Could you come to the bottom of the tower when you are ready please, Simon? Bring your camera with you; you can take a spell in the hide if you like. Over.'

I couldn't believe my ears. I was to be allowed into the inner sanctum, the world of secrets. It was a kind and wonderful show of trust on Hugh's part. Sparrowhawks are nervous birds, and though I had spent a great deal of time watching wild creatures, I had never been so close to such a highly strung huntress. Even though I would be in a hide, I was nervous that I might spook the returning female, but I tried not to let my uncertainty show in my voice.

'Great, thanks Hugh. See you in a minute.'

I hastily gathered my simple film camera (I had recently improved my gear with a basic Pentax 35-mm SLR body and a bulky-but-cheap 500-mm lens, both of them second-, or more likely third-hand) and set off at a brisk pace towards the hide. For a horrible moment on my return journey I found myself lost, the appearance of the trees and woodland paths having changed dramatically since the half-light of dawn. Fortunately, though, I rediscovered my path before having to admit my incompetence over the radio to Hugh.

As I approached the tower, I saw the female sparrowhawk flash from the nest, and quickly made my way to the tower base.

'I'm here,' I said over the radio unnecessarily, since Hugh would of course have seen the departing bird and heard my approach.

'Great. Be right down,' came his response before the back canvas of the hide flapped open and he began to lower the first of his gear to the forest floor on a rope. I released the bundle and Hugh repeated the action until he and all his kit were safely down.

'Right-ho, your turn, Simon. I've left my chair. You just need your camera and the radio. I suggest you have a pee before you go up. It's pretty tricky doing it from there.'

I quickly followed Hugh's wise advice, and by the time I was back at the base of the hide, he was standing with rucksack on his back, and all the rest of the heavy gear in his arms or on his shoulders.

'Up you go, quickly now. We don't want her to be away for too long. Get your kit sorted, then let me know you're ready. When she first comes back, don't move. She'll be watching for anything new. You'll soon see when she has settled.'

I shot up the tower, pulling up into the hide after me my bundle of gear, which Hugh had attached to the rope. The whole transition was so swift that I didn't really have time to consider the height until I looked back for the last time to Hugh, and gave him the thumbs-up. Ten metres suddenly felt like an awfully long way from the ground!

With camera on tripod and lens poking through the green netting that shrouded the window of the hide, I listened to the faint cracking of twigs that traced Hugh's retreat to the car. My view was obscured by the netting – an essential scrim against the piercing gaze of the hawks – but I was astonished at how close the nest appeared to be. I felt that if I reached out through the window, I would be able to touch the three tiny white fluffy chicks that lay motionless in the bowl of sticks that gently swayed in the breeze. I tried hard not to wriggle, for fear that a creak or rattle from the seat might scare the parent birds, who would almost certainly be watching and listening from a nearby tree just out of sight.

This was my first real taste of the anticipation felt by the wildlife cameraman before he becomes privy to a revelation from a parallel world. My view was narrow, my immediate environment claustrophobic and cramped, but my imagination was flying through the trees at a thousand miles an hour. The world of the sparrowhawk was occupying my every thought, and my concentration on the tiny, lattice-covered portal into its private life was absolute.

And then she was there. With the flick of a shadow, the female hawk arrived at her nest, and the burning fire of her sunlit yellow eyes drilled into me. I was transfixed, pinned by her gaze, which seemed to look through the net, through my eyes and into the back of my head. Had I made a mistake and not pulled enough of the netting around the lens of my camera? Was she able to see me clearly, and was her startled form a whisper away from shooting away into the forest, proving me clumsy and incompetent in this first serious test of my character and field knowledge? Her whole body was tense with the anticipation of flight, her yellow talons tightly gripping the sticks on the nest's edge. I dared not blink. I dared not breath. For what felt an age (which was I'm sure no more than minutes), I was held in her stare, feeling both anxiety and exhilaration in equal measure.

Slowly, almost imperceptibly, her gaze began to soften. The tension in her killer feet ebbed away. I realised the chicks at her feet had started an incessant cheeping, begging for her attention, a call that both she and I had been deaf to during our moments of mutual scrutiny. Their begging muted the intense fire in her eyes, and she roused herself, shaking her feathers to settle more comfortably.

I still didn't dare move, but watched as she fiddled with nest material and scraps of long-finished meals. This was it. With a sudden clarity and certainty I knew at once this was how I wanted to spend my days: watching, interpreting, unravelling the unseen world that runs and scuttles, swims and flaps all around us. This one nest, one family of hawks, was the tiniest fragment of the world beyond our gaze; a world of drama, tenderness, fury and calm that plays out each and every day in myriad quiet corners of the earth. The lives of these wild spirits was every bit as compelling as any human drama; perhaps more so, since the secrets of their world were given up so reluctantly. Hugh's generosity had poured fuel onto the flame of my passion and now I had a real target in my sights. I wanted to become a wildlife cameraman.

The trouble was, I was as yet pretty useless with the camera. When I did finally get around to taking some shots of the sparrowhawk on the nest, they all turned out to be horribly underexposed. Though the photographic results were disappointing, I was more than content with the experience of watching the hawks at such close quarters, and, later that evening, once back on terra firma and sipping a mug of tea in Hugh's cottage, could not stop talking about everything I had seen and done during my spell in the hide. Over the next few days, Hugh took me along as his assistant to each of the subjects he was following. I watched at dusk for the dumpy silhouette of a woodcock performing its roding display flight, and by day helped Hugh to another hide, this time on the forest floor where he had discovered their nest. He showed me a spot on the woodland edge where fallow deer ventured out to graze in the lemon light of evening. I helped carry his gear and was allowed to look through the camera eyepiece at distant birds brought near by his telephoto lens. At one point, Hugh gave me a tutorial around the Arriflex camera he was using, and allowed me to take a shot of deer on a forest clearing. Naturally he had set most of the technical parameters for me, but for the twelve seconds that I allowed the film to pass through the gate,

I felt an immense sense of privilege. This was the first shot I had ever taken on a professional film camera and, as a kind gesture, my father ensured it made it into the finished film, despite it being very average.

Ambitions to approach the natural world through academic study started to fade, and instead the adventure and variety that the career of a wildlife film-maker seemed likely to provide began to feature ever more prominently in my thoughts. Going back to school after the spring break was a real wrench. Though I enjoyed most of the lessons and respected many of my teachers, I had less and less inclination to continue with my formal education beyond the obligatory O-levels. I think this came as something of a shock to my parents, especially my mother, who had worked her way out of the poverty of her childhood home in Glasgow's Gorbals with a sharp mind that earned her a scholarship to a grammar school. I had long and weighty conversations with her about the consequences of not continuing with school, and about what would happen if I should falter or fail in my chosen path. But I reasoned that my passion for wildlife would never diminish and I would find some way to indulge it. That was naive perhaps, but heartfelt, and my parents both gave me their reluctant blessing.

The next couple of years included the occasional appearance in TV dramas, lots of homework, a great deal more rambling in the woods, music and girls. I precociously started my first 'serious' relationship with a schoolmate when I was fourteen years old; a very close and exclusive friendship that lasted almost two years. The journey to my girlfriend's house involved a walk, or more usually a run, through the local woods, and in my eagerness to reach her I found I ignored the calls of kingfishers and woodpeckers for the first time in my life.

As the examination season loomed, I continued to seek some form of apprenticeship with a film and TV company, hoping to develop my skills as a camera operator; very fortunately I was offered a place with a wonderful man who owned and ran an independent media company in Bristol, Michael Wagen. Michael was enormously generous with his knowledge and informed me that, once I had finished my exams, I would be able to come and work with him for the summer.

So it was that at sixteen, armed with a bundle of modest results from my O-levels, I started working with the South West Picture Agency. I learned how to print a black-and-white still image and send it over the wire to a newspaper. I was shown how to load the film magazines of a number of 16-mm and 35-mm movie cameras. We worked on commercials for caravans and promotional films for public schools, and all the time I soaked up what I could of the technicalities and operational skills. Most of the time, I was a runner on location, a pair of hands that could help fetch the tea or dash to the car for some fully charged batteries or more film, but as the days progressed I was given ever greater responsibilities.

Loading film magazines for a commercial shoot was a daunting prospect, since I knew that one slip and the whole day's work would be ruined. 'Slip' was the operative word in many cases since, at the time, film was divided into either negative or reversal stock. News shoots and any other project that required a very fast turnaround used reversal film (the movie equivalent of slide film in stills), which had a very slippery emulsion. Since the whole procedure of loading a film magazine was conducted blind, with your hands inside a black cloth bag, any mishandling had very serious consequences, and the reversal film seemed to take on a life of its own once out of its tin. It felt like trying to remove a blancmange from a bowl and place it into another whilst keeping it in one piece, with your eyes closed. Fortunately, I rose to the challenge and managed to get by without causing any great catastrophe.

Whilst I was enormously grateful to Michael for the opportunities he offered me, I grew a little frustrated by my lack of contact with the natural world. Whenever possible, I still explored my local woodland and any other rural spots, and set about trying to beg and borrow bits of film equipment so that I could practise with a camera. I was lucky enough to be loaned a basic Bolex 16-mm film camera and a couple of lenses by Mike and, with short ends of film stock, attempted to film any and all local wildlife. My shots would find their way into the processing bath of whichever project was currently under way with the company so I could see my results. By and large, they were still pretty ropey, but I was getting better.

I was still in close contact with Mike Kendall, with whom I had made the *Man and Boy* series, and he very sweetly helped to orchestrate my first contract as a wildlife cameraman. The BBC Natural History Unit was compiling a bird identification guide that was to be sold on video, but the library had many gaps in its species list. I was given ten rolls of stock and a list of species to try and capture on film. I was still too young to drive myself around the countryside, so either my father, with whom I was now living from time to time, or anyone else I could convince, would drive me into the countryside around my father's house, south of Bristol, in search of yellowhammers, reed buntings or one of the other species required by the producers of the guide.

After a couple of weeks of trying to fulfil my remit, I handed in the exposed rolls of film and waited for the report. I'm not convinced that the results really merited it, but I received a very kind response from the then head of the unit thanking me for my work and saying how nice it was to have someone working on the project who could tell his chaffinches from his bramblings! On reflection, everything I filmed was very average, but those complimentary words and the idea that I had contributed to a professional production gave me an enormous boost.

Chapter 4

The Great, Great Tit Watch

After making a film for *The World About Us* in the foothills of the Costa del Sol in Spain, back in the UK I started a more homespun project for Westward Television in Plymouth; a simple, low-budget journey through the countryside of southwest England called *King's Country*. I could film anything and everything I came across, and the series of six half-hour shows was narrated by me. It was a wonderful brief, the more so since I was only twenty-one years old. In effect, I just had to indulge my hobby, film what I saw, and get paid (very little) for it.

Foxes at the den, kingfishers, boxing hares and mating slugs all featured. I was always on the lookout for the commonplace doing something unusual, whether it was garden snails in an amorous embrace or a puffball fungus releasing its spores in a rain-shower. As early autumn approached, I decided to visit the coastline to try to film some of the birds of prey that follow the flocks of wading birds that come to Britain to overwinter, which in turn forage on the vast expanse of mud flats that grace the country's shores. I chose to bend the series location brief a little and journey to a reserve I already knew well: Farlington Marshes near Portsmouth. My grandparents on both my mother's and my father's side lived in Pompey, as it is known locally, and I often explored the marsh after a visit to my folks. I now had the use of an old Series 1 Land Rover, which we had painted in the pattern of a dry-stone wall with ivy crawling over the roof – very discreet – and the freedom to travel wherever I wished. My filming visit to the marsh would have been unremarkable but for the story of the black toes.

A few months earlier I had started a relationship with a beautiful, petite, intriguing woman, four years my senior, and together we were renting a flat in Bristol. Kim enjoyed the natural world, though not with quite the same degree of focus as I did. We found common ground in the completely unrelated worlds of music and fashion. It was the era of the New Romantic, with bands such as Spandau Ballet and Adam and the Ants leading the trend for medieval, flowing shirts and heavy eye make-up. When I wasn't dressed top to toe in khaki, I would go out with Kim sporting the most outrageous (and, with the benefit of hindsight, comical) outfits, and I had cultivated a number of skinny braids from the neckline of my mop of curly hair. One of my dandy uniforms included calf-high suede boots with an exposed toe. To finish the look, I had painted my toenails black, not something that would get in the way of my day-to-day work, but a bit of a giggle on the weekend. I thought I could keep my interest in the New Romantic dress code completely separate from my work as a wildlife film-maker. Only the plaits were a bit of a giveaway, and more often than not they didn't show clearly in anything but a view of the back of my head.

Back at Farlington, I met with the reserve warden, a

burly chap with a handshake of steel that I tried, and failed, to match. He was very helpful, allowing me to put up my portable hide along the edge of the high-water mark to film the wading birds, and to roam in otherwise excluded zones in search of hen harriers and merlins. Thereafter, he left me to it, and I had a wonderful day following amorphous clouds of swirling waders and picking off shots of low-flying harriers.

It was approaching dusk when I spotted the warden's Land Rover driving along the track on the top of the sea wall. He had very kindly decided to give me a lift back to my own vehicle in the car park about a mile away. With the filming done for the day, I packed my camera kit into my rucksack, pulled the load onto my back and headed for the car. I had almost reached the vehicle when I realised we were separated by a water-filled ditch, about three metres wide and half a metre deep. The water would certainly flood over the tops of my wellies so, without a thought, I whipped off my boots and socks, clutched them in one hand, and waded across to the spot where the warden was by now standing outside his car.

'How was the day?' he asked as I sploshed alongside.

'Marvellous, really excellent, thank you!' I answered enthusiastically, whilst feeling a little uncomfortable at the change that was slowly coming over the warden's face, which had gone from smiling and open to stern with a furrowed brow. I realised then that he was staring at my black-painted toenails, exposed for all the world to admire, and was taking one or two steps back towards his vehicle. I tried in vain to dig my toes into the mud of the track and so camouflage my unconventional adornment, but whatever opinion the warden had of me, it had now been coloured, quite literally, by what I'm sure he took to be evidence of cross-dressing. I did my best to focus the conversation on the events of the day, but he had become rather quiet, and, though civil, couldn't get me back to my car and say goodbye fast enough.

Watching the reaction of someone who clearly felt that such frivolity made me somehow dangerous or less credible was a bit of a disappointment, and suggested to me that if I was going to be taken seriously by the inner sanctum of wildlife enthusiasts I would have to conform – or at least appear to conform – to expected norms. However, quite the opposite was true about the people I met whilst engaged in some of the other camera work I was doing at the time. To earn a few bob, I volunteered to light and film some of the music videos that my father directed and produced through his company. These were short, intense shoots of perhaps two or three days at a time and – given the duration of the finished product, which was just as long as the music track lasted – were much better funded than any wildlife film. The extra budget enabled me to play with new technology, some of which would prove to be useful in wildlife productions later. I worked with artists such as Judie Tzuke, Demis Roussos and David Essex. All were characters larger than life and a lot of fun to be around. I shared meals with Demis, who loved his food, wolfing down freshly cooked Atlantic prawns complete with their heads, legs and shells. I did the same in his company, which earned me his respect!

One video we shot for David accompanied his Christmas song 'A Winter's Tale', which made it to number two in the charts. As a result, the video played repeatedly across the festive season, though as someone whose tastes were rather more allied to The Clash and The Cure, I didn't boast to my friends about it!

The music videos were a fun but brief departure from my more usual work in the world of natural history. Now, at twenty-one years old I was getting more and more work outside my father's company with both independent TV channels and the BBC. I starting presenting a few shows for the Natural History Unit in Bristol and turned my hand to the camera whenever I was able. A series with which I had been involved from its earliest days, and which proved to be a precursor of programmes like *Bird in the Nest* and *Springwatch*, was *Wildtrack*, a magazine show about British wildlife that was presented by Mike Jordan and Su Ingle. I was asked from time to time to film sequences of wildlife that would then be played into the show for the presenters to comment on. I was phoned by Mike Beynon, the producer of the show, for one such task he felt I would be suited to.

'Hi Simon. We've filmed a sequence of Mike Jordan watching a badger, a pretty special one actually. It's very pale ginger you see – well, erythristic they call it. Very rare. Trouble is, we didn't film the badger. Thought you might be the lad for the job.'

I was flattered by the request and the confidence placed in my abilities, and immediately agreed to take on the project. The shoot was to be spread over two days, the first to try and film the elusive ginger-coloured badger, the second to attempt a 'two-shot' with Mike, getting him in frame in the foreground with the badger foraging in the background.

I travelled to the location and, during the course of the first evening, was lucky enough to get some very reasonable views of this curious brock. Phase one a success, then. I cheerily phoned the producer to inform him that I had filmed the badger.

'Great Simon, that's great! I'll send Mike down to you tomorrow for the two-shot. What time should he be with you?' he asked.

'Could he make it here by four thirty p.m. at the latest, please?' I replied. 'We need to be settled at the set at least a couple of hours before the badgers are likely to emerge, just to let things calm down.'

I knew I was being overcautious with this time margin, but I didn't want there to be any risk of disturbance at the set, especially since I would now be held responsible for the success or failure of the sequence. This would be a real test of my field skills and ability to succeed where others had been less fortunate.

I spent the day preparing the area around the set for filming, carefully moving sticks and leaves from the approach path and picking the best place for Mike and I to sit in the evening to film the emerging animals. Mike arrived a little before half past four, and we chatted by the cars before heading up to the set. Mike had a reasonable knowledge of badger-watching but nonetheless I rather presumptuously briefed him on the order of play.

We would make our way very quietly to the set and settle into position. Once seated, it was imperative that neither one of us moved, and walking or changing position during the vigil was out of the question. I warned him that he should be prepared for a wait of some four to five hours, so to make himself comfortable. I hadn't eaten since breakfast that morning, and aware that a noisily rumbling stomach wouldn't help our cause, I bolted down an apple and glugged a pint of milk I had bought from a nearby post office store a little earlier. Then, armed with camera, and cushions for comfort, we set off.

Mike settled down between the badger set and me, whilst I found the best position for both camera angle and concealment. Within ten minutes of arriving, Mike and I had nestled into as comfortable a spot as was possible from the lie of the land, prepared for a long wait. It would be another hour at least before the badgers would emerge. Plenty of time to think. And, within half an hour, all I could think about was the pint of milk I had gulped down before leaving the car. What on earth had I been thinking? Here I was, having laid down the law to someone who I'm sure knew perfectly well how to watch badgers, sternly telling Mike that any movement would undo our chances of seeing the pallid brock, and all I wanted to do was fidget to relieve the increasing pressure on my bladder. After an hour, and still no sign of a badger, Mike was a picture of control and patience; stock-still, staring at the nearest entrance hole. I, on the other hand, was in agony.

By now it felt as though a bathtub's worth of water was trying to escape my tortured system. I had broken into a cold sweat. Another five minutes and it felt as though my eyes were going to burst out of their sockets. I simply had to move. I persuaded myself that I could do it quickly and quietly, and hope that my footfalls were not detected by the badgers. I was just preparing to push myself into a standing position when the nose of a badger tentatively checked the air from the set entrance. It was him! Behind his twitching snout came his broad head, with pale ginger stripes through his eyes where his more regularly coloured cousins would be black. I could see Mike tensing a little, aware that this was the opportunity we had been waiting for, the reward for the hours of discomfort. I knew he would be expecting me to have my eye to the camera behind him, poised for action. I knew that even flexing a thigh would cause an embarrassing accident, and so I was stuck, half sitting, half kneeling.

There are times in life when you have to make sacrifices for your vocation and this was, I decided, one of them. I slowly pulled myself to the camera and started to film, resigned to the fact that there was absolutely nothing I could do about what was by now an astonishingly satisfying release of pressure. The badger performed wonderfully, snuffling about the set within a couple of metres of Mike, giving me ample opportunity to secure images of him in the same scene as this curious critter.

Only once the erythristic and other badgers from the set had left to forage in the fields beyond us did Mike turn to smile at me and we prepared to leave. It was almost pitch dark by the time we reached the cars. I was cripplingly embarrassed by my predicament, but hoped that the darkness would shroud the very obvious and extensive dark patch on my trousers. Which it would have done, had I not stood in the glare of the interior light of the car, which shone an accusatory beacon on my groin. I saw Mike's eyes flick down, then swiftly back to my face.

'I shouldn't have drunk that milk,' I said sheepishly, undoubtedly blushing like a beacon. 'I didn't want to disturb the set, so just had to, well, let it happen.'

Mike gave me a conciliatory grin. 'That, Simon, is what I call dedication! Poor you. Well done for sticking it out.'

Mike's kindness helped alleviate the embarrassment a little, but to this day I cringe when I picture shaking his hand to say goodnight, trying desperately to act as though nothing untoward had happened.

I also contributed to the *Wildtrack* series in rather less stressful ways from time to time, with soap-style family histories on buzzards, foxes and other national favourites. Particularly popular characters turned out to be a family of great tits, which nested in an urban garden in Bristol, and whose entire life cycle had been covered by the series, with cameras revealing the hidden world within the nest box, and round-the-clock coverage of every mini-drama the avian family experienced. A key event in the lives of the tit chicks would be the day they flew for the first time, and I was employed to get it on film.

The nest box in question was in the back garden of a house that had been split up into separate flats, in a region of Bristol that, at the time, was somewhat run down. The elderly couple who owned the ground-floor flat and who had kindly called the BBC to tell them about the tit family nesting in their garden were, well, idiosyncratic. They seemed to pay the minimum of attention to household hygiene or domestic chores, as was made apparent by a stack of washing up in the kitchen basin that had been there for so long that a fine mould had grown over the residue of meals long since consumed. Their pet budgerigar was very nearly forced to the top of its cage by a pile of its own droppings that rose, pyramid-like, from the floor of its prison.

I was grateful, of course, for the offers of lunch and cups of tea from the residents, but – in the circumstances – chose to depend instead on my flask and sandwiches as I waited for the moment the little birds poked their heads out of the nest hole. Although we knew when each of the eggs had hatched, we couldn't pinpoint exactly when fledging might occur, so to ensure nothing was missed, I waited in my hide, staring at the nest hole from dawn to dusk. Naturally I had to emerge from my canvas hide from time to time and brave the owners' lavatory; I won't describe it, but I had to carry out a complete disinfecting of my hands after each visit. My occasional journeys to and from the flat did not escape the notice of the residents of the first-floor flat who were, as far as I was able to establish, all young and female. I should point out at this stage that the property was in the heart of a region that had a reputation as a red-light district. I have absolutely no idea if any of the apartments 'did business', but I was often jeered at and greeted with calls from the girls such as, 'Yer luv, wanna see moi sister's melons?'

To which I would reply, with a mixture of amusement

and embarrassment, 'I'm sure they're great, but I'm afraid I'm a bit busy,' before diving back into my canvas hide. I must have been an eccentric and curious sight, even in this neighbourhood, given that I appeared to be living in a tiny green tent in the garden.

At last, the big day came. With first light, the chicks started fluttering up to the nest hole and staring out into the world beyond. Their excited parents hopped and chattered in the bushes, brandishing tempting beak-loads of tiny green caterpillars to try and coax their young family into making their maiden flight. By seven o'clock in the morning, the first of the chicks was out, and within half an hour, the whole brood was twittering and flicking in all corners of the garden. The moment of fledging had been filmed, but now I had to try and follow the family during these first few hours of life in the big wide world, a period fraught with danger from domestic cats and passing cars. This is when my real adventure began.

Within an hour, the great tit chicks had started to leave the confines of their natal garden. The first of them managed to scale the roof of the building and drop out of sight. I quickly followed, through the ground-floor flat and into the street with my camera and tripod on my shoulder. Homing in on the chick's calls, I found it hiding under a parked car, but no sooner had I filmed it in this predicament, than it flew out and over the terraced buildings that lined the street, out of sight once more. I knew that there were a number of large plane trees in the back gardens of the houses, and guessed that these were where the chicks would end up, calling to be fed by their parents.

I was puffing and panting from the effort of carrying the kit up and down stairs and running down the street, when I rang the doorbell of the first house where I thought I might be able to get a view of the trees. No answer. I rang the next. The voice of what sounded like an elderly lady came over the intercom. 'Hello, yes, can I help you?'

'Hello, yes, I wonder if I might be able to come into your flat? I'm trying to film the tits,' came my breathless response.

There was a click, then silence.

I rushed to the next house and once again found a door bell with an intercom. 'Hello, my name is Simon. I wonder if I could please film the tits from your window?' I asked as politely as I could.

Another click. More silence.

The penny started to drop when the same thing happened a third time. Here I was in the city's red-light district, charging around with a camera in the most brazen fashion, looking for tits. This would take a rather more delicate approach.

I eventually found a flat block with public access to the stairwell and so to the doors of each flat. Identifying those which might have a view across to the trees, I knocked on several, before one opened a few centimetres. Across the top of a security chain peered the eyes of a very pretty – and very heavily made-up – young woman.

'Hello,' I began my revised speech. 'My name is Simon King. I'm filming for a wildlife programme, and I think the baby birds I've been watching could be in the trees behind your apartment. Would it be possible to come in and take a look from your window to see if they are there, please?'

The girl stared at me without changing her expression. 'What kind of birds are they, then?' she asked, her eyes narrowing a little.

'Umm. Urr. Well, they are great tits actually,' I stammered, fully expecting the door to be slammed in my face.

'Ha! No *way*! All right then. Come on in and take a look. No one could make that up!' came her reply as she unhitched the door chain and the door swung open.

'Thank you so much,' I spluttered gratefully. 'Which of your windows overlooks the trees?'

She pointed across the hallway with a long painted nail. 'The bedroom. It's just through there.'

Out of respect for her carpets I kicked off my shoes and carried the camera through to her bedroom. She joined me and leant with both hands on her windowsill.

'So, can you see your tits?' she asked with a cheeky smile.

I blushed at this point, suddenly acutely aware of the ludicrous situation I was in. 'Um, no, not yet. I wonder if I could open your window to listen for their calls?'

'Sure,' she answered, leaning forward to undo the latch and push the window open.

I cast a quick eye around the room. It was very neat, and very ornate, with chintz on the bedspread and faux gold bedside lamps. Shiny and scented, just like her.

I was brought back to the moment by the chattering call of a young great tit coming from the foliage of the tree some fifteen metres from her window.

'There they are!' I said excitedly. 'Thanks so much, this is brilliant!'

The girl looked a little crestfallen, and headed off for the kitchen, offering to make me a cup of tea.

I filmed brief snatches of the young family as the chicks hopped through the branches and the parent birds came and went with beak-loads of grubs for their now itinerant babies.

After some twenty minutes or so, and a very welcome cuppa later, the girl came into her bedroom and asked rather anxiously: 'Is this going to take much longer? It's just that my boyfriend will be back soon, and he may not be that happy to find you here.' She pointed at a photo- graph perched on her dressing table of a heavily built chap wearing thick gold chains around his neck and wrist.

'He gets very jealous,' she added, biting on the skin of her thumb and looking up at me from beneath her false eyelashes.

'Nearly done,' I said, feeling a little nervous suddenly myself and already trying to think of convincing ways to explain why I was in his girlfriend's bedroom with a camera. 'Actually, you know, I think I've got enough footage, thank you very much,' I said, hastily picking up my gear and heading for the door. 'You've been very kind.'

'You're welcome, any time,' the girl answered as she saw me out of the flat. The last I saw of her was her star- tling red fingernails, uncurling from the door jamb as she pushed it to a close.

Once back on the street, I was joined by a colleague

who had been rallied to record the sound of the birds as they moved through the neighbourhood. Together, armed with camera and large microphone, we trotted from one street to the next, following the chicks as they flew perilously amongst the traffic from the trees behind.

I became vaguely aware of a car, a very smart white Mercedes with tinted windows, driving slowly past us. The same car returned a few minutes later, coming from the opposite direction, this time even more slowly. Eventually it pulled up on the opposite side of the road.

'I think we're being watched,' I whispered to the sound man. 'That car has been following us.'

'Let's hide the gear!' he urged. This, of course, was impossible. You can't simply stuff a large film camera complete with telephoto lens and tripod down your shirt.

As we dithered, the rear passenger door of the Mercedes slowly swung open, and out of it stepped the legs of a well-pressed cream suit. The cream jacket set against a black shirt followed, and a tall gentleman, with dreadlocks, heavy gold jewellery and mirror shades, unfolded into the street. Confidently ignoring the traffic, he walked straight towards to us, arms loose by his sides.

I noticed a movement in the darkness of the car behind him. His friends were obviously keeping a close eye on the proceedings.

'Hello,' I beamed, doing my very best not to look guilty or intimidated.

'How ya doin', man?' he flashed with a startlingly white grin and a rich West Indian accent. He walked right up to me, into my personal space, and looked me in the eye.

'So, what y'all doin' round here wid dat camera and tings?' he asked, the smile suddenly evaporating.

'We make wildlife films and we're filming a family of birds that have just fledged,' I babbled nervously. 'There, you can hear one of them now.' I pointed in the direction of the shrill cheeping calls coming from a bush nearby.

'So, you not filmin' any of da people rond here, den? Dat would'n be a good ting to do, you follow?'

'No, no, just the birds. They're great tits, actually.' I couldn't believe I'd just said that. Here I was, almost certainly addressing one of the neighbourhood pimps, and he now knew I was looking for tits.

'Dat's great, man. I just love dem animal shows, wid da lions and da tigers an' stuff. You ever film any of dose lions?' His smile was back and he was warmly reaching to shake my hand.

'Well, no, not yet, but I hope to some day. Just great tits at the moment,' I answered with a grin as I took his hand.

'Excellent, man! You carry on. You won't get no trouble. Great tits, eh? Dat's fonny. Wait till I tell da boys. Great tits. Ha!' He turned with a flourish and sauntered back to his car, once again stopping the traffic without a glance.

The Great Great Tit Show went out a few weeks later, a compilation of all the events that had occurred over the weeks, distilled into a half-hour programme. It attracted a good audience: partly wildlife enthusiasts; partly, I'm certain, young men who were probably initially disappointed, but hopefully ultimately intrigued by the birds' dedication to family life.

Chapter 5

Return to Africa

Whilst I continued with projects for the BBC's Natural History Unit, I still worked with my father on at least one film a year. Together we had established a strand known as 'Animal Dramas', fictitious stories that nonetheless maintained factual integrity about their animal stars. From a trilogy of three films featuring a buzzard, a fox and a Dartmoor pony, we went on to produce one drama a year for a further twelve years, which were usually shown during the Christmas or New Year period. The story of Carna revolved around an orphaned otter cub that was later released to the wild.

In common with all of the 'Animal Dramas' I made, the production period was a little under one year, and so for the plot to cover several years of an otter's life, I had to work with a number of different animals that would appear in the starring role. Young Carna – or Flow as she was known to her carers – was a genuinely orphaned otter that had been brought into the care of the Hessilhead Wildlife Rescue Centre in Ayrshire, an extraordinary facility run by Gay and Andy Christie, who dedicated their lives to nurturing sick and injured wild animals back to health. Flow was a charming little character, and I spent hundreds of hours with her as she grew and developed ever-greater independence. By the time she was ten months old, she was spending most nights in a natural holt on the edge of a disused flooded quarry close to the rescue centre.

The lake had a population of fish – perch and eels mostly – that Flow chased and chewed with alacrity. Because she was so tolerant of human beings, I was able to swim alongside her, using scuba gear, and film her hunting in the shallows of the pool. One of the scenes I wanted to capture was that of an otter investigating a lobster trap. These simple creels, if set too shallow, can kill otters that unwittingly enter looking for an easy meal; like the crustaceans within, otters become bamboozled by the funnel entrance, drowning within minutes. It was a conservation point I wanted to make with dramatic impact.

To recreate the marine environment, I had large amounts of seaweed shipped in, a couple of tonnes of pebbles and sand and a huge plastic liner that I could submerge in the quarry pool and use to build the set. It took several days to get the scene to appear convincing, despite it only covering a few square metres of the shallows. Once the environment was looking close to the real thing, I prepared the lobster trap. I didn't want to risk Flow actually entering the trap for real, so had clear Perspex discs cut and secured to the entrances; invisible to the camera, but an effective barrier to an inquisitive otter.

On the day of filming, I spent the morning swimming alongside Flow as usual, fully kitted out in dry suit and scuba kit. She was as playful as ever, belting after her fishy prey with serpentine grace, and then returning to flaunt her prize in my face, pirouetting and tumbling in a stream of silver bubbles.

Once I felt she was in the mood for a game, I swam over to the marine set and waited with my camera trained on the lobster trap. Within a minute or so, Flow had joined me and, after a cursory investigation of my camera, which she had seen many times before, writhed amongst the seaweed in the set. Things were going well, and I was hopeful that soon she would nose into the trap, meet the wall of invisible Perspex and withdraw: action enough to make the point I wanted. Once Flow found the trap I was surprised by just how curious she was about this new object in her watery world. She clung to the netting sides with her forepaws, and nosed against the mesh. In no time she found one of the two entrances and stuck her head in it. The plan worked and she pulled back from the invisible barrier. Then, in a flash, she swung around to the second entrance, and I watched in horror as she pushed hard into the Perspex disc and, dislodging it, broke her way into the trap. I didn't think twice, dropping the camera, and lifting the trap from the lake bed. The water here was very shallow, and by standing up I was able to lift the trap, with Flow inside, clear of the surface. This clearly shocked and scared her, but there was no way I was going to risk her being trapped inside and getting short of breath. With my free hand, I undid the door of the lobster pot and the otter leapt back into the water and away from me, a stream of bubbles betraying her subaquatic path.

Both she and I were rattled, and I cursed myself for not making the barriers to the trap more secure, feeling it would be best to stop filming for the day and just spend some quiet time with Flow so that she would forgive me my stupid mistake.

Having removed my scuba gear, I waited by her holt, gently talking to her the whole time, and hoping I hadn't undone the months of work it had taken to win her trust. After half an hour or so, she popped her head out and blinked in the sunlight. So far, so good. Gingerly, she came up to my feet, then put her forepaws on my leg and sniffed me. Everything seemed fine. It was as though she had not had a fright at all, and certainly didn't associate me with the incident.

The following day, I decided to check Flow was comfortable with me before trying to film her, and this time wore my diving dry suit, the same as I'd been wearing when she had entered the trap. She had spent the night in her enclosure, a large open run in which she had dug several holes as sleeping quarters. I knelt down close to the burrow she was in, and chatted away to let her know I was there. Two button eyes blinked in the dark burrow entrance, and, a moment later, her broad muzzle and fluffy head poked out.

'Hello Flow, my lovely, did you have a good night?' I cooed in soft tones to put her at ease. 'Everything forgiven for the other day, is it? I promise I shall never do that again,' I said whilst reaching down to stroke her head. That was my mistake. I hadn't given her sufficient time to be comfortable with me dressed in the dry suit since the accident, and my reaching towards her must have reminded her of the splash and panic twenty-four hours earlier. In a lightning blur of brown fur, she lunged forward, bit onto my index finger, and immediately started to retreat back down her burrow, tugging on my digit. I quickly fell forward and tried to give her slack on my hand so that she wouldn't feel any resistance, but her progress down the burrow was fast, and in a few seconds I had my whole arm in the hole, my shoulder forced against the entrance and still she was pulling on the finger. I could feel her teeth grating against the bone, and images of a colleague, Terry Nutkins, who had lost one of his fingers to a bite from a tame otter, flashed through my mind.

I had been bitten many times by my foxes, and had long since learned to resist the urge to pull away, but with my arm in the hole, I had no option but to lie still, and hope that Flow released her grip. She didn't. I could feel her whole bodyweight tugging against my finger, her teeth slicing through the skin and sinew. Suddenly, she broke away. At first I thought she had taken the tip of my finger with her, but when I withdrew my hand I could see it was still there – just. I could also see the bone running from the last joint of the finger to the tip. She had sliced clean through the skin and popped off the end, leaving a deep gash in my fingertip. The attack was entirely my fault, and I felt very embarrassed that I had misjudged Flow's mood so gravely.

It took a couple of weeks for the swelling on my fingertip to subside, and with it the astonishing amount of pain for such a small injury. I had only felt numb during the incident, but in the days following, if I so much as tapped my fingertip against the camera or tripod, which I did the whole time, of course, it felt as though I was receiving a severe electric shock. To this day I have limited feeling in my right index finger, though disappointingly only the slightest of scars to show for such a painful encounter.

My swollen trigger finger made the process of filming a bit tricky for a week or so after that, but I managed to patch things up between Flow and me over the following days. I also had the time to chat with Gay and Andy Christie, the owners of the rescue centre, and hear some of their extraordinary tales about creatures they had cared for in the past. One of my favourites concerned a hand-reared magpie that was brought to them in a cardboard box. Its guardian had found it abandoned as a young chick and caringly nurtured it to adulthood. Unfortunately, it had become aggressive, and started attacking both its owner and other folk, and, so it was brought to Gay and Andy in search of a solution.

Magpies, in common with most of the crow family, are marvellous mimics. Their natural vocabulary includes all manner of squeaks and warbles they pick up from their immediate wild neighbours. This magpie had been exposed to a very different set of influences and was able to perfectly mimic the human phrases it heard most often.

With the box containing the errant magpie placed on the kitchen table, Andy reached inside to try and gently hold the bird and check it over to assess its condition. Feeling around inside the box, he skilfully found the magpie and took it in his grasp. Immediately, a very human screaming came from within.

'Aaaaaah! Aaaaaargh! Owwwwww. No, Nooooooo.

Aaaaargh!' These were clearly sounds the magpie had heard often during its attacks on hapless victims. Amused but unperturbed, Andy brought the bird into the light.

Still screaming, the magpie struggled to try and peck, bite or scratch the hand that gripped it firmly. Unable to get any purchase on Andy, it reached its foot forward as far as it was able and grabbed its own neck.

'Got you, you *bastard*!' the magpie yelled at the top of its voice. 'Got you, got you, Aaaaaaargh!!'

It was all Andy could do to keep his grip he was laughing so hard.

The magpie was later housed in an aviary, given space and care, and in time calmed down to become a friendly member of the rescue centre community. I imagine it learned to repeat some rather more demure human phrases too.

As well as working with Flow in the rescue centre, I spent several months filming wild otters for the Carna project. I chose to work in a spot on the west coast of Scotland, a beautiful estate with a very healthy population of otters that lived alongside sea eagles, wildcats and red deer. The animals were shy, but I slowly built up a reasonable knowledge of their habits and in time was able to follow them for hours on end as they foraged in the shallows along the shoreline.

During a midwinter filming trip, I spotted the otter family I had been following about a kilometre along the shoreline from my lookout point. A bitch with two well-grown cubs was fishing just off a headland that required a brisk run to reach it, and I decided to go for it before she finished her foraging and went back to her holt. I had the choice of cutting inland through an ancient oak wood, where I would lose sight of her; or, instead, negotiating the rocky shoreline and trying to keep her in view. I chose the latter, and set off in her direction at a brisk pace, complete with all my camera kit.

Many of the rocks sloped perilously down to the edge of the sea, and below the high-water mark they were slick with algae. I did my best to avoid the blackened, slippery slabs, but from time to time lost my footing and came down heavily on my knees, all the time trying to keep the camera from falling to the ground. After five minutes or so, I had closed the distance by some 500 metres and, whilst I took a breather, could see that the otter family was still hunting close to the headland. Eyes fixed on my subject, I set off again, careful to avoid the slippery lower section of the rocks. What I didn't take into account was the ice. It had been very cold the night before, perhaps ten degrees below freezing, and I had noticed that puddles of fresh water had frozen solid. I didn't think that the coastal rocks, covered by salt water twice a day, would be affected. I hit a sheet of black ice with my right foot, and came down hard on my right side. My camera and tripod, which I was carrying on my left shoulder, smashed down onto my left temple and knocked me out cold.

I have no idea how long I was there. Unconscious, I had slipped further down the rock to the sea, and when I woke, head bruised, scratched, and still sandwiched between the camera and freezing stone, the rising tide was lapping at my feet. At least my skull had softened the fall for my gear, which was all in good order. The otter, of course, was long gone.

It was during this period that Kim and I had decided to start a family, and in April 1986, aged twenty-three, I became the immensely proud father to my first child, a beautiful son, Alexander. I simply adored being a dad. I was of course naive, and I'm sure made many errors in fatherly practice, but Alexander, or Baggy, as we very quickly dubbed him (a fairly rapid and inexplicable evolution from Alex, to Alybagdad, and ending with Baggy, a name he keeps to this day for his nearest and dearest), was and is a constant source of deep joy. And so it was with enormous emotional turmoil that I had to make a very difficult decision that winter.

Alastair Fothergill, the chap with whom I had made *The Great Great Tit Show*, was a young, foppish Harrovian; he and I had instantly hit it off. Al was dynamic and full of enthusiastic energy, and I loved his unashamed passion for birds and his ability to enthuse people about the most commonplace creatures. Al and I had made other programmes together, including in 1985 *Bird Brain of Britain*, in which we set blue and great tits various challenges, and which had attracted an astonishing 13 million viewers. Now Al had been asked to produce a half-hour programme for *Wildlife on One*.

This series was the BBC Natural History Unit's flagship, a showcase of eclectic wildlife subjects from around the world, and Alastair, still as charismatic and full of energy as ever, had suggested a story about a little-known bird called a white-fronted bee-eater. They are striking to look at, with flashes of scarlet, black and white across their faces. But it was their extraordinary cooperative breeding behaviour that tickled Al, and, after one of his bouncing sales pitches, when he was asked by the series executive, 'Who are you going to get to shoot it?', to my eternal gratitude, Al suggested me.

'Isn't he – well – a little young?' came the response, which was curious since Al and I are not that far apart in years.

Al assured them that he felt I was up to the task, and once he had their blessing, he called me.

'Si, I'd love it if you'd work with me on my next film. It's about bee-eaters. We'd be based in East Africa for a bit . . .' I have no doubt Al said a great deal more, but my imagination had started to fly at mention of the location. East Africa, Kenya. My birthplace, and home to so many of my dreams. This was it. This was my opportunity to revisit the country that had always held a magic for me, and hopefully to prove myself as a fully fledged wildlife cameraman.

But there was a huge problem. The breeding season of the white-fronted bee-eater fell during the rainy season that spanned December and January. Through Christmas. My son's first Christmas.

I thanked Al profusely and asked him if I could have twenty-four hours to think it over, a request that he graciously understood, assuring me I could have longer if needs be.

84

Kim and I discussed the implications at length. Though she didn't relish the thought of my not being around at that time, she kindly assured me she would be able to cope and that, after all, Alexander wouldn't know a great deal about it given that he would be just eight months old. My internal struggle – weighing up the professional opportunity of a lifetime, against the personal significance of my son's first Christmas – ensured I had a sleepless night. But by early the next day, I had made up my mind. If I were to turn down this opportunity to travel to Kenya and make a film, I might be branded as unavailable, and a chance like this might not come around again. I would celebrate a belated Christmas with my family on my return. I would accept Alastair's offer.

One of the most powerful sensory experiences in my life was arriving back in Kenya after an absence of twenty-two years. To be more accurate, it was not the bustle of Jomo Kenyatta International Airport, or the drive from there to a hotel dayroom to freshen up, but the view as we drove from Nairobi – overlooking the Great Rift Valley – that caused a flood of emotion to surge through me. Whether I was overwhelmed by the fulfilment of a child-hood dream, or genuinely having my subconscious nudged by a myriad mnemonics – from the light, to the smells and sounds – I cannot say. What I can be certain of is that, perhaps for the first time in my life, I truly felt I had come home. My eyes relaxed to gaze at a horizon that was perhaps more than thirty kilometres away, across vast plains pocked by the mounts of long-dead volcanoes. We passed roadside vendors selling pork-pie hats made of sheepskin, the very same design as the ones I had played dressing up with as a child in the UK. I knew the bitter scent of those tanned-hide hats without having to stop and check. Other small kiosks offered hand-carved animals, which again I could have identified in the dark from their bitter-sweet sap smell. The odour of diesel fumes from the vehicle in front, mixed with the dust and occasional waft of mangoes or bananas, came crashing in to my subconscious like an awakening. I absolutely knew this place. I knew its rhythm, its sounds and its light. It was in me and I was very, very happy to be reacquainted with its three-dimensional, tangible form once more.

All this happened in relative silence, sitting next to Alastair, who was driving the rather shabby Renault 4 that we had rented for the production. I was mildly disappointed that we didn't have a strapping, forest-green Land Rover for the journey, but quite understood that where we would be filming, there would be little need for an off-road vehicle, and we had to keep the costs down.

We were to focus the production on a few colonies of bee-eaters that were the subject of a study by researchers from Cornell University. All the birds were marked with small plastic tags so that they were distinguishable as individuals in the field, and the study groups lived in an area around Nakuru, northwest of Nairobi. Alastair had managed to secure the rental of one of a handful of houses used by researchers within the boundary of the national park as our base for the eight or so weeks we would be in Kenya filming, and the thought that we were going to be living in the wilds excited me enormously. The drive was long, and over roads whose potholes could swallow our little car in its entirety, but I loved every minute of it. From time to time, we were flagged down at police roadblocks and asked to reveal the contents of the camera cases, then ushered on our way once it was clear we were unlikely to part with any of it.

Everything felt exotic and familiar at the same time, but it was not until we passed giraffes browsing on road-side acacia scrub, and at one point a dead zebra that had come to an undignified end as roadkill, that I truly felt as though we were in a relatively untamed part of the world. When at last we arrived at our house in the park, it was already dark but, with ears ringing from the constant drone of the car engine, I was still able to soak up the barrage of new, yet comforting sounds of the night. Crickets, frogs and distant birds proved emphatically that I had entered the tropics.

The following day, I lost no time in organising the camera gear and, once properly prepared, went to discuss with Alastair our immediate plans.

'Si, the colonies we're going to be working with are on farmland, a few miles outside the park, but before we get stuck in to working with them, let's have a bit of a look around here,' suggested Alastair.

I was delighted by the plan and bundled my film camera and tripod into the back of the car.

Driving on the dirt tracks through the park, we passed waterbucks and giraffes in profusion but, aside from some warthogs, not much else. No lions burst out of roadside bushes, no cheetahs streaked across the plains in front of us. I knew, of course, that the difference between the action highlights condensed into an average wildlife film, and what in fact occurs hour by hour, day by day in the natural world, are two very different things. Nonetheless, as we pulled up under the shade of a sprawling yellow acacia, I felt a small twinge of disappointment.

'How many lions are there in the park, Al?' I asked.

'None that I know of,' he replied. 'There was a very crabby old male, who used to attack cars, but I think they got rid of him. Just as well,' he observed, 'since this is where we get out.'

Alastair had visited Kenya before on one of his 'expeditions', as he liked to (and still does) call them. Compared to me he was an old hand and, as he stepped out of the car to help with the kit, I felt comfortable that he was across any dangers we might face.

He suggested we walk down a slope, too steep and treacherous for our little Renault to cope with, to a pool where he had been assured by the research team that the bee-eaters sometimes gathered to bathe and feed. Permission had been granted by the park authorities for us to go on foot, and there was nothing much to be concerned about. I packed a rucksack with spare batteries and film, humped the camera with telephoto lens and heavy tripod onto my shoulder, and followed Al down the slope. The pool was out of sight, over a kilometre away through long yellow grass and scrubby acacia, and, as Al strode ahead, I felt a tingle of anxiety. Even with no

Ten years old, with
Nipper the fox and
big hair.

Michael Kendall, Tia and I in *Man and Boy*.

Eighteen years old, going through my 'New Romantic' phase. Black toenails optional.

With my father, John, and my first Land Rover after its paint job.

Barn owl on the
Somerset levels.

Drift the mute swan.
She packed quite a punch.

Rannoch's softer side.

Filming a cobra in Sri Lanka for *Aliya the Asian Elephant*.

Bath time, for both Aliya and me.

Grey reef sharks, and me trying the Sir Lancelot look in the Bahamas. The chainmail on my head and arms was insurance against unexpected nips.

Filming close details of whooper swan flight with imprinted birds.

Defa and Papa the dingoes, watching me prepare a burrow to film them digging.

A beardy me trying to escape the heat with the dingoes.

With David Breed driving in the Masai Mara for *Big Cat Diary*.

Filming the Marsh Pride.

Notch – the main man.

Tamu the lioness, an outcast from the Marsh Pride and a superb mum.

homicidal lion lurking in the bushes, I knew that leopard, rhino and buffalo all roamed these plains, and puff adders and cobra surely lurked in the grass. It was disconcerting and exhilarating to be walking in an environment where I could not take for granted the idea that I was safe from attack from other living things, however remote the risk. Here, unarmed, I was most certainly not top dog.

As I considered these things, I noticed Al slowing down. I soon reached his side.

'Just there, up ahead,' he whispered. 'A couple of buffs. Not to worry, though,' he assured me. 'They'll soon clear off when they see us coming.'

My gaze cast across the shimmering grassland and settled on two dark hulks some 300 metres away, oblivious to our presence. I knew buffalo had a fearsome reputation and were responsible for many human injuries and deaths in Africa. I suspected, though, that most of these came as a result of people surprising lone bulls that, when suddenly confronted by their human nemesis, attacked as a means of defence. Here, the buffalo were in open country, as were we, and they would have plenty of time to see us coming.

Al and I strode forward and, to be certain the buffalo knew we were on our way, started calling to them to move on. I strained my eyes to try and read their body language in an attempt to predict an attack and, soon enough, two great horned heads rose up from their grazing to pinpoint the source of the oncoming ruckus. Al dropped behind a little as we closed the distance between the buffalo and ourselves but, rather than stop in the open with nowhere safe to run, I felt that the best course of action was to give off an air of confidence. To further encourage them to move aside, I started banging one of the metal tripod legs with a stick, a sound that would carry more clearly than a human voice.

In perfect synchrony, the two bulls started to walk, heads high, staring down their noses at us, but, rather than taking off in the opposite direction as we'd hoped, they began to pace towards us. By now I had developed tunnel vision, concentrating hard on the still distant buffalo and trying to predict their next move. I thought it wasn't so unusual that they might wish to see who was on their patch and, like a herd of inquisitive cows, they would surely take a few paces towards us before taking off at speed in the opposite direction.

That's when they started to gallop; great muscular flanks shuddering with every footfall, and tails held in a twisted knot of anxiety and aggression. Disturbingly, they still came straight towards us.

'What do you think we should do?' I hissed to Alastair, but there was no reply. My eyes were fixed on the thundering goliaths, which were covering the ground far more swiftly than their great frames might suggest they were capable of.

'Al, what now?' I asked again, this time with a lot more urgency. I turned to where I thought he would be, but he had disappeared. I swivelled on my heels, and saw him running up the slope, back in the direction of the car.

Ah.

Now what?

I considered my options. Quickly.

I could drop the gear and leg it, but by now the distance between the buffalo and me had closed to about a hundred metres, and it was very clear that in a flat sprint, they would definitely outpace me. I scanned around for the nearest tree; nothing higher than a couple of metres, and all covered in thorns longer than my fingers. I could now hear the thundering footfalls of the approaching bulls. I suddenly felt astonishingly clear headed and light on my feet, despite the burden of the camera gear. This, I supposed, is what a proper adrenalin rush does for you. I made my decision. Bashing the tripod legs together as hard as I could, I started to walk, then run towards the oncoming hulks. I'm not entirely certain of my reasoning, beyond some kind of misplaced sense of indignation that these animals were threatening to run me down. I heard a strangled, involuntary roar coming from my throat as I picked up the pace. With fifty metres to go, a flash of common sense hit me, suggesting that this, perhaps, was not the best course of action. But by now, I had no choice but to continue. I was able to see clearly the buffalos' eyes, and drool running from their mouths – or, at least, my well-fuelled imagination had fixed these images in my mind's eye.

With less than thirty metres' gap between us, the lead bull, then his companion, peeled off course and, without slowing, crashed off through the grass and scrub to be swallowed by the vegetation. Over my rasping breath, I could hear their progress as they bulldozed their way into cover and, from their point of view, safety.

So, this is Africa then, I thought. My fingertips tingled, my legs started to shake. And I was completely, profoundly happy. I had never felt more alive, or more in touch with the earth. What for some might have been a dreadful first encounter with the harsh realities of living alongside creatures that have the capacity to end your life, was, for me, a new beginning. I knew then that I was not only back where I had physically been born, but also that I had returned somehow to an ancestral link in my evolutionary chain. Whether this was attributable to some Jungian collective consciousness, or simply the endorphins charging around my body after the encounter, I knew that this place was a part of me, and I a part of it, and that I wanted it always to be so.

Chapter 6

Birds and Bees

Whilst the buffalo were a thrilling brush with raw, untamed nature, their close cousins – who were to be my near constant companions for the rest of the trip to Kenya – couldn't have been more domestic. The main nesting colonies of white-fronted bee-eaters were based on farmland that was predominantly used to graze dairy herds. Not only were these placid milk-producers anything but wild, they weren't even exotic. There might have been a hint of tropical colour had they been Zebu or Borana stock, but no, these were common-or-garden, pied-as-you-like Friesians. Were it not for the heat and unfamiliar bird calls, I could almost have been on a Devonshire hillside.

The bee-eaters dug their nest burrows into the sandy soil of seasonal watercourses on the farm, and these areas at least looked a little more untamed. By and large, though, my days were taken up with sitting in a hide looking at the nest holes of the birds, accompanied by the sound of lowing cows. Only when it was too dark to film, and all the birds had settled in their burrows for the night, could I venture out of the hide and return to our little house in the national park. I looked forward to these brief encounters with a wilder Kenya with increasing enthusiasm.

From time to time I spotted jackals crossing the track ahead, caught momentarily in the car headlights, and once a honey badger bounded along the dirt path, reluctant to give way to my little Renault. Given the badger's stubborn and fierce reputation, he probably had a reasonable chance of coming out on top if he decided to take me – and the car – on in a scrap.

Even with a limited twelve hours of daylight, every working day lasted well in excess of fifteen hours, and though I wanted to explore the park by night, I had neither the permission from the park nor the energy to do so.

After having worked to this regime for a couple of weeks, I returned to the house one evening and, after a quick supper of soup, I turned in for the night, completely exhausted. My room was large, and equipped with the bare minimum of furniture: a simple chest of drawers against one wall, a wardrobe against another, and the single bed – somewhat lost and lonely – near the centre. The door to the room opened on to a corridor, in which there was another door that led to the veranda. Apart from geckos, I had neither seen nor heard anything of the wild world that lived beyond the house, but imagined always that, once the sounds of human life within the four walls fell to a whisper, leopards and other night wanderers would begin to prowl in the shadows nearby. With these somewhat fanciful imaginings, I slumped into bed, hit the light, and before long had fallen into the deepest of slumbers.

I have no idea how long I had been unconscious when

I was wrenched from a coma-like sleep into adrenalin-fuelled wakefulness. Something had hit my bedroom door with enormous weight and power, and the explosion of splintering and cracking timber snatched me instantly to a heart-racing sweat. There was no moon, and the room was so inky black I couldn't even see my hand in front of my face, let alone what had burst in. Another shattering bang against the door was followed by a loud and guttural growl. The thump of my pulse in my ears meant I wasn't able to hear the soft shuffling footfalls I was certain were making their way across the polished cement of the bedroom floor towards me. I hardly dared move, lest I attract the invader to pounce all the more swiftly. As minutes passed, and no attack came, I was able to hear a coarse, rasping breath coming from the corner of the room. At least whatever was there was staying in one place for now.

I gingerly pulled the bed sheet from my face, and strained to make out any shapes in the darkness. I could just see the darker bulk of the chest of drawers and the wardrobe in the gloom, but no hunched form of a beast appeared from the direction of the breathing. For an achingly long minute or so I simply stared at the spot the noises were coming from. With still no sign of an invader, I swung my slightly wobbly legs over the edge of the bed and tiptoed across the room to the door. I allowed my hand to run across its timber and was amazed to find that it was intact. How could this be? Had I dreamed the splintering wood? If so, what on earth was now lying just beyond my door in the corridor, and how did it get there?

Whatever it was, the sounds it was making were definitely very, very real, though the growling and heavy breathing had reduced in volume. I thought of all the cheesy horror films I'd seen, where a terrified maiden tiptoes to the curtains and gingerly pulls them back to reveal the bloodshot eyes of a vampire or werewolf staring back at her through the window. It always annoyed me intensely that the maidens didn't just leave the curtains alone and curl up under the eiderdown, or, better still, go in the opposite direction, away from any suspected danger. Yet here I was, compelled to open my bedroom door to discover what horrors lay beyond. I began to understand the compulsion of the vampire victim.

Keeping one foot firmly planted on the floor a few centimetres behind the door, in a rather naive attempt to prevent any sudden charge from an animal bursting in, I slowly turned the handle and pulled it open a fraction. A dim light glowed down the corridor from the main living area where we left a single lamp illuminated overnight to guide the way to the loo. Once my eyes had adapted to the gloom, I could see that there was nothing in the corridor, but that the sounds seemed to be coming from the door that led to the veranda. This was less than a metre from my own bedroom door, and explained why, in my fear-enhanced and sudden awakening, I had thought the whole thing was going on in my room. Emboldened by the discovery, I quietly opened my door a bit further and reached for the light switch on the wall of the hall. The stinging yellow light revealed that the door had been hit hard by something very heavy from outside; its tongue-

and-groove timbers had imploded and splintered, though not given way entirely. I was certain this was no human invader, or, if it was, he or she was in a very bad way just the other side of the door, judging by the sounds I could hear.

There were no windows in the corridor overlooking the veranda; the nearest of those was in the living room just around the corner. Hastily covering up with a kikoi, I made my way to the living room to try and get a glimpse of the source of the drama. There I found Alastair, hopping from foot to foot in nothing but his boxers.

'Bloody hell, Si, I've never been so bloody scared in all my bloody life.'

'Me too,' I whispered. 'What the hell is it?'

'Come and look at this,' Al answered, and gestured for me to go into his room and look through the window onto the scene just outside.

No more than a metre the other side of the glass, its hindquarters pressed up against the shattered door, and lying on its haunches, was an adult bull waterbuck. Its mouth was agape, and beneath its belly I could see a large pool of fresh blood.

'I thought they were in my bloody room,' Al said.

'Me too! What the heck happened?' I asked him.

Alastair described what he had seen. 'They must have been scrapping. Two thumping great bulls. I woke up when this one must have copped it. Got rammed right against our door there. Sounded like a bloody gun going off! I just saw the other one trotting off into the darkness. Looks like this poor bugger's in pretty bad shape. Must have copped a horn right in the belly. I reckon he lost his footing on the cement floor.'

I felt vaguely embarrassed first, that I had thought my life had been in imminent danger and, second, that I hadn't been able to tell the difference between a distressed antelope, albeit a big one, and a big cat. I comforted myself with the knowledge that Al had been pretty shaken too.

'What are we going to do about him?' I said, pointing to the stricken buck. 'We can't just leave him there, can we?'

The rest of the small hours were spent with Al and me driving to the rangers' headquarters, trying to raise some help, and returning to the house with some rather disgruntled and bleary-eyed wardens. When we arrived, we all strode through the living room to reveal the scene of devastation just outside the window, only to find that the buck had disappeared. Sadly, the proof of his predicament was only too obvious, with the large pool of fresh blood still glistening on the veranda. We all assumed that he had hauled himself to his feet and limped off into the darkness, and the rangers assured us they would try to find him the following day. My guess is that a leopard or other night hunter would have beaten them to it, and we never did hear what became of him.

With my contact with really wild Africa limited to nocturnal doorstep dramas, I got my teeth into filming the bee-eaters by day on the farmland. Crucial to the story of the birds' cooperative breeding behaviour was to reveal the secret elements of their family life. Since they dug long burrows into steep sandy banks and laid their eggs in the gloom of a chamber at the end of them, the only way to get pictures of this was to dig a much larger chamber behind their nest, and, with painstaking care, expose a tiny section of the chamber. Then, with a small square of glass as a barrier between my filming chamber and the nest, I could introduce light and eventually film the hidden world of the birds. Much of the work was very physical, digging huge pits behind the colony in short bursts so as not to disturb the birds and, once these were large enough to take my entire body, adding a plywood roof with a trap door so that I could continue to work unseen. This next phase of the task was incredibly hot and filthy, working in near darkness through the middle of the day, at first with a small shovel and then, as I approached the back of the nest chambers, using a dessert spoon to carefully scrape away the earth. I had used the same technique in the past to film European kingfishers and bee-eaters in the nest, the latter being colonial nesters like the white-fronted.

Unlike their European cousins, however, these birds were very jumpy. This meant that I had to take the introduction of lights and cameras even more gradually and cautiously than usual, and it was weeks before I was finally able to film the first views of the rather grotesque, naked chicks being fed by the adults. This was the key to the story we were telling; the fact that it was not only the mother and father, but older siblings too that helped with the rearing of the new brood. This cooperative breeding was made graphically clear by the coloured tags that had been attached to the birds' backs by the research team, each of which bore a distinct pattern and colour and so identified otherwise identical individuals.

Though slow, the filming of bee-eater family life was going well. By contrast, we had a bit of a problem illustrating what we had assumed would be a very straightforward facet of their world: feeding. To be specific, bee-eaters, as their name so patently suggests, eat bees. Not exclusively, of course; they are partial to virtually any flying insect up to the size of a large dragonfly, but they have a knack for snatching honey bees in mid-flight, returning to the nearest perch and then, with a deft swipe or two of the beak, rubbing their victim against the branch and, in so doing, ridding it of its offensive sting. That's what the books said. That's what we wanted to film.

Hour after hour, day after day, I recorded our avian stars flitting from a low perch and grabbing flying bugs, only to return with some of the most exotic flies I had ever seen, but no bees. We could have relocated to a more bee-infested region and perhaps improved our chances of getting the sequence we wanted, but then the birds would have been unmarked and irrelevant to the story we were trying to tell. No, we wouldn't be happy with any old bee-eater catching bees, it had to be one of *our* bee-eaters. After over a week of bee-less filming, Al came up with a brilliant idea. He would bring the mountain to Muhammad or, to be more accurate and on a more modest scale, the bees to the bee-eaters. Once the area around our bird colony hosted a thriving bee population, surely our avian family would snaffle them up with alacrity?

Alastair contacted a local apiarist, who was more than happy to loan us an active hive. That bit, at least, was simple. Rather more tricky was how we would transport the bees from a farm, an hour's drive away, to the bird colony. Even if rendered semi-comatose by the beekeeper's smoke, the bees were still likely to be pretty aggressive once their treasured home, complete with cargo of honey and offspring, was shifted wholesale across the country. It was decided that Al and the beekeeper would together bring the hive to the location in our little Renault; but to ensure the men's safety, they would each be fully dressed in protective beekeepers' outfits.

So it was that a little white Renault 4 with a driver and passenger dressed like astronauts came to be flagged down at the police stop on the outskirts of Nakuru Town. It has to be said that these same police had given us quite a hard time up to this point. Every day we would pass through the police check. Every day they would flag us down and inspect for faults a vehicle they had seen twelve hours earlier. And every day they would find a problem and try to fine us for it. Both Al and I would get indignant about what we considered a fairly unashamed attempt to prise a bribe from us, and would state, calmly but insistently, that there was no problem with the car, that it was entirely legal and that the gentlemen involved were wasting their time. We were always waved on once it was clear we didn't plan to part with any cash.

On this occasion, however, the police probably had a reasonable point. Driving a car wearing a beekeeper's hood may not be expressly illegal, but it probably does constitute driving with restricted vision. The officer who flagged down the car he had seen every day for a month swaggered slowly and with obvious relish towards Alastair, who waited for the inevitable tap at the window and the request to open the door and step outside.

'Open the window,' demanded the officer.

'I canff offn da wnnnowwww fir, da vmmcle if fllll ov beeeeees' was the muffled reply from Al which, roughly translated, meant, 'I can't, the car is full of bees.'

'OPEN THE WINDOW,' insisted the policeman firmly.

Not wishing to incur the officer's wrath further, and risk a lengthy spell at the station dressed in very hot beekeepers' gear, Al decided to comply.

As Al slowly wound the window down to expose the first few centimetres of air, the bees were galvanised into an escape bid. A stream of very angry, very noisy insects poured out of the car, looking for the nearest victim upon which to wreak their revenge. Which was, of course, the officer. Never had a policeman so swiftly demanded that a window be wound back up and a vehicle move on.

The beehive having survived its adventurous journey to the nesting colony of bee-eaters, we set about filming a veritable bee feast. I had positioned my small canvas hide on a ridge above the site, overlooking a tangle of native trees and shrubs that would provide the birds with lots of suitable hunting perches. The hive had been deposited by Alastair and the beekeeper some twenty metres or so from my hide, just out of sight down the slope to my left. It was only a matter of time, surely, before the birds caught on to this new abundance and indulged in a sting-wiping, name-earning frenzy.

I waited, baking in the now sauna-like temperatures of the hide, for the birds to start plucking bees from the air and doing their thing in front of me, but although plenty of bee-eaters were flitting from the trees to snatch insects on the wing, they seemed to be concentrating on every bug in Africa apart from the bees. As dusk approached, it was clear our plan had not worked, and a careful observation of the hive the following morning revealed why. The bees, quite probably sulking after their recent move, had closed down shop. None was leaving the hive, so none was available for the birds to prey upon. On the third day of zero activity, Alastair decided that they might need a little encouragement.

As I adopted my usual post in the hide, just down the slope, out of sight from me, Al was about to execute his plan. Dressed in full protective gear, he aimed to remove one of the honeycombs from the hive, and shake the bees that clung to it into the air. This should start off a flow of traffic that in time would catch the birds' attention, leading to one or two insects being caught and consumed. It seemed like a good idea at the time.

The day had warmed to a sultry thirty degrees centigrade, and I had already stripped down to nothing but my shorts in the heat-trap of the canvas hide. My view of the outside world was restricted to what I could see through the narrow camera port, so the only way I could chart Al's progress was from the sounds he made. I heard him arrive in the car, the door close, and his footfalls coming up the leaf-littered slope towards the hive. A scraping of wood, some bumps and clunks and then a stillness. I waited, poised, for the first of the bee-snatching dramas to occur in front of me. Nothing. Then the sound of more clunking, wood against wood, and I figured Al was trying to liberate a few more bees. Still nothing. Perhaps ten minutes passed before I heard more wood scraping, followed by an almighty crash loud enough to make me jump. The brief stillness that followed this startling development was pierced by Alastair's voice.

'BLOODY HELLLLLLLL!' he screamed. 'BLOOOOOODY *HELLLLLL!!!!*'

I could discern his heavy footfalls as he ran down the slope back to the car, the door opening and closing hurriedly, and then the vehicle starting up and driving off.

I was very confused and a little nervous. What on earth had happened? Had Al been attacked by a buffalo that had somehow found its way out of the national park to mingle with its domestic brethren? Perhaps he had been assaulted by bee-nappers, who had dashed off with the hive and our car? I was contemplating getting out of my hide to see what was going on when I noticed an ominous droning sound; the approaching throb of a hundred thousand tiny wings. As the reality dawned of what was responsible for the sound, they were already upon me. Bees. Thousands and thousands of bees, launching an all-out assault on the hide.

It was like living in a scene from a Hitchcock movie, the light dimming as their bodies cloaked the tiny canvas tent in an attempt to vent their wrath. I could see their stings piercing the roof and walls all around me, and tiny drops of venom fell onto my naked arms and legs. The camera window was shrouded in green scrim netting, but this was not enough to prevent such a heavy swarm from entering the hide. One, then ten, then fifty bees joined me in the gloom of the interior, and my pulse began to race.

I had been stung by bees in the past and knew that a single shot of their venom was painful enough. I knew too that multiple stings could be fatal, even without an allergic reaction. To leave the hide now was to run into a certain barrage of many thousands of furious bees. It just was not an option. I remained perfectly still, more through lack of any alternative than a conscious strategy. Many of the insects landed on my naked skin, but – remarkably – none of them stung me. One or two perched on my face and started to wander close to my eyes. I carefully raised one hand and ushered, rather than brushed, them away. I was sweating heavily, as much through fear as the ambient temperature, and some of the bees busied themselves with the task of collecting the moisture from my body. I felt that this was a very reasonable compromise under the circumstances.

Gradually the fervour of the attack diminished, and the tempest of stinging insects peeled away from the exterior of the canvas. With their departure, I opened the netting in the camera port a little; the increased beacon of light encouraged those bees that had found their way inside to join their squadron, and leave too. After twenty minutes or so I was left with no more than a handful of rather sickly individuals, which had apparently lost their stings to the canvas and were to perish as a result. With no sign of Al, I settled back to the task in hand, and over the next couple of hours managed to film several of the bee-eaters, including a couple of the tagged individuals we had been following, snatching bees and expertly ridding them of their stings with a swift wipe along a branch. In a rather roundabout way, the plan had worked.

As evening brought a lemon light to the sky, Alastair drove back to the hide and came up the slope to help me with the gear. Hearing him approach, I undid the back flap of the canvas and popped my head out to greet him.

'Hi, Al. What on earth happened? And why are you still wearing your bee-keeper's kit?'

'Blimey, Si. Are you OK? That was pretty spooky, I can tell you. Have they all gone?' came his worried reply.

'What happened?' I asked him again, still completely baffled.

'I was trying to pull one of the combs out of the hive,' Al explained, 'just to liven things up, when the whole bally thing came crashing down on top of me. Next thing I knew I was completely covered in bees. They were pretty pissed off too,' he added glumly. 'I got stung about five times on my ankle – look.' With this Al lifted his white protective trouser to reveal a nastily swollen lower leg, peppered with red welts. 'They chased me all the way to the car, and followed me down the track. I thought I should try to lead them away.'

'They came back,' I told him with a wry smile. 'I don't know quite how, but I didn't get stung. The whole hide was covered in them.'

Enraged by their hive being tipped over, the swarm had been hellbent on attacking any foreign body in their vicinity. When the car had driven off, they had not been able to keep up, and so had turned their attention to the next large dark object in the area: my hide. I had read that bees tended to target the darker areas of their victims, which naturally tends to be the most sensitive and vulnerable spots, like eyes, ears and mouth. Those individuals that had entered the hide had probably been confused by the gloom that, fortunately for me, had suppressed their aggression, despite the miasma of aggro-inducing pheromone that must have been emanating from their pumped-up colleagues outside.

'I think I got a couple of foraging shots. I could definitely see the birds wiping off the stings,' I added. 'Do you think we should return the bees to their rightful owner now?'

'That sounds like a very good idea,' Al concurred with a nod of his netted head.

Christmas Day, 1986, was hard for me. I spent most of it crouched with my camera in a hot dusty hole filming the interior nest activity of one of our bee-eater families. Rather than take a break, I chose to keep my head down and work, reasoning that if I was unable to be with my baby son, Alex, and Kim, then I had better make the most of the time professionally. This was the first of many emotionally difficult choices I had to make, torn between the demands of my young family and my professional commitments, filming the wildlife of the world. I did my best to pick myself up during the day and appreciate my extraordinary good fortune in being able to work in such a wonderful country with exotic wildlife, but, despite my best efforts, I found myself sinking into a self-pitying gloom, shedding tears in the darkness of the earthen burrow.

In the evening I tried to phone home, but contact with the UK was limited to calls made from a land line in the researchers' HQ, where the connection was so poor we had to conduct conversations as you would a radio exchange, saying 'Over' at the end of a sentence to allow the other person to speak. The result was strained and dissatisfying for all of us. It would perhaps have been better not to speak at all, and depend instead on the more considered and thoughtful medium of letters, although these sometimes took weeks to reach their destination.

Once the 'festive' season was over, I perked up and reconnected with the thrill of being in Africa. I still spent most of the time on the farmland outside the park, but I did manage one or two visits to the banks of Lake Nakuru. From a distance, the shallows and soda-encrusted shoreline appeared to be tinted with pink paint but, as I got closer, the roseate shores manifested themselves as thousands upon thousands of flamingos. The spectacle had been described as one of the seven natural wonders of the world, and, with a low evening sun, and the air echoing to their guttural croaks and the yelping calls of fish eagles, I could see and hear why.

By the end of the two months' filming I was quite ready to go back to the UK, though. I had lost about five kilos in weight, was utterly exhausted and very happy to return to my baby son and Kim. But, despite the pain of being away from loved ones, I was very happy, too, to have completed a project in East Africa with a degree of success. I hoped that this would lead to me being trusted to work on other projects with wildlife abroad, so that I could continue a life of adventure and discovery.

Chapter 7

Painted Wolves

My next trip to Kenya was to film African hunting dogs –
or 'painted wolves', as they are also known – for part of
the David Attenborough *Life* series. *The Trials of Life*
concentrated on behavioural themes shared by most animals,
from mating to raising a family and finding a meal.

David and the producer of the episode called 'Talking
to Strangers' wanted to feature a story that had only recently
come to light through an extensive study of the dogs and
Thomson's gazelles in the Serengeti National Park. If a
pack of hunting dogs appeared on the plains, virtually
every mammal bigger than a mouse would break into a
blind panic and take off at speed in the opposite direction. You might think that getting as big a distance as
possible between themselves and their nemesis would be
the priority, but the researchers noticed that some gazelles
'stotted' rather than galloped away. Stotting is a stiff-legged,
bouncing gait where all four feet of the gazelle leave the
ground at the same time. It is very eye-catching and a clear
visual signal, but a significantly slower way of getting
around than a flat run. Just what the gazelles were 'saying'
by stotting was the question, and the research showed that
it was likely the gazelles were making a statement about

their level of fitness. 'Look at me! If I can bounce this high on all four feet at the same time, just imagine what I could do if I really wanted to get away!' It was suggested that the dogs could read this 'language' and target the less proficient stotters.

So, no Friesian cows for me this time; no long hours spent in hot, dusty holes in the ground. This was my first taste of what was to become a way of life for me for part of almost every year thereafter: following the great predators of Africa around the savannah in a four-wheel-drive vehicle and documenting their dramas and their charisma on film or tape.

The four-wheel drive on this occasion was a modest Suzuki; about the size of a Mini, but nippy and great for negotiating areas of rocks. I worked with a wonderful chap called Paul Kibochi (sadly, Paul was killed some years later by a charging elephant). His ready smile and exhaustive knowledge of the Masai Mara and its wild inhabitants were a joy and inspiration to be around. Paul drove the car whilst I filmed from a purpose-built mount welded to the roof, or another that was bolted to the passenger side of the car in place of the door.

Once I had settled in to the camp by the Mara River and prepared the cameras ready for filming, Paul drove me into the reserve for the first time for a quick evening's game viewing. We passed vast herds of wildebeest, zebra and gazelle, most of which barely lifted their heads as we drove by. I had never seen such an astonishing profusion of large wild animals, and was thrilled by the spectacle, but tried not to show it. I fatuously thought that if Paul realised just how inexperienced I was, he might not take what it was I was trying to do with the filming of the dogs seriously enough. After half an hour or so of driving, Paul turned to me grinning and said, 'Ha, over there, Simba. Want to see some lions?'

'That would be great, Paul, thank you,' I answered. I kept up the façade of casual interest rather than reveal the bubble of overwhelming excitement that was building in my chest.

This was to be the first time I had come into contact with lions in the wild, and it was one of my childhood ambitions realised. The closest I had come to this was my trips as a kid to Longleat Safari Park and Bristol Zoo. I had been captivated by the great cats then, but always felt a little uncomfortable staring at them through bars or a car window, whilst they stared back, through and beyond me, into the middle distance of excruciating boredom, or perhaps towards an ancestral memory of an imaginary horizon broken by flat-topped acacia trees and processions of wildebeest and zebra.

Paul drove towards a small cluster of tourist vehicles that had half encircled the lions and were shielding them from our view. It wasn't until we drove past the last car that I realised just how close we were to the cats.

The pride had killed a zebra very recently, and were tucking in to their supper no more than twenty metres away (a distance I now know is closer than park regulations allow, but which is rarely enforced). Before I knew it, I was below the eye-level of the nearest lioness, who was standing off from the kill, with nothing between us but the camera door, which was just a plank of plywood that came midway up the opening. The rest of the females, an adult male and a gaggle of cubs of different ages were locked in a tangle of claws, teeth and shoulder blades around the carcass, and the scene was accompanied by a rhythmic bass, grunting growl coming from a couple of the females who were arguing over the same choice cut. The lioness closest to me started to move in towards the fray, and I noticed at least one of the others lifting her head slightly and glaring with an intensity and menace that oozed aggression. The lone female took another step that elicited a deep, chest-rattling growl from her rival at the kill.

I became sucked in to this primeval scene, lost in the raw, visceral power of it all, when suddenly it exploded. The growling lioness launched an attack on the newcomer, charging in the direction of the car with a terrifying utterance so mighty I could feel it reverberating in my own chest. As she sprang forward, I felt myself involuntarily springing in the opposite direction, halfway across the car and almost into Paul's lap. I was to discover that the scuffle between the lionesses was pretty standard as far as table manners go in leonine society. But a wildlife cameraman jumping into the lap of his assistant was not. For a moment I thought I might just have got away with hiding my shock and fear of the moment, but one glance at Paul revealed I hadn't; he was sporting the biggest grin, which soon broke into an all-out giggle, suggesting that he might just have seen through my bluff.

'Phew. That made me jump!' I said unnecessarily, trying to sidle back into my own seat with a minimum of fuss.

'Don't worry,' chuckled Paul 'They don't want to eat a *mzungu* [white man], just their zebra!'

The incident with the feeding lions taught me that if I didn't know much about a subject, I should not try to hide the fact; instead I should try to glean as much information as I could from those about me who had a far greater knowledge than I did.

Paul had watched hunting dogs on many occasions, and assured me that for most of the day they would sleep, hunting from first light until soon after sunrise, and again at dusk if they were still hungry. To satisfy my own curiosity, we spent the first few days watching the snoozing pack from a distance, but I soon realised that it was a pretty safe bet that they would follow the activity pattern described by Paul. When they did get up and go, the atmosphere was charged with their charisma and power as a hunting unit with a singular objective: securing enough meat to feed the pack. And with over forty dogs to satisfy, that was a lot of meat.

Two of the adult dogs in the pack had been radio-collared by the research team, and with the help of these collars we tried to find them before first light each morning. Despite the telemetry, this was no simple task, since the dogs sometimes travelled over twenty kilometres overnight; the further away they were, the weaker the signal from their collars. Knowing where to start looking for them in the darkness and chill of pre-dawn Africa was more of a lottery than a science. Sometimes we only picked up a signal long after sunrise and would find the pack replete from a morning's foraging, while we had driven for hours to try and track them down. There were days when we didn't find them at all, and it soon became clear that filming them hunting was not going to be easy.

About two weeks into the trip, we followed the research team out of camp at four thirty in the morning as usual and, after no more than thirty minutes, were excitedly informed that they had picked up a strong signal from an area of open plains just outside the reserve. We found the dogs huddled in a patch of rock-strewn grassland, still dozing and blinking in the lights of our cars.

I prepared the camera kit and waited for the cue that they were going to head off for a meal, which always took the form of a pre-hunt ritual known as a 'twitter'. One of the more dominant dogs would rise from its slumber and wander to a colleague. A little face-licking ensued, an act that was clearly infectious, rippling through the pack so that, within a minute or so, all the dogs were up, sniffing, tails wagging and licking each other. A few minutes more, as first light revealed a stencil-sharp eastern horizon, the whole pack broke into the twitter. This term perfectly describes the social frenzy that the dogs indulged in just before they headed off to hunt: jumping over each other, twisting on the spot, tail-wagging and much face-licking were all accompanied by a rising crescendo of high-pitched whining and whistling calls, making them sound more like a bunch of squeaky toys than one of the most efficient killing machines on the face of the planet. Once this display had peaked, the lead dogs suddenly broke off and trotted with intent across the plains, followed by the rest.

If their voices were not menacing, their dark forms appearing over a rise in a united front most certainly were. Lions, cheetahs and leopards are almost always mobbed when they are spotted by their prey species. When creatures that may feature on the menu of the great cats see their enemies, they turn to face them, and snort in defiant alarm. They may even approach to within remarkably close range of the cats, so confident are they of being able to escape them, so long as they have them in view.

Not so with the dogs. A range of creatures, from wildebeest and zebra to impala and other antelopes, flee the moment they see the wall of dark force approach, and from a distance this gives the impression of a wave of life parting. Though the dogs might look like a relatively unassuming gang of mutts, their prey species know a thing or two. Once the dogs pick their target, they are relentless, running at a steady pace of about forty kilometres an hour with astonishing stamina. No matter where their quarry goes, which way it turns, it is pursued, and in the final stages of the hunt, its escape is often cut off by other members of the pack as they converge on the exhausted victim.

I had witnessed the early stages of this drama a few times already, and every time I had been unable to film the climax of the hunt. Either it had occurred just over a rise, out of view, or else been too far ahead of our vehicle to see until the dogs had already finished the meal. This morning, Paul and I planned to try and keep ahead of the action, by second-guessing the dogs and moving 500 metres or more ahead along their path to catch them coming into view. Nice plan. Much easier said than done. The dogs change their course in an instant depending on the evasive action of their quarry, and frequently chase their prey into rough ground that is impossible to access with a tank, let alone a little four-by-four.

Today, they started in at a trot towards a herd of fleeing gazelle, and then the lead dog broke into a run. Paul was off, foot to the floor, making a wide, arcing loop ahead of the running animals to get me into position to film the oncoming pursuit. I was standing on the back seat of the car, exposed to the elements from the waist up, clutching the tripod head with one hand, the rim of the roof hatch with the other. My face was being hit at speed by low-flying bugs and I felt a flash of sympathy as I shared the punishment received by your average car windscreen. The camera was nestled at my feet on the back seat of the car, padded by a couple of pillows to soften some of the worst blows dealt by the bumps and rocks we hit.

Paul turned the car through forty-five degrees and switched off the engine.

'Get your camera ready, they're coming,' he beamed. He clearly enjoyed a spot of rally driving.

No sooner had I set up the camera on the roof mount than they came into view. First the gazelles, four or five females and an adult male. All had long since given up any idea of showing off their fitness level by stotting, and instead were in a flat gallop, mouths agape, eyes wide. Close behind them came the dogs. A mob of five dogs had splintered from the main pack to chase this herd, and the gap between predator and prey was closing. They did not appear to be travelling at great speed, but as the first of them came past the car, the heavy thudding of its paws on the dry earth and the intensity of its mission made clear that it had in mind an early breakfast. In seconds the whole circus had thundered past us, and the moment I looked down at Paul he started the car and was off again at a blistering rate.

Once again we drove well wide of the animals, attempting to get ahead of the action whilst at the same time ensuring that we had no effect on its outcome. Since I was half out of the vehicle, I have no idea of the speed we were doing, but judging by the squashed bugs on my forehead, it was quite quick. As I looked to my left I could just make out the lead dog closing in fast on the male gazelle, which had started to run in zigzags, a sure sign it was tiring and that it was just moments before the group of dogs would close their trap. Paul pulled the car round to the left, and made a beeline for the action, which was still 400 metres or so away.

My eyes were fixed on the commotion ahead when there was an almighty crunching sound from beneath the car, accompanied by a shudder and a sense of weightlessness. I knew this was not good, but hadn't the time to work out that the rock we had hit had sent us skyward. The brief flying sensation was abruptly terminated with a near dead stop as we hit the ground, the front right wheel burying deep into a warthog burrow.

I had been involved in a couple of car accidents in the

past, which had fortunately not resulted in serious injuries to anyone. In the past, however, I had been strapped in with a seat belt. This was an altogether different experience. My legs were thrown forward so that both feet flicked up to kick the inside of the car just above the windscreen. The top half of my body was thrown forward and down so that my nose hit the roof on the outside. Fortunately, I managed to bring my arm forward to protect my head from the bare metal bars of the camera mount. In effect, I was the bread around a car-roof sandwich. After a moment of remarkable flexibility, I was lurched back into the rear passenger seat of the car, staring through the windscreen at the distant dogs that by now had caught up with their meal and were making short work of consuming it.

'Are you OK, Paul?' I asked, looking at his shoulders hunched over the wheel. He turned to reveal his familiar grin.

'Sorry for that. Aih, aih aih! That is a biiiig hole!' he answered. 'What's wrong with your nose?'

A minor nosebleed and some very attractive shades of blue and purple along my stomach and arms were all I had to show for the incident. But I had most definitely learned to sit in a more secure position once we were in the heat of a pursuit.

Over the following month I did manage to film the dogs taking one or two gazelles, and, more importantly, the gazelles stotting their socks off when they spotted the dogs on the horizon. With the sequence reasonably secure, and just days before we had to leave the Mara, things took a very unpleasant turn.

One morning we discovered a lone dog, calling soulfully for the rest of his pack, who were nowhere to be seen. It was not unusual for members of the gang to become separated during a hunt and to relocate their clan by 'whoo' calling – a soft-toned, yet far-carrying contact hoot. This was different, though. It was still very early in the day and unlikely that the dogs had hunted yet. And something about this dog looked wrong. As we watched, it started to bite at the grass and soil, before looking very lost, with sunken eyes staring into the darkness. These were the precursor signs of a terrible blight that was to affect the whole pack. Rabies.

Being such social creatures, with regular mouth-to-mouth contact, it was inevitable that if one dog had been exposed to this incurable disease then it was just a matter of time before the whole pack would be struck down. Hugh Miles, my friend and mentor, was arriving in the Mara to continue filming the pack for another project just a few days after I had to leave. It was his sad task to record the dying days of the last resident pack of hunting dogs to roam the plains of the Mara. All forty-two of the dogs died over the course of the following month, and to the date of my writing this, no pack has returned to spread their awesome black menace across the plains.

The savage splendour of East Africa was now well and truly embedded in my being. My vague infant memories had by now crystallised into a very real and unwavering passion for the place, its people and, of course, the wildlife. Leaving the Mara was an almost physical wrench, but the promise of time with my partner and young son was building a bubble of anticipation and joy in me as I took the night flight back home.

We had moved to a house in the heart of the Somerset Levels, a place where the skies were of a scale to rival those in Africa, and with wildlife which, though more subtle than the great herds and predators of the Mara, had a modest and delicate charm of its own. My love of watching and working with British wild animals was undiminished and, to that end, my father and I had started work on another of the 'Animal Drama' series of films. This time, we were showcasing one of the most familiar and accessible of birds, the mute swan, and the location for much of the film was my own doorstep. Literally.

Our house lay along the banks of a small river that lazily wound its course through the flatlands of the moors. Soon after we moved in, we noticed a rather curious male mute swan that would watch the house from the safety of the water. Keen to get to know the locals, I started spreading grain across the lawn and, within days, he was clambering up the bank to feed just outside the dining-room window. After a week or so, he introduced his mate to the ready food source, the two of them making a somewhat grand contrast to the blue and great tits that fed on peanuts hanging just above their heads on the bird table – the nation's biggest birds alongside some of the smallest.

Drift the Mute Swan, as the film was to be titled, followed the fortunes of an adult female raising her family in the heart of the Levels. A key facet of the storyline would hinge on the development of the chicks up to the point they learned to fly, so spending a lot of time at nest sites would be imperative. Unfortunately, my graceful neighbours chose to nest in a site that was not particularly picturesque, and so I looked a little further afield for the perfect location. I found two active nests within a couple of miles of the house and began working with both. One was accessible from a land bridge, but the second – and most attractive – could only be reached using a boat.

It was at this latter nest that I wanted to reveal life from the chicks' point of view, especially at the point they were hatching, and with this in mind had purchased a newly developed piece of kit called an angle-scope. It allowed me to attach a wide-angle lens at ninety degrees to the camera on the end of a series of tubes. This gave me the facility to poke the lens through the hide and about half a metre outside, looking straight up at the sky, or, as I hoped, at the belly of the sitting swan. My plan was to get the adult swans so used to the hide that they would tolerate it sitting on the rim of their nest platform. I would then carefully work the lens into position through the nest material so that it rested amongst the brood. When the magic day for hatching came, I would be able to record a unique view of the proceedings without disturbing the adults in any way.

I took the hide introduction very carefully, despite the robust nature of the birds. Actually, they never did more than half raise themselves from the clutch to threaten me with a hiss and wings held up over their backs like sails in the wind. However, the display was impressive enough to jog memories of what I took to be the mythical might of an angry swan, which, as many will know, is reputed to have enough punching power to break a man's arm. Just how it was supposed to achieve this feat of strength and agility I never knew, but quite apart from not wishing to upset the birds, the reputation gave me an added incentive to ensure that they remained relatively calm in my presence. The moment I settled the hide into a new position, they nestled back onto their nest with much fiddling and rolling of the eggs using their bills.

After a little over a week, the hide was in position, and I had already introduced the lens into the nest without causing the least bit of disturbance. The view was extraordinary. When the female sat tight on her clutch it was, of course, inky black; not a chink of light permeated the toasty enclave of her breast feathers. But when she lifted up to roll her eggs, I was treated to a view of her reaching down into the lens as though the camera itself were part of the clutch. This was precisely the view I hoped would add a new and exciting dimension to the day the chicks hatched.

Although I knew when each of the eggs had been laid, I still had to start a relentless vigil from the hide from the earliest possible day of emergence. From first light, day after day, I waited, camera ready and in position, for a little chip in the calcium armour that would herald the cygnets' struggle into the world. On the fourth morning, my persistence was rewarded. As I reached the hide, the female bird lifted up to challenge me and I could clearly see that one of the eggs had a small but detectable hole in the shell.

I quickly entered the canvas tent and settled the camera into position. I do my best to keep the sense of personal excitement under control when I'm filming – unchecked, it tends to lead to shaky hands that do nothing for the quality of the camera work; but having put so much energy in to this venture, the adrenalin was starting to work its way through my system. What would I see? Would the female lift up from the eggs during the hatching, or would she sit tight, making the whole exercise fruitless from the filming point of view?

I need not have worried. After twenty minutes or so, she rose to inspect her emerging family, gently reposi-tioning each egg, and staring down into the lens of the camera. It was the perfect opportunity for me to film the early stages of hatching, and I gently started to move the camera a little in order to adjust the framing to accom-modate the mother towering above her brood. I was not aware of the fact that my head was pushing up against the canvas at the base of the hide, creating a small, slowly moving bulge close to the feet of the mother swan. She shifted again, lifting her head a little higher and I changed my position once more to better the view. I did notice her rising up a little further than usual – and then I received the blow. It came like a hammer through the canvas wall, straight into my right temple, knocking me to the floor. I was vaguely aware that she was shuffling back down onto her nest before I lost consciousness.

I awoke, a minute or so later, with a thumping pain in my head and an egg of a bruise swelling nicely on my temple that would not have looked out of place in a Tom and Jerry cartoon. I slowly pulled myself to the eyepiece of the camera and stared down it. The blackout confirmed that the female swan was back brooding her clutch, just as she should be. Still a little dazed, I realised that she must have seen the bump made by my head on the canvas as I tried to film and decided that it needed discouraging, using the best method she knew how; by using all her might to hit it with the carpal joint of her wing. I now had first-hand – or, to be more accurate, first-head – knowledge of just how powerful a blow from the wing of a swan could be. And, under the right circumstances, it quite probably could break your arm.

I spent the rest of the day feeling a little sore, but thrilled by the revelation of the new family and the close care and attendance displayed by the parent birds. At about midday, the male swan came up to the nest to inspect the results of this year's labour, grunting softly to his mate and brood. Given that he was even bigger and more powerful than his partner, I was very careful indeed to ensure no part of me pushed against the hide's wall.

Working close to home was wonderful in many ways, challenging in others. Being 'on location' the whole time meant that any day the weather was fair I felt I ought to be out filming, regardless of it being a weekend or not, and I was constantly torn between work and spending time with my growing family. My first daughter, Romy, was born in the early May of 1989. Her beautiful, sanguine and gentle demeanour perfectly complemented her blue eyes and golden hair: a real-life angel. The greatest challenge in my life: that of balancing my commitment as a father with my passion for the wild places on earth was now even more difficult. The juggling act of trying to reconcile both was a near constant concern for me. I considered starting a new career; I flirted with the idea of buying some nearby lakes and managing them as day-ticket coarse-fishing venues, or perhaps starting a wildlife film-making school, but the travel bug was deep in my core and the drive to get back to my birthplace still nagged at me.

I was well aware that my career as a wildlife film-maker would probably stagnate if I restricted the subjects I filmed to within a ten-mile radius of my Somerset home, and I knew that if I were to continue to grow professionally, I would have to take on more overseas assignments.

Before long I was planning my next trip to Kenya, this time to film some of the very creatures that had captured my imagination so completely as a kid. Having proved that I was at least able to negotiate customs and immigration in East Africa, I managed to convince the commissioning editors at the BBC that the next 'Animal Drama' should showcase lions, and to achieve this I would be spending at least three months of the year back in the Masai Mara.

Chapter 8

Meeting the Marsh Pride

The build-up to the first trip for the production of *Kali the Lion* was full on. It was the first time I had set up a shoot of this scale, and I arrived in Nairobi utterly exhausted in the early morning after a night of little sleep, having been forced into the foetal position of an economy seat for nine hours. Amongst the throng in the arrivals hall, I spotted the dimpled grin of David Breed.

David was a young but very experienced and talented stills photographer and guide, born and raised in Kenya, and it was with him that I would be working throughout the project. Dave was to be my guide and driver, having converted his old Toyota four-by-four into a film-friendly vehicle, with custom-built camera doors and roof mounts. His knowledge of the Mara, and of the big cats in particular, was remarkably deep, having worked as a guide for camps and other film projects in the past. Together, we made the dusty journey from town to the bush; a seven-hour run that was fraught with hazards, most of which came in the form of lorries thundering towards us on the wrong side of the road.

We reached the camp in the Mara just on last light, to discover that the tents that were supposed to have been allocated to us had been occupied by tourists, and that we would not be able to move into them for a couple of days. I was beyond tired, and a more than a little annoyed that our booking, made months before, had been so casually ignored, but was assured by the camp manager that we would be housed very comfortably in his own quarters, whilst he would move into other staff accommodation until our tents were ready.

With aching limbs, and dry, stinging eyes, Dave and I plodded to the small thatched stone hut that was to be our home for the next couple of days. Once inside, we were relieved to see that the beds looked clean and comfy and that warm water ran from the taps in the bathroom. After showering and bolting down a light supper, we retired to our respective single beds on opposite sides of the hut and collapsed.

With the lights out, I was at last able to reflect on my astonishing good luck at once again finding myself about to embark on six weeks following some of the greatest predators on earth. I had been so busy in the days leading up to departure, and depressed at leaving my young family, that it had been difficult to find the headspace to fully appreciate my fortune at being able to indulge my passion.

The wave of wellbeing that was flooding through me was given a further boost by the sound of distant thunder. An African storm was approaching; dramatic, innocently violent and utterly beautiful, like so much in this great land. The first heavy drops of rain started to fall onto the grass roof of our hut, and I allowed my exhaustion to sink into the sounds of the night, sleep creeping into my every fibre. Just as I was dozing off, I felt a fine mist of moisture on my face and bare arms. This was what it was all about: the atomised spray from the rainfall outside was finding its way through the thatch and softly coating my body. It was warm, very faint, and felt like an embrace; a gentle welcome from the skies.

I breathed in deeply, the better to appreciate the scent of the dust in the rain, and was jerked out of my reverie by a sudden and overwhelming smell of ammonia. My eyes snapped open, but I could see nothing in the darkness of the hut. I was vaguely aware that I must have been dreaming, since there was no sound of rain on the roof, but, inexplicably, there was most definitely a fine, strong-smelling drizzle falling on my face. I fumbled for my torch by the side of the bed and shone it into the rafters. Directly overhead, hanging upside down from the inside of the grass roof, were hundreds of small brown bats. Disturbed by the torchlight, they began to pour from their temporary roost and out of a small gap in the roof. I realised with some discomfort that I must have imagined the approaching storm in my sleep, and this construct had creatively explained the shower of bat urine and droppings that now coated me. Dave stirred on the other side of the room.

'What's going on, Si?' he mumbled.

'I'm covered in pee,' I answered, then, thinking I ought to explain further, 'bat pee. There are hundreds of the little blighters over my bed.'

A sound that I thought at first was sobbing, but then very obviously became uncontrolled laughter, came from the darkness. After a moment's indignation, I joined in, and soon both Dave and I were curled double in opposite corners of the hut with an exhaustion-fuelled, eye-watering fit of the giggles. Dave's bed had thankfully been spared the golden shower treatment, and I ruefully suggested that his must be the spot where the manager normally slept. I dragged my bed across the floor in a bid to avoid a further soaking, scrubbed the worst of the mess from my face and arms and once again slumped into the deepest of sleeps.

The next day, Dave and I drove into the reserve to search for the nearest pride of lions to the camp, affectionately known as the Bila Shaka (meaning 'without doubt', in reference to the ease with which they were generally found) or the Marsh pride by many of the driver guides. They were not physically different from any other lion – no webbed feet or snorkels – but in the heart of their territory lay the Musiara Marsh, an area of water that remained throughout the dry season, attracting animals from far and wide in search of a drink. This made it a productive hunting ground for the cats all year round.

One lioness in the clan caught my attention right away, a female that was somewhat ostracised by the rest of the pride, but which still seemed to be very much in favour with the pride male. Within an hour or so of meeting her, she had snarled at the car twice and made a sudden mock charge at us, earning her the name Kali, which means 'fierce' in Swahili.

Our routine from that day on was based around the hours of daylight and the activity cycle of the cats. I knew of the lions' reputed capacity for sleep, and this was borne out by the incredible number of hours the great felines could invest in their slumber. On some days it seemed they did little else, having hunted successfully through the night and wisely saving their energy through the heat of the day. If we were lucky, we found them at first light returning from a successful hunting trip on the plains to the heart of their territory. From time to time they would collect around the car and, as the heat of the sun started to make them uncomfortable, seek the nearest shade. More often than not, we were it. The car provided a cramped sanctuary for the large cubs and some of the females trying to escape the direct rays, and we sometimes ended up with ten or more lions vying for a place beneath our vehicle. They often argued over the best, coolest spots, and there was much clanging of heads against steel and thumping of bottoms against the running boards of the truck. This was all very amusing, up to the point when one of the cubs decided to chew through the brake pipes and Dave had a humorectomy. From then on, the moment it looked as if they were going to shuffle under our car for shade, we drove away in the opposite direction.

Bit by bit, I learned to read the cats' body language and subtleties of behaviour that would help me predict a potential fight or hunt. I soon learned that I could not afford to look away, regardless of how comatose they appeared. A distant crack of a twig made by a clumsy warthog would snap Kali and the other females into action; pulling themselves slowly from the prone position into a tense crouch, all focused eyes and ears. Some hunts developed from nothing and were over within minutes. I had to be ready the whole time to react with the camera.

We were generally well looked after at camp, once we were established in our own tents, but from time to time my delicate Western stomach suffered from an introduction of new and exotic bacteria. These bouts only lasted a few days at a time, but were very inconvenient when sitting in a car for fourteen hours at a stretch. I did my best to hold on for as long as possible, but there were simply some moments when I had to visit the bushes. Quickly.

On one such occasion, Dave drove some five or six hundred metres away from the pride, out of sight of the cats over a small rise, and close to a dense thicket of croton shrubs. I was already very uncomfortable, having held on as long as I was reasonably able, and the need to leave the car had become terribly urgent. I had followed this procedure before, taking a roll of paper and a shovel with me to do what I must as discreetly as possible. Entering thick bush did bring with it the risk of bumping into a buffalo or other dangerous animal; to counter this, I picked up a stone and started banging the shovel with it to herald my approach. I reasoned that any animal lurking in the shadows was best warned of an oncoming human, rather than being surprised by him.

With the need to deal with my predicament ever more pressing, I went into the thicket in something of a hurry, bashing away at the shovel and whistling as loudly as I could. I now really, really needed to go. Just at the point where I felt I was sufficiently well hidden if any tourist vehicles happened past, I heard a low, rumbling growl. The bushes were so dense that I could see no further than a metre or so into them, but, as I strained to pinpoint the source of the sound, I found myself staring into the eyes of an adult male lion, whose fiery stare pierced the gloom and drilled into me. I knew I shouldn't run, but truthfully I don't think I could have done even if I'd wanted to. I was glued to the spot with fear. There was no more than a couple of metres between this huge predator and me, and I was armed with nothing but a small shovel and a very dodgy tummy. He growled again and then, with a great gravelly grunt, leapt up, tail lashing, and bolted away from me deeper into the bushes.

I was frozen to the spot, spade raised in one hand, roll of paper in the other. And – remarkably – cured of my urgent need. What could have gone so horribly wrong in so many ways had in fact proved to be a miracle cure for a gippy tum. I slowly backed out of the bushes and walked, somewhat stunned, to the car, where Dave was waiting, discreetly facing in the opposite direction.

'Did you see that, Dave?' I enquired as I reached the car.

'See what?' he replied. 'I didn't think I should be watching, especially after the sounds you were making. It sounded awful!'

'Never mind,' I answered. 'I'm much better now. Come on, let's get back to the rest of the pride.'

Dave looked at me quizzically for a moment before driving off.

*

During that first trip filming the Marsh pride, their fortunes turned. When we arrived there were large numbers of zebra visiting the marsh each day, providing easy meals for the lions during the night. But, as the weeks passed, and the zebra headed south to greener pastures, the cats were forced to tackle more challenging prey, and to do so whenever the opportunity arose, night or day.

Buffalo are among the largest creatures killed by lions, and the cats do not take on these leviathans lightly. Only when there is little else to choose from do they take the risk of tackling quarry that may weigh up to 900 kilos – about the same as a small car – and which is armed with heavy, sweeping horns and a temperament to back up their malevolent looks.

One crisp morning, a couple of weeks after the last of the zebra had left the marsh, we spotted the lions eyeing a group of four old male buffalo that were grazing close to the riverine forest on the west side of the marsh. First Kali and then the eldest of the lionesses, who we called Bundu, started to walk towards the herd with intent. They were soon joined by the other five adult lionesses that made up the female contingent of the pride, leaving the nine cubs to watch the developments from the safety of the marsh edge.

The lions had done this many times before during our stay, and so far these tests had come to nothing more than a brief squabble and flexing of muscles by both the lions and the buffalo. But there was something in the body language, particularly of the lead two cats, that was different today. They had a purpose, a determination I had not seen before. Just as I made ready to run the camera, it all kicked off. Kali and Bundu made a headlong charge at the buffalo which, startled by the lions' sudden aggression, took off towards the forest rather than turn to face their foe. Dave did a terrific job of positioning the car to allow me to film the chase, but as the bulls crashed into the forest with the lions hot on their tails, we lost sight of the whole circus. We followed, manoeuvring slowly through the trees and switching off the engine.

Some way into the thicket, we could hear a crashing of branches and the occasional low growl, suggesting either that the lions were fighting amongst themselves or else they were having a showdown with their giant prey. Dave started up and gently nosed the car between the trees until we rounded a dense bush and were presented with an extraordinary scene. In a small clearing, the seven lionesses had encircled a lone bull buffalo that they had separated from the herd. There was no sign of his colleagues; they must have run on, confused by the thick cover and scent of lion all around. Because of the dense vegetation, the only way to see what was going on was to be right on the edge of the clearing, which was of course very close to the centre of the showdown.

Dave managed to position us so that I was able to film the scene from the passenger door mount, putting me within a few metres of Kali as she rounded on the bull. First one, then another of the lionesses tried to tackle the buffalo from the rear, grappling his hocks and attempting to knock him off balance. Each of them was repelled as their quarry spun round, wildly thrashing his horns and stamping with his forefeet. During one such counter-attack, the bottom of the buffalo came perilously close to the front of our car, his tail brushing across the front bumper, and, feeling that there was something behind him, he turned on us and gave the front of the car a half-hearted knock with the boss of his horns. I had never before witnessed such a battle of the titans, and was torn between feeling sorry for the buffalo and admiring the guts and tenacity of the cats.

The bull backed away from the car, followed by his phalanx of tormentors, while they began to ramp up their attempts to tackle him. One of the younger females made a sudden leap onto his back, and this emboldened two others, which each took a rear leg. With a deep bellow the bull came down onto his knees and other lionesses leapt onto his back. I thought that now it was just a matter of time before the buffalo succumbed to the great predators' claws and teeth. I was wrong. His bellows had been heard by the rest of his gang, which suddenly burst into the clearing amid splintering timber and flying leaves. In an instant there were cats and bull buffalo running everywhere, many within a whisker of the open-sided door where I was poised with the camera. One enraged bull eyed the door for a moment or two, before deciding to vent his wrath by charging at one of the lions instead, much to my relief. All the lionesses managed to sidestep the bovine cavalry, but they had lost their chance of securing a meal. Their target quickly leapt back to his feet and – accompanied by his buddies – thundered off deeper into the forest.

It was an electrifying and at the same time terrifying

event, but in its aftermath I couldn't help feeling very sorry for the lionesses who had expended so much energy and all to no avail.

The Marsh pride didn't fare much better over the following weeks, and I bore grim witness to the younger members growing listless and bony as they were forced away from whatever meagre pickings were obtained from time to time by the more able members of the pride.

There was talk from the reserve wardens of supplementing the lions' diet by shooting topi or other antelope. But, though tormented by the sight of these beautiful cats suffering so much for want of a meal, I just couldn't endorse this practice. Starvation, however harsh it is to our eyes, is one of the few perfectly natural controls of lion populations. One of the reasons the adult females aggressively take their share before they allow the cubs to feed when times are hard is precisely because they can survive to breed another day, whereas the cubs still have a long way to go and many hurdles to cross before they are of a breeding age. The youngsters are, to put it bluntly, expendable. I adopted the maxim that we were in their kingdom as observers, not as players, and I try to stick to this philosophy still, however personally tough it may be to watch their suffering. Who are we to judge whether an antelope should live or die to feed a pride of lions, simply because we spend more time watching the lions than we do the antelope? The only exceptions I have made have been when the cause of the suffering is as a direct result of human interference – with a snare, for example, or a road accident – in an attempt to try and redress some of the harm caused by mankind.

That first year alongside the Marsh pride of lions was the beginning of a relationship with the cats of the Mara that was to be enduring. I have watched many feline dynasties rise and fall since then, but never tired of being in the presence of these magnificent predators.

Chapter 9

Dramas on the Wild Side

Whilst my appetite for working in Kenya alongside such charismatic megafauna was undimmed, I still loved tackling subjects back in the UK. The next character I wanted to showcase in the 'Animal Drama' series was one of the country's best-loved mammals, the badger.

Much of the material shot for *Dusk the Badger* was filmed at wild sets – some in Essex, some in Somerset – but there were a few scenes I wanted to include that would be impossible, or immoral, to film with wild badgers. One such centred on an all-too-frequent occurrence in rural Britain at the time: that of 'stopping' an earth or set. This practice, once common in fox-hunting country and not unheard of today, involves the blocking of any holes in the ground that are large enough to harbour a panicking fox being chased by hounds. By keeping the fox from finding refuge, the hunters get a more protracted chase, the main point of the horse-and-hound exercise.

Badger sets are obvious targets for this practice and, despite assurances that all holes are cleared of their barriers after a hunt, I have found many that have remained blocked. I once came across a scene that told a sobering tale. A badger set had been made impassable with concrete blocks and rubble. The badgers within had dug a great trench to one side of the barrier in order to escape. Fortunately for them, the soil was friable enough to achieve this, but it made me wonder how many more had been buried alive in the past. Of course, I couldn't tell who had blocked that particular set or why it had not been cleared, but I wanted to highlight the distress caused to these sensitive animals if the entrance to their home was barricaded, and so searched for badgers being kept in captivity with which I might be able to work in a controlled and stress-free manner. This quest led my research team to Burstow Wildlife Sanctuary in Surrey, one of the most extraordinary places I have ever visited.

Burstow was set up by a marvellously committed woman called Penny Boyd, and was unlike any other wildlife sanctuary I had ever seen. Where most took in poorly hedgehogs and foxes, Penny went one step further. In fact, she went several great leaps further. For, in addition to lavishing her care on the sick and injured wild creatures of Britain, she dedicated her time and grounds to much more exotic beasts that had, for one reason or another, outstayed their welcome in previous homes.

The first time I visited Penny to discuss the possibility of working with her and her badgers, I had a bit of difficulty finding the place. If I'd been told to follow the jumbo jets I might have had less trouble, since it lay directly under the eastern approach to Gatwick Airport.

I left my car near the gate and walked into the main yard, trying to time my calls of greeting between the thunderous roars of the landing aircraft. I approached the smouldering remains of a large bonfire, where old straw and bedding from the cages was incinerated. I had almost passed it by when I noticed the vague acrid smell of burnt hair. Looking more closely, I saw that part of the blackened heap was in fact made up of two Vietnamese pot-bellied pigs lying in the cinders, and thought for a moment that they were fresh carcasses, but when one stirred and opened an eye to scrutinise me, I realised that they were very much alive.

I backed away from this slightly surreal scene and carried on with my search for Penny. I spotted a long barn of a building whose sliding door was open a little, and made my way towards it. When I was within ten metres or so of the door I was stopped in my tracks by a loud, metallic rattling sound coming from my right. I turned to see an apparition of fury bolting straight at me: a border collie – whose upper lip was so fully raised he wasn't just baring his teeth but virtually peeling his nose up and over his forehead – was charging for my throat. I instinctively recoiled, but with nowhere to go and no time to go there, I braced myself for the inevitable savaging I was about to receive. When no more than a couple of metres away, the slavering hound was suddenly stopped short by a chain attached to his robust leather collar at one end, and his kennel some five metres away at the other.

Having been cheated of his kill, the collie proceeded to bark and growl wildly, straining at his shackles. Not trusting the reliability of the collar, or the steel chain, for that matter, given the fury with which it was being tested, I gave the dog a wide berth and continued to make my way to the barn. A little shaken by the attack, and not knowing what to expect next, I rather gingerly stepped inside the building.

'Helloooo. Penny, are you there? It's Simon King here, I've come about the badgers. Helloooooooo.'

'Hi there,' came a reply from the far end of the building. 'I'll be right with you. Just feeding the coati.'

I rounded a series of stable-like enclosures to see a tall, slim, blonde woman, wearing jeans and a jersey, holding an adult coati – a long-nosed cousin of the racoon – in her arms.

I reached out to shake her hand, then realised her hands were full of coati so simply greeted her instead. 'How do you do? I'm Simon. I' m sorry to burst in on you – you're obviously so busy . . .'

'I'm always busy,' Penny replied in a soft Scottish accent. 'Just a mo, I'll feed this fella and then I'll be with you.'

With that she scooped a tin of dog food into a bowl and, after kissing the coati, which responded by shoving its nose halfway down her throat, she allowed it to trot back into its enclosure to eat breakfast.

'That's a pretty unusual animal to see in a British wildlife sanctuary,' I noted, nodding in the direction of the coati.

'He wasn't wanted at the zoo where he was raised. Didn't have a home, so I offered him one. A lot of the animals here are the unloved or uncared for. Did you meet the collie?' she asked.

'Um, yes. I don't think he liked me much,' I mumbled sheepishly.

'Oh yeah, sorry about that, I meant to warn you about him when we spoke on the phone. He doesn't like anyone much, apart from me. I rescued him from a farm where he was beaten daily. He thinks the whole of the human race is going to hurt him, so he tries to get one in first.'

With this, Penny continued her rounds of the cages, scooping tins of dog and cat food into bowls for a collection of critters ranging from hedgehogs to foxes. From time to time, she popped a spoonful of the mashed-meat mix into her own mouth.

'I don't have much time to stop and eat. I have to do it as I go along. This stuff isn't bad, you know. If it's good enough for them, it's good enough for me.'

I told Penny I'd take her word for it.

'So, you'd like to meet the badgers then? Give me a mo and I'll take you to their enclosure.'

Penny was a blur of activity and energy, mucking out one cage here, feeding one of her charges there. I offered to help, and a broom was thrust into my hands; I swept the loose hay in the barn gangway into a heap.

'Right then,' she said, once the last creature, a chinchilla, had been fed and watered. 'Let's go.'

The psychotic collie glared at me and uttered a constant low growl, baring his fangs in a Hammer-Horror grimace.

'Enough now!' urged Penny to her dog. 'The man's not going to hurt you.'

At hearing her voice, the dog was transformed into a lovable family pet, wagging his tail and bouncing on the spot for her attention. Penny went over to him and bent down to ruffle his neck fur with her hands. He couldn't have been more benign looking, but as he caught my eye over Penny's shoulder, he gave me a steely glare and raised his lip in warning. I was more than happy to respect his preference for his owner, and gave him a very wide berth.

On the way to the pen that housed the badgers, we passed an astonishing variety of exotic animals, including marmosets, a balding capuchin, meerkats and a gibbon. As we went by each resident of the sanctuary, Penny gave me its potted history. Most had come from zoos that no longer wanted them in their collection for one reason or another. The bald capuchin was not sick, just getting on a bit but, since it looked scruffy, the park where it had lived wanted rid of it. The meerkats were a spill-over from a too-successful breeding programme in another collection. Some of the creatures were here because they were surplus to requirements or not deemed fit for public display, others because of behavioural problems. The gibbon, I was assured, was unpredictable, and had become too much of a handful for its keepers.

I marvelled at the selfless, non-judgemental way in which Penny dealt with each of these so-called redundant creatures, believing that – just because they had outstayed their welcome elsewhere – they should not be relegated to the scrapheap. I could see that her resources and time were stretched to breaking point, but there wasn't a hint of self-righteousness or self-pity in her rhetoric.

The badgers, two of them, were housed in a moderately sized pen, and looked to be in very good condition. They had come to Penny as orphans and she had hand-reared them to adulthood. She had a plan to try and rehabilitate them to the wild, but for now wanted to ensure that they had as good a life as possible in her care. I suggested that we might be able to help by building a large, badger-proof enclosure on her grounds, which would suit the filming I wanted to do and at the same time give them much more space, and an outdoor run to get used to a life back in the wild. Penny seemed thrilled by the idea, and it was agreed that work on the ground to erect the fence and build the artificial set would start the following week.

'Do have a look around, Simon,' Penny kindly suggested as I prepared to leave. 'I have to get back to feeding the rest of the gang. Just be careful of the dog.'

I left Penny pushing a wheelbarrow full of hay across the yard as I made my way back to the car. En route, I passed by the cage with the gibbon and paused to watch it a little more closely. It noticed me, and with the most soulful and imploring of hoots, put one hand through the weld-mesh side of its cage, looking at me with deep brown eyes.

'Hi there, little fella,' I said. 'What happened to you then? Nobody love you any more?'

I took a couple more steps towards its cage, and it responded by inverting its hand, palm to the sky in a very human manner, apparently urging me to come closer.

'You can't be that bad, can you eh, mate?' I said as I took another step, still keeping what I thought was about a metre distance between me and the ape.

With that last step I had obviously crossed some sort of invisible line, since this was a cue for the gibbon to change his strategy and temperament, completely and dramatically. He snapped from a lost and hopeless waif into a muscular and determined thug. His arm flashed out of the cage and appeared to extend beyond all physical possibility towards me, grabbing the lapel of my jacket and locking on to it with a vice-like grip.

'Whooooaaa. Nice gibbon, let go please. No, no, don't pull!'

The strength in such a long, skinny arm was breathtaking. He pulled me closer to the mesh of the cage and stared into my eyes with what I can only describe as wicked glee. I didn't want to yank too hard on his hand for fear of injuring him, but in truth I need not have been concerned; he was well able to look after himself. Once I was a few centimetres from the cage, he suddenly tugged at my jacket with all his might, pulling my shoulder and cheek up against the mesh with extraordinary force, then released me a little, then repeated the action so that I was beaten several times against the cold steel. Afraid that he might try to pull me tight up against the cage and bite me, I used all my strength to unpick his locked fist from my lapel, and broke free, almost falling backwards into a muck heap with the release of pressure.

'That wasn't very nice,' I said as he sank back on his haunches, looking very pleased with himself, his charade of an innocent, pitiful beast in need of company having worked perfectly to dupe this gullible new boy. I understood now why his keepers might have been a bit exasperated by him, and found even greater respect for Penny for having taken him on. The truth was, of course, that he had every right to display such antisocial behaviour, having been given a life sentence without having committed a crime. I begrudgingly respected his spirit of revenge.

The badger enclosure took the best part of a week to finish and, once complete, really looked the part. With the help of my assistant, Matthew Thompson, we had created a little slice of deciduous woodland that would match the badger sets I had been filming in the wild. Now it just remained to introduce the tame badgers to their new home and, after a couple of nights settling in, film the sequence.

The idea was that we would encourage one of the pair of badgers into the set with food, then carefully block the entrance with stones and cement blocks, just as someone might who was trying to prevent foxes using the hole. The big difference of course was that Penny would be on hand the whole time to ensure that her badger wasn't stressed and, if he had too much difficulty getting out, we would move the blocks for him. I felt that illustrating the hardship wild badgers were sometimes put through justified giving this fellow a bit of a work-out for his supper.

It took several hours to set up the lighting rig on the night of the shoot, with large lamps covered in blue gel to simulate moonlight positioned all around the enclosure. We gave the badgers plenty of time to sniff our feet and the base of the tripod so that they were familiar with all the changes to their environment before we considered shooting the scene. The weather forecast had been good, but as I adjusted the last of the lights there was an ominous rumble of thunder. A bright flash of lightning sent the badgers scuttling for cover, and it became clear that a storm was very much on its way — and soon. I hastily switched off the filming lamps and covered them with heat-resistant plastic gel to protect them from the worst of the rain, and was just dealing with the last of them when the heavens opened. Stair-rods pummelled into the soil all around and burst off the lights in great plumes. I was soaked in an instant, and barely able to hear Penny, who was waving and signalling for me to join her in one of the sheds in the yard. Matt dashed to the shelter of a lean-to, and I ran to join Penny.

'Come in, quickly Simon,' she said above the drumming of the rain on the roofing felt. 'I have to close the door.'

I was drenched and very grateful of the refuge. Once inside, there was absolutely no light whatsoever; the inky blackness was permeated by the musty scent of animals and hay.

'Quite a storm,' I offered, a little awkwardly.

'Yeh, that's a biggun,' came Penny's voice close to my left-hand side.

I managed to find the wall of the shed and rest my back against it.

A small window in the opposite wall allowed a little light into the gloom but, try as I might, I could not see Penny, or even my hand unless I held it up to the window.

The rain was getting heavier now, building up to a deafening roar on the roof, when I felt the hand stroke my left thigh.

Blushing furiously, my mind raced. I was flattered by the attention, but it had come so unexpectedly. Fortunately

I did not have time to open my silly, vain mouth before there was a flash of lightning that revealed Penny – a good couple of metres away from me – standing by the opposite wall of the shed. Why on earth I had thought for one moment she might want to stroke my leg, I have no idea.

I was silently kicking myself for being such an idiot when the thought struck me: something *had* stroked my leg, and if it wasn't Penny, then what was it? On cue, the thing now took my thigh in a firm grip and, knowing full well this was not Penny making a pass, I felt it was reasonable to ask her what she thought it might be.

'Ah yes, that'll be the wallaby. Don't worry, he's blind, he just wants a bit of company.'

Another flash of lightning (this storm had theatrical timing) revealed the marsupial in question clinging onto my left thigh with both forefeet and thrusting his hips against my shin in a very suggestive fashion.

'He's very friendly,' I stammered. 'I guess he hasn't had a lot of company recently.'

The storm had reached a climax now, with a strong wind gusting through the gaps in the roof. Once again, there was a perfectly timed brilliant flash followed by a mighty clap of thunder. This snapshot of light revealed another creature huddled in the corner of the shed, a lamb with wide, anxious eyes.

'Oh he's not alone,' answered Penny. 'I have a lamb in here too. She only has three legs but they keep each other company.'

With the next lightning flashes I saw the lamb struggle to her three hooves and move to the far corner of the shed. I pictured the scene in here once we had left; the blind wallaby feeling his way around the walls of the shed and the lamb hobbling just out of his reach to avoid an over-amorous embrace. No wonder she had a worried look in her eye.

Once the storm abated we were able to strike up the lights and start filming with the badgers. My concerns that we might stress the one we worked with soon evaporated when I saw the power with which he pulled the stones we had placed in the set entrance out of his way. He struggled just enough to make the scene work for the purpose I intended in the film, but was out and munching peanuts and dog biscuits a minute or two after we started.

Penny and her badgers helped with several other scenes that I wanted to create for the film, including a fabricated – but I hoped powerful – brush with the illegal and obscene practice of badger baiting. Throughout the filming, the tame badgers remained perfectly content and were never stressed, and I sincerely hoped that by bringing such revolting activities to the public's attention we might somehow help bring them to an end.

Whilst continuing with the 'Animal Dramas', I also started work on the most ambitious series I had ever undertaken. *Walk on the Wildside*, which aired in 1992, took a look at marvels of the natural world, categorised by a series of headings that I felt related to our own world in some way. Topics such as sleep, waste, hygiene and temperature all came in for a populist treatment as I and a team of researchers and assistant producers scoured libraries and the most recent scientific journals for new, engaging stories to illustrate some of the more unexpected elements of the natural world. I was producing, writing, presenting and directing the series, as well as filming a good percentage of it, which, with the benefit of hindsight, was bonkers. It was a ludicrously large workload over a two-year period, but some of the opportunities the filming trips represented were, frankly, unmissable. Canada, several of the American states, Sweden and Kenya were just a few of the locations earmarked for key sequences.

The shoot in the United States was scheduled to cover several stories that featured a wide range of subjects, from beavers in Minnesota to hibernating frogs in Quebec and southern sea otters in California. Sea otters are one of the most charming of all sea mammals, and unlike any other otter species in that they rarely, if ever, come onto land. They are so perfectly adapted for a life at sea that they even sleep on the waves but, to prevent being washed away on the tide, they secure themselves before nodding off by wrapping up in fronds of live seaweed anchored to the sea bed.

It was this behaviour I wanted to film for the programme in the series which featured the science of animal sleep, but I wanted to bolster the story by showing how they fed. Uniquely amongst marine mammals, sea otters use a tool, an anvil they brace on their chest as they float on their backs, which they use to break open hard-shelled prey like clams and abalone. Some carry their favourite anvil stone tucked under their arm for days on end, and one otter I watched, in the harbour of Monterey Bay where

I went to film them, used an old Coke bottle, which he took with him wherever he swam.

Filming underwater is a rewarding but technically and physically testing endeavour, and I was lucky enough to enlist the help of a local expert in sea otter behaviour and a diver who had swum with them many times before. The otters that were most used to seeing people, and which would be easiest for me to film, lived near the marina in Monterey, so I sought, and was granted, special permission to film in this busy waterway.

Rather than try to follow the otters underwater, believing that I would quickly lose track of them, I decided to take with me a bag of fresh clams to a spot where the otters often foraged, laying them out on the sea bed and hoping they would attract some visitors. Before we started the dive I discussed the tactics we would deploy for filming with my assistant, Chip. I planned to lie still on the sea bed, with the clams spread across the sandy bottom in front of me. If the otter approached from my front, I would see it coming, but if it came from behind I would not have time to get the camera running before it came into view. To address this, Chip and I worked out a code. He would kneel on the sea bed just behind me, facing in the opposite direction. If he saw an otter approaching, he would tap me twice on the ankle. Feeling the tap, I would run the camera and so, hopefully, film the otter as it swam over the lens and into view.

With a game plan and bag of incentive at the ready, Chip and I entered the water close to a small group of otters resting in the bay and prepared to film. The dive was not deep, but we wanted to limit our bottom time to under an hour to prevent any unnecessary risk of nitrogen build-up in our systems, or 'the bends', as it is more popularly known. After five minutes or so, I was surprised and delighted to feel a tap on my ankle: Chip's signal that an otter was on its way. I concentrated on framing the area in front of me that held the clams, and ran the camera. I was still using a film camera in those days, which had the advantage of getting very high-quality slow-motion images. I expected the action to be swift and so had set the camera to record at three times slower than life – seventy-five frames a second. The only problem with this was that the maximum load of film – 400 feet – would run out after about four minutes. Every second counted.

Despite having received the signal, the seconds were ticking by and the film was being used up with no sign of an otter. I was just about to switch off when the signal came again, but this time rather more urgently and halfway up my leg. I figured this was Chip's way of telling me that there really was an otter nearby and that I should keep filming, which I did. A few seconds later, he tapped me again, but this time on the bottom.

This was getting strange. I appreciated that he was keen to let me know that we were on the verge of getting the shot, but this was just a bit too familiar. I didn't have time to turn to see what was going on before he held onto my air tank and pulled it, then put both hands on my head and squeezed firmly. Now things had gone beyond weird. Still puzzling over what this new development in our code was supposed to mean, I suddenly found myself staring into the face of a large male sea otter. It was holding onto my head with its forepaws and peering into my mask upside down, finally revealing the source of the mystery tapping code. A quick glance at Chip revealed that he was gripped by a fit of the giggles; inaudible, but clear from the stream of irregular bubbles belching from his regulator.

I knew sea otters were bigger than the otters I was used to working with in the UK, but this guy looked huge – about one and a half metres long and probably weighing about forty-five kilos. He twisted round and grabbed the regulator in my mouth with his forepaws, tugging so hard it burst from my lips and vented a violent stream of bubbles. Thankfully, this was enough of a shock to cause the otter to drop it, allowing me to hastily replace it in my mouth for a much-needed breath.

Over the course of the next few minutes, the otter performed marvellously; scouring the sea bed for the clams I had hidden in the sand and sticking them under his armpit to carry to the surface where he could smash them open at his leisure.

Within forty-five minutes I had filmed all I needed beneath the surface, including, in addition to the foraging, a view of a mother and her baby wrapping themselves in kelp for a rest. A week later, the sequence was complete and I was off to my next location, Florida.

Chapter 10

'Them's gators'

Some books suggest that it was manatees that sailors used to confuse for mermaids. An interesting theory, this. If you have ever seen a manatee, you would have to agree that a chap would have to have been at sea for a very, very long time to think that these great gentle beasts of inland seas and rivers could be temptresses. They may be endearing, but pretty they ain't! Like so many aquatic mammals, they have the ability to sleep underwater, and for the same programme on sleep behaviours in which I had featured the sea otters, *The ZZZZ Factor*, part of my *Walk on the Wildside* series, I wanted to film manatees snoozing on a river bed: eyes closed, breath held for minutes on end.

The Crystal River system in Florida provided the best location to capture the shots I needed. Manatees congregate there through the winter months to feed in the relatively warm, fresh water that rises up from underground springs.

Because I was on a very tight schedule, I decided to work with a small group of captive manatees. These were kept in a huge underwater pen at a natural pool in Homosassa Springs State Wildlife Park, a spring feeding into the Crystal River system. Here they were completely used to seeing people in the water and so, I thought, would be relaxed enough to fall asleep in my presence. Rather than using scuba gear, which I thought might be too noisy to allow the manatees to snooze close by me, I chose to swim with a snorkel instead. I figured that I could hold my breath for long enough to get the shots I wanted and, anyway, the creatures lived in very shallow water, so I would be able to get a lot of filming done simply by floating on the surface.

After chatting through the plans with the head ranger of the park, I donned my wet suit, rigged the film camera in its underwater housing and walked into the bay where the manatees lived. Most of the area they used was perfectly natural, fringed with trees and running directly onto the Homosassa River beyond. Only at the mouth of the bay was there a barrier of robust, vertical bars that prevented the manatees swimming out into the river, but allowed fish and other aquatic wildlife of all descriptions to enter the pool. Amongst the group I was filming were a couple of well-grown calves, which were significantly more curious than their parents. One youngster in particular seemed to take quite a shine to me, following me around as I finned across the pool to find the most photogenic spots and look for sleepy individuals.

He may have been an adolescent, but he was still big, probably weighing 150 kilos and measuring a good two metres from the tip of his shovel-like nose to the end of his spatulate tail. I filmed him feeding on aquatic vege-tation; he was so confiding I had to keep backing away to keep him in focus.

After an hour or so of gentle swimming, I noticed one of the adult manatees resting on the floor of the pool, both front flippers and tail tip daintily touching the soil. I dared not approach too close, too fast, for fear of disturbing his peace, and so finned very gently in his direction, then allowed myself to drift. As I got to within five metres or so, I could see that his eyes were closed and he was indeed sleeping. Not exactly the most thrilling spectacle I had ever witnessed in the natural world, but a great illustration of how different creatures adapt to catch forty winks, even if they have to hold their breath to do so. Because I was using the snorkel to breathe, there were no noisy bubbles to wake him up and I was able to film without risk of disturbing him. Or I would have been, if I'd been left to the task in hand.

As it was, I was clearly still a thing of great interest for the adolescent member of the clan who, unseen by me, had been following me around the whole time, staying just a metre or so behind me. Now that I was hanging motionless on the surface, he plucked up the courage to investigate this newcomer more closely. At first, I could feel his prehensile lips working along my fins, then his head and chest pushed down on my legs so that he could swim further up my body, pushing me underwater as he did so. Next, I felt his front flippers gripping me around both legs, gently but firmly. All this was pretty amusing at first. I was certain he did not mean to do me any harm, but just wanted to solicit some sort of game out of this new boy on his patch.

He started to swim away, still holding me very firmly

and taking me with him. I started chuckling down the snorkel; this was, after all, a pretty amazing experience, and a privilege to be accepted so readily by these gentle giants. But manatees don't allow for the fact that human beings, or this human being at least, cannot hold their breath quite as well as they can. As we cruised down the central channel of the pool, my new friend started to roll over onto his back, taking me with him. Anticipating what was about to happen, I took a deep breath just before the snorkel was forced underwater, and I was propelled, looking up at the surface of the pool, half a metre below the surface. I didn't want to scare the manatee, having spent time building his trust, but at the same time, after forty-five seconds or so, I was beginning to feel the need for a bit of air. After a minute, my lungs were burning and I was getting desperate. I decided to risk an escape, twisting my body to face my captor, and talking to him with a stream of bubbles

'Pbbbbbleeesbbbb bbbbleeetbb goooooggggggggg!', which translated from bubble language meant, 'Please let go!'

The sight of my face and the strange sounds pouring from my mouth in a silver stream of air were enough to startle him. He released my legs and made a surprisingly violent and powerful down-stroke with his tail, surging straight over me and spinning me in circles. For a second or two I had difficulty working out which way I should swim for the surface, but soon found my bearings and kicked hard with my fins. Never had sucking in the warm, humid air for a breath felt so good.

*

To maximise productivity during my stay in Florida, I hoped to target several other subjects besides manatees during the shoot; events like mullet jumping clear of the river surface to rid themselves of lice for the programme on hygiene, and wood storks defecating down their legs to cool down in the heat of the day for the episode about temperature. For this latter show I also wanted to film a curious creature called an anhinga, a cormorant-like bird that spends a lot of time diving in the cool waters of the river system looking for fish. It lacks efficient waterproofing to its plumage so to warm up after a prolonged hunting session, they perch with their wings open, exposing the black feathers that run down the middle of their back to the sun, so helping to bring their body temperature back up to normal.

Filming the birds sunning themselves was quite straight-forward – it was not uncommon to see them perched on low branches overhanging the river margins – but filming them hunting underwater was another thing entirely. This time, I had to work with totally wild birds – there were none in captivity that I knew of – and for this I settled on a location known as Rainbow Springs. I had special permission to dive at the headspring in the early morning and was aided in my quest by a local diving operation and their staff.

I was not a very experienced diver at the time, but had had the good fortune to work in the Caribbean and at other world-famous dive sites. I didn't expect a pool of fresh water to begin to compare with any of them. I was wrong. As I dropped below the surface, I simply couldn't believe my eyes. The basin surrounding the spring was perhaps seventy metres across but, despite this distance, I could see the far bank underwater as clearly as I could above. I had never witnessed such amazing clarity. Colour, of course, dropped away with distance, so that the large-mouthed bass that appeared to be flying past me shifted from green-brown when they were close, to pastel blue as they cruised away towards the far bank. I knelt on the river bed, utterly mesmerised by the beauty and peace of this alien scene. I could see every detail of every creature within the pool: a large snapping turtle here, a cormorant or an alligator garfish there. This was definitely a fantastic location for underwater filming.

If only the anhinga had agreed. They, it seemed, were about the only creatures on the whole river that were in the least bit concerned about a human being sharing their subaquatic world. Over the following days I saw them in the distance, fishing around the base of the emergent reeds, but every time I tried to approach, they would paddle away from me. After four days diving with no result, I decided to change tactics and lie in wait for the birds to come to me.

The dive buddy I had been working with was due his leave, and was being replaced by a local chap with a very broad Floridian accent, called Jim. Alarm bells rang when the guy I had been working with took me to one side and said:

'Simon, I really hope you have luck with your filming. I'm so sorry I can't stay on to help you. I'm sorry, too, that you've got Jim with you now.'

Jim and I were scheduled to meet at a car park by a mall just before first light. He was bringing the dive kit, and I had the camera gear in my car. As I approached the rendezvous, I spotted a man leaning casually against a large black pick-up.

'Morning. You must be Jim,' I said cheerily. 'I'm Simon. Thanks so much for coming out this early. Let's stop at a drive-through for a bite to eat,' I suggested. 'It could be a while before we can have lunch.'

Jim barely looked up from beneath the peak of his oversized baseball cap. 'Don't bother me none,' he mumbled in his Southern drawl. From this somewhat unenthusiastic response, I guessed he was not a morning person.

Jim and I drove in convoy to the headspring and decanted the gear into our dive boat before heading upstream towards a spot where I had watched anhingas fishing on previous days. There was not a great exchange of pleasantries between us and, after a couple of attempts to warm the atmosphere, I decided it was best to shut up and get on with the job.

'Whad y'all filmin' here anyhow?' Jim eventually asked as we puttered upstream.

'Oh, didn't they tell you back at the dive centre? It's anhingas – snake birds. I'm trying to film them fishing.'

'Anwhatchamas?' he replied, screwing up his nose. 'You don't get any anwhatchamas round here. I been brought up on this here river, and I ain't never seen any anwhatchamas.'

'Oh you do though – look, there's one,' I said, pointing

at a convenient example of an anhinga that was sunning itself on a jetty as we passed by.

'That there's a catamaran,' said Jim with a deadpan expression.

I supposed that this was his attempt at humour, and accordingly I forced a laugh. This was met with an equally deadpan expression, so I rapidly straightened my face and coughed a few times. 'Oh. A catamaran,' I nodded. 'Really. That must be a local name then. Sorry. Anyway, it's those birds I want to film underwater.'

'What the heck y'all wanna do that fur?' Jim spat his response into the water as he looked away. This was going to be a very long day.

As we rounded a bend, he suddenly became very animated. 'There ya go. A whole mob of them catamarans,' he said at the top of his voice, pointing to a small group of cormorants that were swimming together near the bank. He spun the boat around and aimed straight for them at speed.

'Git yer camera ready boy,' he whooped. 'They ain't gonna wait fur ya ta pull yer finger out yer butt.'

'Um. Jim, they aren't really what I'm looking for,' I said as the startled flock dived in unison at the sight of the rapidly approaching boat.

'Heck, boy. You sure missed that one. Where d'yall learn how to do this stuff anyways?'

I had a dreadful sinking feeling as I responded, 'Here and there. Here and there.'

We reached the headspring and I asked Jim if he would please tie the boat to an overhanging branch and hand the camera in its underwater housing to me once I was in the water, whilst keeping an eye on things from topside. The river margin was very shallow, so the risks of being underwater without a buddy were minimal, and, frankly, having seen the way he behaved with the cormorants, I didn't want him close to me when I was trying to get a view of the rather jumpy anhingas.

Despite being very keen to get a bit of distance between my new assistant and myself, I decided the best strategy now was to wait topside in the boat, but be fully prepared to drop into the water the moment I spotted a bird hunting in the pool. I would then try to swim ahead of its path, hoping to film it as it came past me.

Once everything was sorted and I was sitting at the bow of the boat, there was a long and uncomfortable silence. The stillness was broken by a loud croaking that came from the reeds to our left.

'Them's gators,' said Jim in a matter-of-fact way.

'Oh really,' I answered, genuinely surprised. 'I thought that was a bullfrog. There it goes again.'

Above the loud croaking, Jim sounded indignant. 'Listen, boy, when y'all spend yer whole life on this here river, like I done, y'all know a gator when ya hear it. An' them's gators. Y'all want me to jump in an' catch it ta show ya?'

This was getting really embarrassing. 'No, no thank you,' I said uncomfortably. 'I'm sure you're right.' I stared silently down at the bottom of the boat.

The silence lengthened as the day heated up. Cicadas started drilling their strident rattle from the tree-tops, adding to the oppressive mood.

Jim was the first to speak again. 'Y'all like movies?' he asked.

'Yes,' I offered, trying to be interested. 'I don't get much chance to go to the cinema but—'

Jim cut me short. 'Y'all seen *Arachnooofobia*?' He drew out the middle vowel of the word.

'Um. Yes,' I lied, trying to avoid a lengthy discussion about a recent horror film that featured a plague of spiders, the trailer for which had been enough to put me off ever spending money on going to see it.

'It was just awesome,' Jim enthused. 'There's this guy, an' his family an' they all live in Texas, or maybe it's Louisiana. Anyways. This guy gets his whole house, like, totally filled with these killer spaaaders. But hang on, no, that's not the start. There's this guy . . .'

I started to glaze over and long for the uncomfortable silence again.

About an hour later, Jim was still recounting, scene by scene, the plot of *Arachnophobia*. And because he kept backing up to correct himself, he was only about halfway through.

'Sorry to interrupt you, Jim, but I think I just saw an anhing . . . I mean a catamaran coming downstream. I'd better get in the water.'

I was lying, of course. I just couldn't bear any more of the inane monologue and desperately wanted a bit of time on my own. I dropped over the side of the boat, put the regulator in my mouth and gestured to Jim to hand me the camera.

Fully equipped I signalled to him that all was OK,

which he seemed to ignore, and I swam off on my back with my camera.

I reached the reeds on the far side of the pool and dumped the air from my buoyancy compensator jacket to submerge. An image from a scene in the film *The Graduate* flashed into my mind, when a young Dustin Hoffman escapes the attentions of the crowd at his party by diving into his family swimming pool wearing his scuba gear. Peace at last. Looking around, I noticed a shoal of bass hunting smaller fish and slowly finned towards the scene just in case it developed further. A sudden flash of legs and a darting, snaking neck and beak broke through the silver throng to reveal the very bird I was hoping to film fully absorbed in its hunting. I managed to film it as it dashed after fish within a metre or so of where I lay on the river bed. It was all I needed for the sequence. With the film magazine empty, I surfaced and swam back to the boat.

Once I reached the side, Jim reached down to take the camera from me, but left me to get my rig off and get back into the boat alone.

'Y'all had enough already, boy? Don't got no stayin' power, huh?'

'Actually, Jim, it all went rather well. I think I got some pretty good views of it as it came by.' I assumed he had seen the anhinga from the surface, since his task was to follow my progress from above. From the surprised look on his face, it was clear he had no idea I'd even been underwater.

'Ya mean ya got it?! Well, hell boy, that's gotta be worth

a steak supper!' Jim somehow felt he had been responsible for the success of the shoot, and deserved reward in the form of me taking him out for dinner. I would rather have sawn off my left leg.

As I smiled weakly at his suggestion, a loud, rattling growl came from the reeds close to where I had been filming the anhinga. It sounded like someone trying to start a reluctant outboard motor, but was most definitely from an animal. I recognised it instantly from recordings I had heard. I looked at Jim, whose expression had changed to one of deep concern.

'What in heck's name was that?' he said, more rhetorically than to me.

'Them's gators,' I replied.

After America, I was Kenya-bound again, with a long wish list of sequences for the series. I had narrowed the locations to Nairobi, where I wanted to film some captive bushbabies, which were kept by a family on the edge of town, and to do some night filming in the national park. Nairobi Park is a marvellous testament to the tenacity of wild animals. Given the opportunity, even lion, cheetah and rhino can thrive, despite being in view of tower blocks and having jumbo jets passing overhead every few minutes. Run by KWS, the Kenya Wildlife Service, it offers a slice of wilderness just a few minutes' drive from a bustling, urban centre, and, for me, a spot to try and film a number of night sequences.

With the blessing and help of KWS, Dave Breed and I entered the park at dusk and were allowed to stay until dawn over a period of a week or so. Amongst the sequences I wanted to record were giraffe sleeping, which they allegedly did for only five minutes in every twenty-four hours, wildebeest resting by taking it in turns to be on sentry duty and, of course, lions hunting. The camera I was using would allow me to record images in bright moonlight, so I timed the trip to coincide with the week of the full moon.

Anyone who works a night shift will testify that it does funny things to your circadian rhythm. Personally, no matter how much time I spend working on projects where I am awake by night and sleeping by day, I find myself getting progressively more and more exhausted. The shoot in Nairobi required Dave and me to be busy from about five in the evening to six in the morning, night after night. After six nights of this, with very little sleep during the day, we were both pretty shattered. The filming of the giraffe had gone well, as had the work with the wildebeest herds but, as expected, the lions were proving to be tricky. We found the cats easily enough on most evenings, but keeping up with them in the darkness was tough, the long grass concealing their movements and rough terrain making it impossible to follow them for much of the time.

After a week of trying, we were finally lucky enough to find the pride we had been watching as they rested close to one of the roads at dusk, giving us ample time to rig the night gear in preparation for darkness with the lions in full view. An hour after sunset we moved closer to the cats, which were just thinking about making a move. Amongst the pride members were a couple of young males, about two years old, which by day were rather sluggish and bored looking, like sulky teenagers the world over. By night they were different beasts, though, full of playful energy and mischief and often walking close to the car to inspect us within.

This evening, one of the young males had taken up station on a mound within a couple of metres of the road edge, and Dave carefully positioned the vehicle so that I could film close views of his face in the moonlight. The camera system I was using did not have an eyepiece; instead I had to look at a TV monitor, which I positioned on the floor of the car between my legs to frame the shot and focus. I was lining up a shot with the lion's eyes filling the frame when Dave whispered to me, 'Si, I think we'd better move.'

'Hang on a mo, Dave, I'm just getting this close-up. Why, what have you seen?'

Dave spoke more urgently. 'Look up, Si. We really do have to move. Now!'

I shifted my gaze from the screen and blinked into the night. It took some seconds for my eyes to adjust to the darkness, but as ambiguous blobs morphed into identifiable forms, I realised why Dave was concerned. The second of the two young males had joined his buddy on the mound, and whilst I had been concentrating on filming the first, this second lion had become fixed on staring at my face. Nothing particularly alarming about that, but given that he was no more than two metres away, on the same level as my head, and was shifting his bottom in precisely the same way a domestic cat does when it is about to pounce, I could see Dave's point.

'Oooops! I didn't see him. Right ho, start her up,' I urged.

Dave sparked the diesel engine into life and the lion relaxed a little, his focus shifting away from my exposed torso and into a more generally mischievous gaze at the car. We pulled away from the pride and kept our distance as they stretched and prepared to head off for a night's hunting.

We managed to keep track of them for an hour or so as they spread out into the grassland, at one point targeting a herd of eland, but by midnight they were still unsuccessful and had decided to take a break. Dave stopped the car, about fifty metres from where the lions were now in various states of repose on a patch of open grassland, and switched off the engine. The heat of the day had slipped into the clear sky and there was a definite nip in the air. Both Dave and I were used to this dramatic drop in temperature and had come fully prepared with warm fleeces, jackets and woolly hats. Dave, who was particularly sensitive to the cold, had gone one step further and had brought a balaclava that he now pulled down over his face.

Straining to keep an eye on the now sleeping cats was very soporific. We both knew that the lions could galvanise into action at any moment, so didn't want to look away, but they were barely visible, despite a bright moon, and I began to feel the weight of my eyelids sagging.

I woke to a startling bright light shining in my face.

The rangers' night patrol had come across our parked car and stopped to check that we were all right. They hadn't noticed the lions.

'Hello,' I spluttered as full consciousness returned, 'we're filming the lions. Umm. I'm not sure you should be standing there, they're really quite close.'

One of the rangers looked behind him and stepped closer to the car. The second, the one with the torch, shone the beam on Dave, who had fallen asleep in the driving seat. The sounds and light woke him abruptly, but he was in no position to greet the rangers cordially.

'Si, are you there?' Dave's voice was strained and fearful. 'What's going on? I can't see!'

I was alarmed at first that Dave seemed to have been blinded during his nap, but as he turned to face me I could see the problem. The balaclava had twisted through ninety degrees so that the eyeholes were near his left ear. In his sleepy, befuddled state, Dave had no idea what was happening to him. The ranger with the torch started to giggle and was joined by his colleague and then me.

'Don't worry, matey, it's just your hat,' I said, reaching across to help him straighten up and regain his vision.

Once Dave had surfaced and sorted himself out, he looked to where the lions were now taking more than a passing interest in the rangers standing by our vehicle; a couple were starting to slowly walk towards us.

Dave leant across to talk to the rangers. 'I think you'd better get back in your car. Those simbas haven't eaten yet this evening and they're looking in your direction.'

But Dave's attempts to reassert his dignity and authority

were doomed to failure. The rangers wished us good luck and walked confidently back to their vehicle, without even looking in the direction of the lions, still chuckling to themselves.

Chapter 11

Encounters with Elephants

After a few more nights in Nairobi Park, I still did not have the lion-hunting footage I wanted, but we decided to cut our losses and make our way to the Mara, where the bulk of the filming for the shoot was to take place. Once there I hoped to film lions hunting by day, and a host of other natural events that would complement stories I wanted to tell in the course of the series.

On this visit we stayed at a different tented camp from previous trips, one positioned even closer to the heart of the territory of the Marsh pride of lions. It was perfectly placed for a host of other creatures, too, from baboons to hippos, all of which were on my wish list to film. Dave and I settled into a much more manageable routine of waking before dawn, heading out into the bush to film and returning to camp soon after sunset. The exhaustion that we'd built up from the night filming started to lift and we both loved the marvellous contact we were getting with the vast herds of wildebeest and zebra – and, of course, the big cats.

We had been concentrating on filming the Marsh pride one morning when we received news from one of the other drivers based at the camp that there was a bit of a drama developing there.

All of the rubbish generated by the visitors and staff was disposed of in a vast pit, dug into the soil a few hundred metres away from the tents. It was made secure with a huge steel cover, equipped with a trap door to allow the trash to be tipped in. Someone had forgotten to close this door overnight, and the pit had attracted a visitor – a hyena. We were told that it was perfectly happy, given that it was surrounded by mountains of free food, but personally I was very doubtful that the hyena was comfortable in the pit trap, especially if there were lots of people around trying to get a glimpse of it. Dave and I decided that we should return to camp to see what, if anything, we could do to help.

When we arrived we were greeted by the spectacle of about twenty staff from the camp vying for a peek at the unwitting prisoner. In addition to the human audience, a group of baboons had gathered close by, obviously used to scouring the area for any food scraps that might not find their way underground, but now deprived of their usual forage by the unusually large crowd of people. There were several mature male baboons amongst the troop that were sitting back on their haunches with a dignified air, surveying the scene and waiting for their chance to run in and snatch a meal.

Dave parked the car and together we walked to the rubbish pit. I stepped onto the metal cover and peered inside the open trap door. I was immediately enveloped by a miasma of rotting vegetables whilst I allowed my eyes to adjust to the gloom below, and after a minute or so I was able to make out the sorry scene. The hyena was anything but happy. I took it to be an adult male (though they are notoriously difficult to sex, especially from above and in the dark), and it was curled up in one corner of the pit. It had obviously been in there for some time already, since it had tried to dig its way out, creating a huge overhang of earth around the whole base of the pit. It now looked scared, surprisingly hungry and exhausted.

I turned to Dave. 'We're going to have to help him out. It's not going to be easy. He may be tired but I'll bet he's got plenty of fight left in him.'

Hyenas have some of the strongest jaws in the animal kingdom, capable of crushing through large bones to get to the marrow within. This fellow was unlikely to make any allowances for a human grabbing him, even if it was for his own good. Nope, we needed to hatch a cunning plan. After some deliberation, we thought we had it.

A tractor was called to pull the metal cover from the pit and allow access to its base via a ladder. Meanwhile, I went to the workshop and found a two-metre section of metal tubing, and a long length of stout nylon cord. I ran the cord down the pipe, made a loop, and then returned the cord back along its own length, so creating a noose that could be held, or released, from a distance. Dave sourced a ladder and some manpower and we returned to the pit.

The crowd – both of people and baboons – had grown now. This was becoming something of a theatre. The idea was this: someone would slowly descend the ladder to about halfway down, staying high enough to avoid the jaws of the hyena but low enough to assist with the next stage. That was to carefully introduce the noose, and with the assistant on the ladder using a long stick, gently place it over the head of the hyena. The chap on the ladder would then climb back out of the pit, help tighten the noose and pull the hapless creature from its dungeon. I knew that the neck and shoulders of the hyena would be strong enough to withstand this brief pressure and really couldn't see any other way of getting the job done without a long wait for someone to fly in with an immobilising dart gun. Who, though, was going down the ladder?

I looked at Dave, whose eyes lit up at the thought. 'I'll do it, no problem,' he enthused.

'Are you sure Dave?' I asked him. 'It could be a bit dodgy down there. I think I should go down.'

'No way,' he answered. 'I want to do it, really!'

I could see there would be no arguing with him, so enlisted the help of one of the guys who serviced the tents to hold onto the noose with me, and to pull the hyena out once the cord was securely round its neck and Dave was safely clear of the pit.

As the ladder was lowered, I kept a close eye on the hyena for any signs of an imminent attack. It remained sullen and hunched, with its back to us, looking over its shoulder from time to time, but not making any attempts to lunge at the ladder. I made ready the noose and, armed with a stout stick, Dave slowly climbed about halfway down into the pit.

I lowered the noose towards the hyena's head, and tried very gently to slip it over its nose. The animal remained surprisingly calm, or perhaps just plain exhausted, not flinching away from the rope but instead sniffing it and shifting a little so that I missed my mark on the first attempt. I reset the noose and tried again. I didn't want to startle the hyena, feeling that I might get just one clear go at this; once shy of the rope, the task of pulling him to freedom would be made much more difficult.

This time Dave helped guide the end of the noose over the hyena's head with the stick he was holding, and managed to get the rope under his chin. I pulled gently back to tighten the noose a little, and all the time the hyena remained calm.

'I think we've got him,' I said to my assistant, who was standing behind me, holding the ends of the rope and preparing to pull at my signal. He must have misunderstood my intention though because, as I said 'got him', he tugged hard on the ends. The noose tightened around the hyena's neck and pulled him back a little.

That was all he needed to realise something fishy was afoot. He suddenly leapt up and ran to the opposite wall of the pit, jumping as high as he was able and scrabbling at the earth. Not wanting to loose our hold on him, I shouted to my assistant to hold on, and I put my weight into countering the now thrashing cords, hoping to keep the noose in place whilst Dave made his exit from the pit. Again, my request to hold tight was misunderstood as my assistant, sporting a large grin, started to haul on the rope with all his might. This was not at all the way things were supposed to be going. The hyena was now being dragged backwards, throwing its head violently from side to side and snapping its massive jaws. Dave, seeing that this now crazed critter was fast coming in his direction, held out the pole he was grasping to fend it off. The hyena took the wooden pole in its jaws and, with a single, shuddering bite, snapped it in two.

It's at times like these when everything appears to slow down. I still have a vivid image of the hyena, eyes rolling and revealing the whites, jaws snapping and drool running from its lips, being hauled up the wall of the pit until it was face to face with Dave, who, armed with the short end of a shattered stick, could either hope the angry critter would be pulled past him swiftly enough to avoid being bitten, or to try and escape the pit first. He wisely chose the latter option. In cartoons, when a character is being chased up a ladder, their legs become a blur, and they invariably shoot off the top and continue their ascent into thin air. The same can happen in real life. I know; I've seen it.

As Dave popped up above the edge of the pit, shaken but unhurt, there was a cheer from the human onlookers. The crowd of baboons, on the other hand, obviously thought this was a signal that they could now climb down and take their pick of the morsels below, and started to walk in towards the edge.

I turned to my assistant, and belatedly and quite unnecessarily shouted, 'Now, *pull!*'

We hauled on the surprisingly heavy, wriggling load, and within a second or two the head and shoulders of the hyena popped up into view. If there are moments in time when I wish I'd been filming something, this was one of them, solely to preserve the look on the faces of the baboons which, until then, had been blissfully unaware that a large predator had been within a few metres of them. A Mexican wave of pink eyebrows were raised in alarm, the whole troop rose to their hind legs and, barking in shock and fright, bounded off in unison to the safety of the nearby trees.

With one more haul on the rope we managed to get the hyena completely clear of the pit, but I didn't want to release him right away in case he fell straight back in. In a bizarre parody of a rodeo calf-roping contest, my colleague and I tried to manoeuvre the furious hyena into a safer zone, away from the hazardous fall. It had no idea, of course, that we were trying to help it, and did every-thing in its considerable power to counter our efforts. Eventually, though, it swung away to one side, where there was nothing behind it apart from forest and grassland.

'Let go,' I yelled to my assistant. Nothing happened. I looked back and he was still clinging to the rope with the biggest grin on his face. I turned to the hyena and noticed that it had stopped pulling so wildly and was eyeing us both with a degree of purpose. These are very bright animals, and I knew it was only a matter of time, a very short time, before it worked out who was holding the rope and, instead of pulling against it, would come running at us to encourage us to let go in its inimitable, bone-crushing fashion.

'Let go, *now!*' I yelled at my assistant, who snapped out of his adrenalin-fuelled deafness and dropped the ends of the ropes. I released one side that I was holding and pulled on the other. The noose flopped loose, then pulled away from the hyena. For a moment he stood his ground, staring me straight in the eye, and I thought he might be about to avenge himself for having been so ignominiously yanked by the neck, but after a beat he turned and loped off across the plains.

There was a moment of silence as our breathing returned to normal. 'OK, Dave, let's get breakfast,' I suggested.

I had a superb team collaborating with me on the series, from researchers to assistant producers who helped enormously with the workload, but I was beginning to feel the strain a little as we entered the second year of production. This was exacerbated by an additional project, the next in the 'Animal Drama' series, which left me little time for reflection, or, more importantly, being with my family. We decided to create a story about an Asian elephant for the next docudrama, to be shot on location in Sri Lanka. It was my first visit to the East, and I should have been very excited by the prospect, but the truth was that I was exhausted, swamped by all that I still had to achieve with existing projects. Even though I was well aware of my good fortune, I felt jaded and in need of a break.

Part of the problem was the manner in which this film was to be made. The vast majority of it would be working with captive elephants that worked with their handlers in the forestry industry. This would enable us to shoot scenes more or less to order, but it left me cold in terms of life experience. I was glad of the work, but when it came to job satisfaction, filming captive creatures was my least favourite element. The whole film was made in a little over two months, during which time I spent no more than a week working with the wild herds of elephants that roamed the southern forests where we were based. Were it not for these brief moments I spent following and filming the families around a lake in the early mornings and late evenings, I would have become thoroughly depressed, I'm sure. But seeing these lovely creatures living on their terms, rather than enduring the often aggressive and unpleasant treatment that the logging elephants were subject to, was enough to keep me smiling and sane.

The wild herds strayed far and wide through the forest and into the densely farmed land beyond. As a result, there was a great deal of conflict between smallholders, who were quite reasonably trying to protect the crops that would feed their families, and the elephants, which equally reasonably saw such densities of sweet vegetation as fair game. Every week, humans and elephants died in this war. For every animal killed by a bullet, ten more suffered gunshot wounds that they survived, but which tainted their attitude to the scent of man forever. Once they had received a painful injury, they were more inclined to be very aggressive if they felt threatened.

I was well aware of this when I decided to try and film a sequence of a wild herd bathing and feeding in a beautiful setting on the fringes of a flooded valley. I had watched the herd's movements the evening before and identified the spot where I thought it would be safe to set up the camera and await their bathing session.

I arrived at the spot at about noon and, after a quick search, found a small outcrop of rock with some scrubby bushes and a single dead tree on its crest, no more than eighty metres from the lake's edge. There were signs that the elephants used this area regularly, and I felt comfortable that I would be sufficiently well hidden and out of reach should they come down to the water to play and drink.

With camera set up, I sat on a rock waiting for the first sign of their approach. It came four hours later, with a distant rumble and cracking of twigs from the forest some 200 metres to my left. I have always been amazed at the silent progress made by a herd of African elephants whilst moving calmly through the densest of forests, and their Asian cousins were no different. As they came closer I was able to glimpse the occasional flapping ear and flash of white tusk through the undergrowth before the first of the younger females cautiously walked into the clearing by the lake. Once she was satisfied that the coast was clear, she moved out of the cover and was followed by a spectacular sight. Elephant after elephant poured from the gap in the trees, a stream of goliath life forms whose scale seemed wholly improbable given the close proximity of the nearest farmland no more than a few hundred metres away. Mothers with tiny calves, aunts and sisters, young males, and eventually two immense bulls all made their way to the lake.

The younger members of the mob charged excitedly into the water to douse the oppressive heat of the day from their skins, the older animals adopted a more sedate pace; but once in the lake all seemed to delight in splashing, bathing, rolling and drinking. This was clearly a social highlight of the day, and one that every member of the herd took part in. Having been pretty low for much of my stay in Sri Lanka, working alongside such noble creatures, now subjugated by man, I felt a weight lifting off my chest. These were elephants as they should be, as they have always been, as I hoped they always would be.

One by one, the bathers left the water and started to drift back towards the forest. The vast majority moved back along the path from which they'd come, but a few started to make their way towards the forest to the right of where I was hiding. This was not good. The wind direction had been in my favour throughout their ablutions, but had shifted in the past fifteen minutes, and, if these few continued on their path, they would walk into my line of scent.

I held my breath as the first of them, an adolescent male, reached the point where I thought he would smell me. For a moment I thought I had got away with it but, just as I started to relax, he stopped in his tracks, flared his ears and backed up a pace or two, emitting a low rumble. The signal was clear, and instantaneously affected every member of the herd. From being a peaceful throng of pachyderms, now the whole mob stopped and turned to face me. The first of the young bulls was joined by a second, slightly older male and the two of them started to move in my direction. The adrenalin was pulsing through my veins now, but I still felt that I was in a pretty inaccessible spot, so held my ground. I had little option anyway, since some of the other clan members had moved around behind me, effectively cutting off any escape route.

I looked around for possible hiding places and noticed, rather too late, that the rocky mound I had considered tricky for an elephant to climb was in fact covered with drying heaps of their dung. Not exactly out of reach, then. As the lead bull got closer he lifted his trunk and sucked up a lungful of human scent. He must have had a very bad experience because this heightened his aggressive mood, and he picked up the pace, half running in my direction with his buddy close behind. The other elephants in the herd simply watched their vanguards charge towards me. I was staggered by the ease with which the young bulls scaled the rocks. Despite a forty-five-degree incline, they were up it and on a level with me in seconds, closing the distance between us to less than ten metres. I looked at the dead tree I was standing next to on the mound, my supposed insurance in case things got out of hand. It was now very obvious that the bulls would have absolutely no problem knocking it over if they wished. Not really an escape option.

I was now faced with two very upset elephants, holding their trunks in the air and their ears at right angles to their heads, emitting an almost constant low, rumbling growl. The lead animal took a sudden step towards me, throwing dust and grit up with his forefeet, and I involuntarily stepped back. My movement startled him and he pushed forward another pace. I had moved away from my camera and tripod by a couple of metres, which now stood between me and the bulls. Not much of a defence. I decided that I had better try and talk my way out of this. Starting with a very low tone, I started mumbling pleasantries to my anxious visitors.

'Hello elephants. Nice elephants. Don't worry, I'm not going to hurt you . . .' The irony of the last sentiment almost started me off giggling, a side effect – I'm sure – of raw fear.

The bull raised his trunk and gently allowed it to drift over the top of my camera, testing its scent. I winced, expecting it to be thrown to one side with a single effortless sweep, with me after it, but instead it was treated with astonishing care and gentleness. I caught my breath a little, and continued to mumble sweet nothings to them. They in turn seemed to relax, their ears flapping a little and their trunks checking the ground where I had walked. We entered a strange limbo, a stalemate, where the bulls had me pinned down, and neither party was quite sure what to do next.

I was happy to notice that the rest of the herd had calmed sufficiently to start drifting away; the mothers and calves first, followed by the younger females and eventually the older bulls. But the bulls stood their ground in a face-off that lasted a good thirty minutes, which is a very long time to have adrenalin pumping. At one point a mongoose dashed across the mound between us, startling us all and putting everyone back on tenterhooks, but slowly, after perhaps forty-five minutes, the bulls backed away down the ridge, still facing me, then turned and walked briskly into the forest to join the rest of the herd.

My shoulders were aching with tension and I suddenly felt absolutely exhausted. But at the same time, I also felt a tremendous sense of privilege and a profound joy at having been so close to these sentient creatures for so long, and coming through the encounter unscathed. I put my fortune down to the elephants' fundamental desire not to harm anything, and having allowed, or rather having been forced to let them ponder the perceived threat in their own time and on their own terms. The lenience they had shown me seemed particularly generous in the light of the distressing treatment I had seen their captive cousins endure at the hands of their human masters.

Chapter 12

Life in the Freezer

Once I returned to the UK from Sri Lanka in early 1992, I had only a week or so with my family before heading off on my next filming assignment. When I had accepted the job, I was aware that I might well be a little tired by the time it came around, but I simply couldn't refuse it. *Life in the Freezer* was to be a comprehensive look at the natural history of Antarctica, and the opportunity to visit this true wilderness might only come around once in a lifetime. I should have been buzzing with excitement as I prepared my camera kit and polar clothing, but instead I had a heavy heart. I was going to have to leave my family again.

We flew from Brize Norton Airfield on a British forces supply jet, bound for the Falkland Islands. Along the way we stopped at Ascension Island to refuel the plane; a bizarre stopover of several hours during which we were all held in a chain-link enclosure. Once we arrived in the Falklands, we were transferred directly to Port Stanley, where we were introduced to what would be our home for the next month and a half. The *Abel-J* was a substantial ship, just over thirty metres long, and designed to run quietly so that it did not disturb marine mammals, whilst being strong enough to withstand reasonable ice impact.

Before I knew it, I – together with a team of producers and underwater cameramen – had set sail for South Georgia and the Antarctic Ocean, in search of vast shoals of krill and the throngs of animals that gather to feed on these abundant, shrimp-like creatures.

Ernest Shackleton was, and is, a hero of mine, as is Robert Falcon Scott. Now here was I, not yet thirty years old, about to enter the savage paradise through which those two legendary figures had blazed a trail. I knew that I should be buzzing with the thrill of it all, but still I couldn't pull myself out of my sulk. Outwardly, to the rest of the crew, I think I appeared to be reasonably upbeat, but inwardly I was wrestling hard with my emotions.

After an hour or so out of port, the seas began to swell to meet their Southern Ocean reputation. I donned my waterproofs and went outside to the rear deck to get some air, and privately shed a tear or two. The ship was rolling heavily in the swell, and nosing into the troughs of the waves, and I braced myself against a railing to keep my balance. Looking north across the grey walls of water, I thought of my son Alexander and my baby daughter Romy. I missed them with a physical pain in my chest. The salt spray was sufficient to camouflage my tears when one of the producers came out on deck to see if I was OK, or at least I hoped it was. I assured him all was well and that I was just getting a feel for the sea.

He turned back into the warmth of the cabin, leaving me alone once more. On the horizon, I noticed a stiff-winged bird, appearing and disappearing behind the waves. It didn't flap once, but cruised with no apparent effort towards our ship. Just when I thought it must be nearby, it continued to grow in size, until I realised what it was I was looking at. A wandering albatross, a wild spirit from my dreams, with the greatest wingspan of any living bird. An icon. And I was looking at one. It cruised to within a few metres of the stern of the ship and then seemed to hold its position, staring down at me. I could clearly see its soft brown eye, its powerful beak and its long wings that stretched well over three metres across.

I was lost in its serenity and, despite its size, its fragility in this vast and harsh environment. It seemed to want to stay with the ship, perhaps using an updraught caused by our progress, or else hoping we were a fishing vessel that might provide easy pickings. Whatever its reasoning, it brought with it a change of heart for me. I was lost in its gentle majesty, its mastery of the elements; bit by bit, I found my enthusiasm and joy seeping back. I was one of the luckiest men alive, still am. I reasoned that life would always throw up challenges, and compromises would always have to be made. As long as I was still able to feel the wind on my face and get pleasure from it, I would try to juggle the loves of my life so that none suffered from too great a neglect. I was back, and heading south.

The cruise to South Georgia took over a week, made slower through rough weather and the occasional pause in our progress to film whales. My first attempt at this involved a thrilling scrabble to launch an inflatable boat and jump on board to record some topside views of a group of fin whales we happened upon.

One of the crew of the ship manned the Zodiac inflatable whilst I concentrated on trying to keep the camera relatively steady on the bumpy sea. At one point an adult whale came to within a couple of metres of our starboard side, giving us a magnificent view and graphic impression of its size. Fin whales are second only to blue whales in scale, and I was mesmerised by what seemed to be an endless back, arching alongside our little boat, which eventually ended in a vast tail fluke rising above us like the wings of a light aircraft before the whale dived. We estimated the animal was in the region of twenty metres long, by far the largest creature I had ever seen in the flesh. As it surfaced again nearby, we were positioned just downwind of its blowhole and received a face full of whale breath, which is, I can assure you, very smelly indeed: a heady mix of gases with a fishy undertone. Throughout the filming, I neglected to don a hat, and because I was already follicly challenged – oh, all right then, balding – I suffered the worst sunburn to the top of my head I had ever endured. Ironic given the time I'd spent in equatorial countries without any problems.

Fin whales filmed, we were back under way and heading for the sub-Antarctic islands. If I thought we had already been through rough seas, I was in for a shock. We entered the region where raging monster waves are the norm. Not for nothing are the areas south of forty degrees latitude dubbed the Roaring Forties, Furious Fifties and Shrieking Sixties. With an ocean unimpeded by any landmass, the winds build unchecked to the highest average speeds found on earth, whipping the seas up on a truly gargantuan scale. I wanted to illustrate this for the film, and with the help of one of the producers on the series, created a method of filming from a boat, which I have used many times since.

Back in the UK, before we'd left, the team had tested a number of hi-tech gimbals and image-stabilizing devices, many of which worked very well with small to moderate vibrations, but none of which coped when a platform was rising and falling through a ten-metre swell, and pitching and rolling through forty-five degrees in all directions. I reasoned that the human inner ear was pretty efficient at the job of keeping us upright, and so thought that hand-holding a camera with absolute freedom to move the upper body might be the answer to our problem. We again experimented with a number of mounts and chairs into which a cameraman might be strapped, but in the end, low-tech won the day. By punching the centre and spokes from an old motorcycle wheel rim, we were left with a very rigid, broad hula-hoop. Then, with three ratchet straps equally spaced around the wheel and secured at hip level to the railing on the aft deck of the ship, I was able to stand with my legs spread and move my upper body through any amount of contortion without risk of falling over. With an immersion suit on for safety, and the camera housed in a special splash-proof cover, I took my station at the back of the ship through the worst of the weather, riding the most exhilarating rollercoaster on earth.

It was not just the huge seas I wanted to film, but the

birds that rode the updraughts caused by these rolling monsters. Tiny prions, seabirds about the size of black-birds, travelled in flocks several hundred strong, searching the waters for food. They were accompanied by Cape petrels, giant petrels and a variety of albatrosses, all perfectly at ease in the most savage sea conditions. So massive was the movement of the ship in these storms that it often felt as though we were going to be rolled completely over in the waves, but no matter how crazy the angle, the *Abel-J* always righted itself. Fortunately.

We reached South Georgia on a relatively calm day, and I was immediately taken with its rugged beauty; its great snow-covered peaks lifted up from the sea in a sweeping ridge of terrestrial defiance in this ocean-dominated land-scape. I was profoundly affected too by knowing of its rich history in the annals of human exploration and endeavour, from Shackleton's great southern adventures, to the rather more sobering and macabre legacy of the whaling industry that once used this remote outpost as a lucrative base. Much of the filming we had scheduled was to be conducted from on board ship, searching for the krill shoals and hordes of birds and cetaceans that follow them, but there were a fair few natural stories we wanted to cover on the islands too. One of these was with another goliath of the animal kingdom, the elephant seal.

I arrived after the breeding season, when the bulls, which can weigh over 3,000 kilos and measure five metres or more, had finished defending their harems of females and had entered the moult. The seals are insulated from the chilly waters with a thick layer of blubber, but whilst they moult, blood has to rise through this fat layer to reach the shedding skin and hair. This in turn makes the seals more vulnerable to the cold, and so they spend weeks lazing in scruffy, steaming heaps called haul-outs. There were some of these in several bays around South Georgia, and we settled on a particularly large gathering to illustrate this sedate episode in their year. Like so many of the creatures in this part of the world, the elephant seals had no fear of man, and that had been their downfall in the past when they were killed for their blubber. Now, protected from the shortsighted ravages of human beings, numbers were back up. Fortunately, the seals didn't hold a grudge.

We landed on a beach close to the haul-out with the Zodiac inflatable and decanted all the camera gear I needed for the day onto terra firma. I approached the seals slowly, despite their tolerance, giving them time to adjust to this newcomer on the fringe of their communal bath. From a distance, I could only see one or two seals lifting their heads to watch our approach, but as I got closer I realised that a shallow, muddy pool, about the size of a tennis court, was chock-full of them. They were packed in like huge, festering sardines in a tin, steam rising from them in the cold air. There was little or no movement from most of them, and only when I came to within a couple of metres of the edge of the wallow did the nearest animal, a huge bull, open his eyes and prove that he was in fact still breathing.

I filmed the messy spectacle for a while, snatching moments of good light as clouds skittered across the sun, and then decided to move in for a more intimate view. I attached a wide-angle lens to the camera and, with a small beanbag for support, crawled in on my belly to the edge of the wallow. The closest bull lifted his head a little, but soon flopped back in to the quagmire, uninterested in this puny invader. Before long I had the lens no more than half a metre from the massive rubbery proboscis of the nearest male, gazing down the eyepiece whilst waiting for him to open an eye, or take a breath – probably the most activity I could hope to see under these circumstances. Now that I was so close, I noticed that many of the seals had an unpleasant green slime running from their noses, which I later discovered was a common condition caused by nasal mites. Not exactly photogenic, but again, a part of their world; it would certainly give the sequence I was trying to build an added 'yuk' factor.

As elephant seals can dive to astonishing depths and are so completely at home in their marine habitat, I thought that the wallow made for an interesting counterpoint to their otherwise action-filled lives. I shifted forward, closer still to the nose of the bull, so that he was now no more than twenty centimetres away from the front of the camera. After a minute or two he shifted a little, and I ran the film as he lifted his head and let out a sudden and powerful sneeze. His huge nose rattled with the force of the exhalation, and a shower of the sticky, green mucus burst out of his giant nostrils, covering the camera, and my head and face. I'm not generally squeamish, but the combination of the texture of warm goo and its strong fishy scent, a tiny bit of which had found its way into my mouth, made me feel suddenly nauseous. I sat back, dripping with the stuff, and the bull opened one great watery eye to inspect his work. He must have been satisfied with the job, because he went back to snoozing a moment later.

With the wallow filmed, and me back on board the ship for a much-needed wash and brush-up with disinfectant and a wire brush, we were off to another land-based location, Bird Island.

Lying just off the northwest tip of South Georgia, Bird Island hosts a truly remarkable wealth of wildlife, not all of it feathered. Vast colonies of fur seals vie for position on the beaches, alongside elephant seals and the occasional leopard seal. They are dodged by thousands of penguins making their way to their breeding colonies, and elsewhere on the islands huge numbers of albatrosses, petrel and prions nest. There are many spots where you can quite literally not move for animal life, most of it incredibly confiding in human company. This is one of the breeding sites for the wandering albatross, the giant of the bird world, and we had planned that I should film some courting behaviour.

Reaching the albatrosses meant running the gauntlet of the fur seals on the beach. They had passed the peak of their breeding fervour, but numbers were still high, as were their tempers. One of the downsides of working amongst creatures that have no fear of man is that the more aggressive ones have no compunction about attacking you if they think you are invading their space. Fur seals move remarkably quickly overland, and possess long, sharp canine teeth which they don't hesitate to use on unwary humans. The bulls are large and powerful, and even the cows will have a snap at your legs as you go by. The team and I were provided with bodging sticks – broom handles to you and me – to keep the most persistently aggressive seals at a safe distance, but I found manipulating this effectively whilst carrying the camera kit across the slippery, dung-coated tussock grass really tricky. At the height of the breeding season, two members of our crew sent to cover the action had suffered severe injuries to their lower legs from the slashing jaws of the territorial bulls. I was luckier and managed to avoid being munched.

With the seal defences breached, we made our way up the steep slope to the albatross nesting colonies. It was quite a haul with the kit, but once there all feelings of fatigue evaporated. Wanderers were all around me; some settled on nest mounds, while others stood around the edges of the loose colony. Even without their wings spread they were impressive birds, and now that I was able to study them at very close quarters, I was even more taken with their comical good looks. Their beaks were over half the length of my forearm and tipped with a powerful downward hook – ideal for grabbing and holding slippery fish and squid, and well able to inflict a nasty bite if they so chose.

The rest of the production team continued further up the hill to check out an area where a species of petrel nested that we hoped to film over the next few days, leaving me alone with my camera and the albatrosses.

I set up the gear, then settled back into the grass to

watch the birds, hoping that I would be able to film some of the early stages of pair bonding. Wanderers don't start breeding until they are about ten years old and, once they find a mate, they tend to stay together for life. That can be for well over forty years, so their choice is a pretty important one. They may spend at least three years 'courting', and with so much hanging on choosing the right mate, I expected to see some examples of the way they went about the process.

Before long, a group of four non-breeding birds, three males and a single female, started walking purposefully together, with heads held low, swaying from side to side. One of the males approached the female and, standing in front of her, did the most marvellous avian impression of a flasher. Holding his head high, he opened his wings, as an exhibitionist might open his overcoat, and uttered a bubbling, rattling call. She responded by bowing her head low and clattering her beak. The male obviously took this to be a come-on, and took a few steps forwards, pointing his beak into the air and stretching his great wingspan further, all the time rattling and wheezing at his potential mate. Perhaps this was too forward for her tastes, because she turned her back on him and faced me.

The other males tried to walk in front of her, calling and gesturing with their most seductive repertoire, but she was having none of it. Instead, she waddled towards me, head low and swaying. I took my eye away from the camera and watched her approach. She moved slowly to my left-hand side, walking behind me, and the next thing I knew my woolly hat was being preened by a wild wandering albatross. She crooned a little as she rattled her bill and pulled gently at the hat, nibbling down towards the back of my neck. I was a bit concerned that she might not realise my ears were very much a part of me, and try to rid me of them with her powerful, hooked bill, but I need not have been worried; she was incredibly careful and delicate in her actions. All this time we were being observed by her three suitors, all of which looked somewhat crestfallen. I was very flattered that she had chosen to join me for company, but I had to let her know that this was a relationship that would never work out. I just didn't have the wings for it. I raised my arm a little to show her how puny I was, but she seemed to take this to be a sign of my approval because, far from dissuading her, it solicited a more feverish bout of preening.

I stood up, and she looked up at me with her deep, brown eyes. I hated having to disappoint her, but I had no choice. I picked up the camera and walked away a few metres. She watched me go, then turned to the three males and flirted with them wildly. I think she was just trying to make me jealous.

Later that afternoon, having filmed the albatrosses courting, I walked down to the British Antarctic Survey base on Bird Island. There are quite strict rules about how one disposes of waste – of whatever nature – in Antarctica, or the sub-Antarctic islands, and I really needed to deal with a very personal kind. The base had a loo with a view, a tiny wooden shed that was built halfway down the landing jetty, overhanging the sea. All human waste (and there was not a great deal of that since there were very few people on station) went via this route.

I put my gear safely out of the reach of the fur seals, and went into the little hut to do what I must. Before I settled, I looked through the hole in the seat and into the sea a couple of metres below. My gaze was met by the saucer eyes of a young fur seal, swimming in circles directly underneath. He was joined by a second, then a third, and shortly afterwards a couple of gentoo penguins swam into the fray. I really couldn't put off my appointment any further and, despite asking my audience to move away, had to see to nature's call whilst they had a view I did not envy.

Later, chatting with members of the research team who were based on Bird Island for two years at a stretch, I discovered that during the winter the bay froze over. As a result, there was a gradual build-up of frozen human waste beneath the jetty loo over the winter months. It was traditional for a tote to get under way amongst the team, betting on the date the ice would break up and take their collective offerings out to sea. I marvelled at the ingenuity of the British when it comes to finding fun in an awkward situation.

With a mildly guilty conscience after my visit to the loo, I walked back down the jetty to the beach and found a patch of ground unoccupied by seals on which to sit and watch the world go by. The view was simply breath-taking, with huge numbers of penguins, seals and seabirds buzzing to and fro wherever I looked. This was a world where wild creatures, now protected, reigned supreme, and I felt enormously privileged to be able to witness it. Whilst I reflected, I was joined by a mutt, the nickname of a small scavenging bird more properly called a sheath-bill. At first glance, they look like a stout white dove, but a closer inspection reveals a heavily built, dagger-like beak. They put this tool to good use, scavenging on any carcass that might wash up on shore, or terrorising penguin parents and stealing the regurgitated krill that was meant for their babies. Mutts aren't much loved. They are incredibly confiding, though, and as I looked down at the little fellow that in turn looked up at me, I had a thought. If I were to slip, knock my head and fall unconscious, how long would it be before the first bird plucked up the courage to have a peck at me? I decided to conduct a little experiment of my own, and lay down flat on the jetty decking close to shore. I allowed my eyes to remain a little open, but otherwise remained completely motionless.

Within a minute or so, the first of the sheathbills was walking on the deck close to my side, and making its way to my face. I tried not to move as it stared into my eyes, wanting to see just how bold it would be. It was quickly joined by a second and the two of them strutted closer still to my face. With a dagger beak no more than ten centimetres from me, I decided to blink, just to let them know I was still alive. They stopped in their tracks, but continued to inspect me carefully. Five minutes later, an Antarctic skua, the southern form of a great skua, flapped onto the jetty and walked up to the sheathbills, obviously attracted by their focus on a potential meal. All three birds seemed to be waiting for an opportunity to dig in, and if I remained perfectly still they quickly strode forward, assuming I was not going to put up a fight. More skuas gathered, and then a great flapping of wings heralded the arrival of the real heavyweight vulture of the southern ocean, the giant petrel. More cautious than its smaller colleagues, this powerful relative of the albatrosses walked towards me with wings held outstretched and stared intently at my face. When I didn't move, it took two purposeful steps forward to bring its solid-looking hook-tipped beak within striking distance.

I opened my eyes and sat up, sending all but one of the sheathbills waddling away a few metres. I had the answer to the question I'd posed myself. If I were to fall unconscious, for whatever reason, in this wilderness, the chances of me waking up with eyes would be extremely slim – and who knew how much further damage the scavenging birds could cause? I resolved not to give them the chance to demonstrate.

After a couple of days at sea on a fruitless search for krill shoals, we returned to Bird Island to try and film the nocturnal activity of white-chinned petrels. Reaching their colony involved a substantial hike into the high ground behind the research base, carrying everything from camera gear to a small petrol generator which would power the infrared lights we intended to use.

By the time the crew and I were on site, we were pretty weary, and glad of a breather before darkness fell. We had planned to camp close to the colony overnight, and so had brought the appropriate survival gear too: sleeping bags, food, water and bivvies that each of us could slide into if the weather turned. It was February, the southern summer, but here on South Georgia that could mean anything from a reasonably fair, clear night with temperatures well above freezing, to an all-out blizzard driven by howling gales. We had to be prepared for all eventualities.

The petrels tended to visit their nest burrows after darkness in an attempt to avoid the predatory strikes of skuas, which hunted mostly by day. I rigged the infrared camera in the last shred of visible light, and tested the lights. With all the kit in a 'go' mode, I settled back out of what was turning into a cold, stiff breeze to await the first arrivals. They came unannounced and invisibly; the first I knew of their presence was the shrill piping calls that the arriving bird made to its mate, which was hidden in an undergound nest burrow. Their movement on the ground was clumsy, their legs being set well back on their body, and I could see why they might feel particularly vulnerable if caught in these compromising circumstances by day.

I had managed to film a short sequence of the birds calling and taking turns over nest duties, when the weather turned. That might be an understatement. It changed from a reasonably clement evening to a howling whiteout in seconds. I hastily covered the camera and fumbled for my head torch so that I could get to the lights and protect them from the sleet and wind. With the torch on my forehead, I stood and looked around for the other guys in the crew. I could see nothing but a wall of white driving past my face, so dense was the blizzard. I put one hand out to feel my way in the dark and took a step forwards.

Something hit me with a solid crack in the forehead and fell by my feet. A small seabird aptly called a fairy prion lay in the grass looking bewildered but otherwise unhurt. As I considered what might have happened, I was struck in the head again, this time by something bigger. A white-chinned petrel flopped to my feet to join the prion. As I reached for the head torch I was struck a third time, very hard indeed, enough to knock me off my feet and onto my bottom. Into my lap fell a skua, blinking in the light of the torch, which I swiftly extinguished. All three birds had obviously been on the wing when the storm struck and they had homed in on the beacon of light from my head torch, much as a moth does to a candle. It was a bizarre collection, two frail petrels and their nemesis all sharing the same crisis, and me with a nice collection of bruises on my forehead to show for my stupidity at not switching the torch off sooner.

For most of the rest of the trip we were at sea, sailing well below the convergence – the movable line where the cold Antarctic waters meet the warmer waters from the north – and frequently travelling throughout the night for days on end. We took it in turns to help keep a lookout for icebergs, which were common in the seas further south. Despite the ship being equipped with the latest in sonar and radar technology, I always felt a little on edge when it was my shift, staring into the darkness or studying the radar screens for signs of a big obstacle. I learned that each category of ice had a name, depending on its size and form: growlers, bergy-bits and floebergs had a romatic ring to them, but each carried the threat of damaging a ship the size of the *Abel-J* to a greater or lesser extent. But apart from the occasional grinding of a growler against the bow of the ship, we were expertly steered past all the more threatening lumps by our skipper, Ham, a chap who had many years' experience in polar waters.

The krill continued to play hard to get, only showing up in relatively small shoals. It was enough to keep our enthusiasm high, but frustrating given that we knew the huge shoals had to be somewhere and that the flocks of birds and pods of whales and seals knew where – their lives depended on it. The best we had to go on was the archive of sightings from a variety of vessels, from whaling ships to military fleets, and our own hunches. Matters were not helped by regular storms that made life on board ship very uncomfortable, especially for those of the crew, and there were a couple of them, who didn't sail well. After a particularly rough vigil of three days, our skipper decided we should head for safe anchorage near South Georgia. Everyone, especially Ham, was exhausted and in need of some solid, unbroken sleep. We battled through gargantuan seas until we reached the leeward, western side of the island, and a protected shallow bay that would offer us all a safe and peaceful haven for twelve hours or so. Anchors were dropped, two at an angle to each other just to be sure we didn't slip our mooring if the wind changed direction and blew into the bay.

After finishing the first meal we had eaten sitting down for days, and drunk cups of tea that we could, for once, put down onto a table between sips, we all decided that, despite it still being light outside, our bunks beckoned. I was sharing a dormitory with the two underwater cameramen on the shoot, Doug Allan and Peter Scoones. Each of us collapsed into our respective beds and were out for the count in minutes.

I awoke some time later to a roaring sound. It was dark now, but the glow from one of the lights on the ship cast a yellow shadow through the little portal that was alongside my top bunk. I sat up as far as I was able, which was not far given that the ceiling of the room was less than half a metre above my bed, and strained to look outside. I could just make out the inky water off the starboard side, and could see that it was being whipped wildly by the wind. There was another sound, a grinding groan, that coincided with a particularly vicious gust.

'Sounds like the wind's picking up,' I said into the dark. I was full of priceless gems of wisdom.

'Yup,' agreed Doug from the lower bunk. 'I reckon the anchors are dragging,' he added, which was indeed an impressive interpretation of the sounds we were hearing. 'I'm going up to the helm to see what's going on.'

'I'll come with you,' added Peter, and the two of them slipped on their clothes and left the cabin.

I stayed in my bed, assuming that I had little or nothing to offer the ship's crewmen, who would be dealing with any problems far better than I could. There was no doubt now that the wind had picked up severely, and that it had changed direction through 180 degrees, so that our mooring was exposed to the full force of the gale. I switched on the little light by my berth and tried to read, but kept losing concentration and looking out of the window at what was going on outside.

After half an hour or so listening to the sound of grinding chains and clanging metal, I heard the ship's engines start. I hopped out of bed and pulled some clothes on and made my way to the galley. I was the last person on board to arrive on the upper decks, and once in the galley met with Lance Tickell and Ned Kelly, producers on the project and seasoned polar adventurers. Lance had been one of the first people to start a ringing programme of wandering albatrosses on Bird Island and some of the birds he had ringed when he was a young man in the late 1950s were still looking sprightly and breeding regularly. He had commented to me that it was a strange irony that we humans, who considered ourselves to be relatively long-lived creatures, didn't weather the years half so well as an albatross. There were photographs of Lance as a young man, thirty years' earlier, putting rings on the legs of the very birds that we had recently filmed. Looking at the birds today, you wouldn't be able to discern the slightest sign of the passing years. Lance, on the other hand, had the distinguished looks of a man who had been exposed to his fair share of wind and rain.

'Ham said he's going to make for the other side of the island for some shelter,' Lance offered as I sat next to him with a cup of tea. 'I hope he doesn't choose to go through the Sound. It'll be pretty rough with this wind. Still, he's the boss.'

'The Sound' that Lance referred to was Bird Sound, a very narrow waterway, in places no wider than 500 metres, bordered by jagged rocks that divided Bird Island from mainland South Georgia. By day it could be treacherous, with strong currents and tidal surges funnelling through it, and fierce winds pummelling between the cliffs that towered either side. By night, in rough weather, I imagined it would be impassable. After a while, Lance and Ned said they were going up to the helm to see what the plan was, and deciding there were quite enough people offering opinions to the skipper, I decided to return to my bunk. I had absolute faith in the abilities of the ship's captain and, after Lance's comments about the treacherous Bird Sound, thought that he would very probably plump for the longer, uncomfortable, but relatively safe option of travelling right around Bird Island in the open sea to reach a safe harbour on the eastern side of Georgia.

Once we were in open water, the scale and extent of the storm became very clear. The ship was tossed like a cork on waves the size of a three-storey building, and the pitching and rolling was so severe it was all I could do to stay in my bunk. I wedged my elbows against the sides and stared out of the porthole window. The engine growled and strained as we laboured our way through the storm, and for much of the time I could see nothing but sheets of sleet and snow, highlighted by the lamps from the ship. After twenty minutes or so, I thought I caught a glimpse of rock some fifty metres or so away from the ship and, unnerved by this apparition, clambered out of the cabin and up to the helm.

I found a tense and silent atmosphere amongst everyone present, some of them ship's crew, some from our film team. Ham, the skipper, was at his station, staring into the darkness and keeping an eye on the ship's instruments.

I went up to one of the crew to ask what was going on.

'Ham's decided to go through the Sound. Thinks she can handle it. Not everyone agrees,' came the strained reply. I staggered over to Ham and steadied myself against the control panel. Without me opening my mouth, he told me his strategy.

'Going right around Bird Island would take at least ten hours in these conditions, and if you think this is rough, then out there you'll learn what rough really is. This is a short cut, and the ship can handle it. I dare not touch the controls, though, the auto-navigation will make far better corrections than I can in the dark. It'll be fine.'

I looked around at the faces on deck, illuminated by the yellow glow from the instrument panel. All were very grave and I could sense that there had been words.

'Anything I can do?' I asked Ham.

'No thanks, Simon. This shouldn't take too long. We'll be in the lee of it soon.'

I left the rest of the crew and returned once more to my berth, uncomfortable with the thought of going through the narrows but resigned to the bumpy ride and reasoning that the quicker it was over with, the better. Staring through my little window at the world outside, it was clear that conditions were not getting any better. Once or twice I was almost hurled from my bunk to the floor by the violent lurching of the ship. For a moment I thought I saw rocks passing the window, though the sheets of sleet soon obliterated any view. But there they were again, this time unmistakable: not just rocks, but a wall of rock, jagged and unforgiving, rising and falling past my view as the ship rode the crests and troughs of the waves. They were still twenty metres from us, but from time to time we lurched suddenly towards them, only to be snatched back into mid-water by the same wave.

I had no idea which part of the channel we had reached, but realised that we were only just entering the narrows when I saw that the rocks were now much closer to the side of the ship. I considered going back on deck, but thought better of it. If things did get out of hand, I was sure I would know all about it soon enough and, quite frankly, in these icy waters with such monstrous sea conditions, I doubted there was much any of us could do if the ship did get into trouble. I lay back in my bunk, wedged my arms against the sides to prevent falling out, closed my eyes and thought about my family.

After an hour or so of hellish rolling and pitching, we eventually passed through the channel and rounded the northeastern tip of South Georgia. An hour more and we were in the relatively calm water of a protected bay, with daylight straining to lift the gloom of a leaden sky. Anchors were lowered and the engines stopped.

Like everyone else on board I had had very little sleep and, bleary-eyed, I joined a few of our crew in the galley for a much-needed cuppa.

'That was a bit hairy,' suggested Lance in a classic understatement. 'I'm not sure quite how we came through that one.'

The captain, Ham, walked into the galley, looking absolutely shattered and drawn. 'Well, guys, we made it,' he observed wryly. 'Next time, remind me to go around the long way.'

Chapter 13

Dingo Days, Emu Nights

I stayed in the southern hemisphere for my next film project, but this time plumped for a period on dry land. As usual, the 'Animal Drama' strand was ongoing, and I had chosen Australian dingoes as a good candidate about which to weave the next story of survival. Before settling on a location, though, I wanted to personally check out a number of different dingo hot-spots around the country, and so embarked on a two-week trip there in the early part of 1993.

Among the spots I wanted to visit was Fraser Island, off Queensland's southeastern coast. Being cut off from the mainland, and so removed from any risk of cross-breeding with domestic dogs, the dingoes there were thought to be some of the last pure-blood examples of their kind in Australia.

I was travelling light, with a backpack and bedroll – or swag, as they're known – and this gave me the opportunity to stop and camp wherever and whenever the fancy took me. I rented a small four-by-four and explored the island over a couple of days, driving on the vast seventy-five-mile beach that runs along the island's eastern seaboard, and checking out a number of campsites where dingoes were reputed to hang out looking for scraps they could scavenge from dustbins. It wasn't long before I saw my first dogs trotting with confidence along the beach, but the moment they went into the dense forest, I lost track of them. It seemed likely that this would be the pattern for most sightings, and I quickly realised that this would not be the best spot to try and film the animals for protracted periods. Certainly I knew it would be very hard to record them hunting in these conditions. I decided to camp for one more night before leaving the island the following morning and heading for the interior.

I rolled out my swag on the beach, heated a quick meal on my camp stove and turned in for the night. As I lay looking up at the stars, I heard feet crunching in the sand nearby. Sitting up, I saw in the moonlight a large male dingo trotting purposefully towards me. Without hesitation he came straight up to the foot of my sleeping bag and gave it a sniff. Obviously not put off by a scent that I'm sure would have dissuaded your average human, he carefully grabbed the bag in his jaws and gave it a gentle tug.

'Hey buddy, let go.' I smiled at my new companion's antics. 'I'm too big for you to eat.' I had been very careful not to leave any food scraps around my camp site, but I guessed this critter had been more fortunate in the past with his bold raiding technique.

'Go on, scram,' I said, waving my hand in his direction.

This just seemed to excite his playful streak, making him crouch on his haunches, staring at my face; then he leapt around the sand, spinning in circles and stopping to watch my reaction. This unsolicited game lasted several minutes before the dingo seemed to tire of it, and trotted away up the dune and into the forest.

I settled back onto my swag and fell asleep to the gentle hissing of the waves rolling onshore.

The following morning I woke at dawn, made a quick coffee and packed my gear. But when I reached for my walking shoes, they were nowhere to be seen. I scoured the area and checked the car in case I had absentmind-edly tossed them in the back, but couldn't find them anywhere. I went back to the spot where I thought I'd left them and looked carefully at the sand all around. There were a lot of dingo tracks, one set of which went off in the direction of the dune. I assumed these had been made when the dingo had headed off yesterday evening, but with nothing else to go on, I followed them into the grassy hinterland. I was about to give up this lead when – about 500 metres from my camp – something caught my eye. A scrap of fabric was sticking out of a heavily disturbed patch of sand. When I dug deeper I discovered my shoes, or what was left of them, buried about a metre apart and chewed beyond all recognition. I took this to be my dingo's sense of humour – or perhaps retribution for me not sharing my supper with him.

After Fraser Island, I was back on the road and heading for the great inland desert, about 100 kilometres south of Uluru (Ayers Rock). There I met with a chap who had a great deal of experience with dingoes, having raised several in captivity on his farm in New South Wales for a film some years before. Roland Breckwoldt was an author, politician, farmer and ex-rodeo rider. He was also a witty, bright, inquisitive man, and great company, and we soon became firm friends. Together we drove from the airstrip in Alice Springs to the Aboriginal reserve lands that Roland had already visited on my behalf some weeks earlier and identified as having potential for filming wild dingoes.

We had just three days to check out the area before I had to return to the UK and make my decision regarding the location, but the moment we started driving though the more remote stretches of the desert, I was blown away by its beauty. Great stands of desert oaks stood sentry by dry water holes and long yellow grasses bowed in the hot breeze. Unlike most of the inland desert regions of Australia, this patch had not suffered in the past from the ravages of grazing sheep, and consequently much of the original fragile flora was intact. Another huge bonus was that the indigenous people of the area were benign towards dingoes, largely because their chief considered them to be his totem, and so sacred.

Roland and I pitched a simple camp in the bush, forty kilometres from the nearest water source, and spent the days searching for dingoes by driving around the desert with a rented four-by-four. We saw one or two individuals early on, trotting through the scrub country at a distance, but they seemed wary of the car. This wasn't a good sign, since I knew they would cover vast distances and that we would need them to accept the vehicle as a filming platform, much as the big cats of Kenya had, if we were to have any success filming them.

On our second day, we spotted a dingo, about five

Filming a flat-backed turtle egg laying on Crab Island, off northern Australia.

Lying next to a fresh imprint on the sand left by a saltwater
crocodile on Crab Island.

An orca hunting sea lions in the waters around Peninsula Valdes, Argentina.

One of my greatest inspirations and mentors, Hugh Miles (with the camera), filming polar bears in the Arctic.

A black-browed albatross with South Georgia in the background.

Working in the black-browed albatross colony on Steeple Jason Island,
in the Falklands.

'Room for one more?' The kit arriving on Talan Island, Russia.

All the comforts of home. Alastair Fothergill and me preparing
breakfast on Talan Island.

A south polar skua asking me to leave on Svarthameren, Antarctica.

Waiting for the sea eagles to arrive on Talan.

The meerkat family we came to know so well in Tswalu
Kalahari Reserve, South Africa.

Arnie, the mighty
meerkat, as a baby.

Arnie the meerkat, warming his feet on my back
on a cold Kalahari dawn.

With Toki in his new home,
Ol Pejeta Wildlife Conservancy.

Taking a mid day break with
Toki and Sambu the orphaned
cheetah brothers on Lewa
Wildlife Conservancy, Kenya.

In Speyside, Scotland, for *Springwatch* 2008.

hundred metres away from the car, casually checking out a large rabbit warren. I stopped and watched from a distance rather than try to approach any closer, hoping the dingo would discover us in his own time and on his own terms. He gradually headed in our direction and, after twenty minutes or so, had halved the distance between us. I decided to speak, keeping my voice at its normal volume rather than whisper, to ensure the dog knew we were in his patch and so avoid startling him. Hearing me speak, he lifted his head and scrutinised us for a few seconds, then went back to searching for lizards in the sand. This was a great sign. He was still too far off for good-quality filming, but I felt confident that if he was typical of the dingoes in the area, then we could definitely get them used to us in the car in a very short time.

We lost sight of our dog as he trotted off in the direction of our camp, and we decided to search further afield for others in the territory. During our exploration we encountered wedge-tailed eagles, wallaroos (a small variety of kangaroo) and countless galahs, a type of parrot, but no more dingoes, so after an hour or so decided to retrace our tracks and look for the dog we had seen earlier.

When we were no more than a kilometre from camp we spotted him, or at least we thought it could be him, trotting purposefully towards the hills in the north. Studying him through binoculars, I could see there was something different about this dog and, driving a little closer and checking again, I realised what it was.

'Roland, he looks like he's picked up some paper, or a streamer or something. Where on earth would he have got that from?' As I said this I realised that the only place for miles around that might be a source of human trappings was our camp, but knew we had been very careful to box everything securely just in case the dingoes discovered it in our absence.

'Oh yuk mate,' exclaimed Roland. 'You know what that is, don't you? I'll bet he found one of our loo pits!'

We had of course had to visit the proverbial bushes close to camp, but had been very careful to bury anything we left behind. It seemed that this dingo had discovered one of our buried treasures and had dug it up.

'Oh no! I don't think he's carrying anything in his mouth, it looks like it's stuck to his back!' exclaimed Roland. And he was right; on closer inspection it was clear that the dingo had rolled in his discovery. Now he was modelling his new adornment with an air of great importance.

'Well, at least he'll get used to our scent,' I laughed. 'Remind me never to pat him on the back!'

I returned to Australia a few weeks later, prepared for the first shoot in the desert. In addition to filming the wild dingoes, I had arranged for three hand-reared animals to be with us for the duration of the shoot, to enable some of the more structured scenes to take place. These dogs came from a wildlife park close to Roland's home in New South Wales, and he had managed to cut through the layers of red tape that surrounded these controversial creatures to allow us to travel with them across the various states we had to pass through en route to the location.

I very quickly discovered that everyone in Australia had

an opinion about dingoes, positive or negative, and much of this was coloured by the infamous Lindy Chamberlain case. The Chamberlains had tragically lost their baby whilst on holiday near Uluru. Lindy claimed that a dingo had snatched her baby from their tent and killed it in the rocks behind. A long and drawn-out court case followed, in which Lindy was at first cleared of any wrongdoing, but was sensationally later prosecuted for the murder of her own baby. She served a jail sentence before she was eventually fully exonerated and her name cleared.

Whatever the facts in this case – and having had a dingo playfully try to pull me out of my sleeping bag on Fraser Island, I certainly believe that they are physically capable of carrying a small baby away – it had divided Australian public opinion down the middle.

The journey we made from New South Wales to the desert, with the three tame dingoes in a trailer behind the Land Rover, exposed us to many people along the way. Once they knew we were travelling with dingoes in the car, everyone would offer their opinion about the animals, and most would quickly move on to discuss their thoughts on the Chamberlain case. I soon learned to remain neutral in these brief exchanges, for fear of becoming embroiled in a heated debate, especially since it was usually perfectly clear which side of the fence a person was on by the way they opened the conversation.

'So, mate, what do you think about that Chamberlain bitch? D'ya reckon she done it?' was a common opening gambit from those who clearly believed no dingo would ever hurt a human being. The polar opposite was usually delivered as someone stared at the dingoes in our charge. 'They're killers, you know mate. Just look at that poor Lindy Chamberlain and what she had to go through.'

Roland had in fact been one of many expert witnesses on the character of dingoes when the case was originally heard, and he had said unequivocally that a dingo was both physically and practically capable of killing a human child, especially if its fear of man had been eroded by years of close contact in places such as Uluru. Dingoes there frequently foraged for scraps around the camp sites and over time had become very bold around people.

The fact that a lone dingo might well have taken a small, helpless baby from a tent and killed it did not make all dingoes savage murderers. Certainly, the three dingoes we travelled and lived with for several months across the year were simply marvellous company: independent of spirit but attentive to anyone prepared to show them care and contact. We gave each of them names: Deefur (as in 'D for' dingo) was a mature female; Papa after '*papa inura*', the Aborigine for dingo, was the male; and the last, a young female, we called Inura, literally meaning wild. Inura soon became my favourite of the three, a slightly built dingo but with a super demeanour and full of character. She never once showed aggression towards me and always wanted to be close, unless she was hunting. Despite this, I would not have trusted her or indeed any one of these powerful dogs around children or people they didn't know, but then neither would I trust a large domestic dog under similar circumstances.

Our journey north took us through a wide variety of

habitats, but by far the majority of it was made through the great red desert regions. The gateway from the south to this endless dry landscape is a place called Woomera, in which we proposed to camp for the night. We stopped at a typical outback fuel station on the highway, all flapping sheets of loose corrugated iron and a crusty attendant who answered our questions with monosyllables.

Roland opened proceedings by asking him where might be a good place for us to stay. 'G'day mate. D'ya know anywhere here where we can get a shower and roll out our swags?'

'Yup,' came the answer.

'Wanna share it with us, mate?' pressed Roland, clearly irritated by this unhelpful response.

'Just turn right down here. Some barracks down there have rooms, I think. Pretty basic stuff, but it might do. Are those dingoes?'

'Nah mate, just tan-coloured heelers. Thanks for that. See ya.' Roland had learned to avoid the inevitable discussion about the dingoes when we were pressed for time, and the sun was rapidly nearing the horizon.

With the vehicle fuelled up, we followed the attendant's advice and took the left turn down a rough bit of road that ran alongside the petrol station. A simple, worn sign bore the words 'Woomera 5 km'.

I didn't know what to expect, but thought that at best we might find a ramshackle collection of buildings and perhaps a sheep station where we could replenish our water supply, give the dingoes a walk on their leads and sleep under the stars. After a few kilometres we crested a small rise; below us was Woomera village. I couldn't believe what I was seeing: a green oasis, with neat rows of modern family houses stretched across the plain below. As we entered the town, the road became immaculate, with no sign of a pothole or shred of litter anywhere. Two-storey clapboard houses lined the street and their neat lawns were bordered by white picket fences. It only needed a child waving in slow motion from a tricycle to put the finishing touch to the impression that we had entered the set of some sinister David Lynch movie.

We pulled in at a tidy collection of shops to ask where we might be able to find a place to wash, and were cordially directed to a large building alongside a sprawling complex of warehouse-like structures. This, it turned out, was the barracks we had been recommended by the man at the fuel station, but where they were once used exclusively to house military personnel, now a large section was devoted to tourists and travellers looking for a room for the night.

After checking in to a simple but perfectly comfortable cabin, we walked and fed the dogs and then, in the last shred of light, explored the village.

Woomera was developed during the Cold War as a closed village or, more simply put, a secret location from which the British government could test nuclear warheads on long-range missiles. The very name, *woomera*, had been adopted from the Aborigine word, which describes a device used for throwing a spear. This legacy was on show in pride of place in the village centre, comprising a collection of decommissioned missiles set at jaunty angles on great iron plinths. Now I thought about it, I had vaguely heard of the Woomera Test Range, but I still found the whole principle of the town's origin disconcerting, especially since it obviously had a modern-day role and was full of American servicemen and -women.

After checking the dingoes and putting them on their leashes for the night, Roland and I decided to explore the area around the barracks a little. We bumped into and joined a couple of guys walking towards the warehouses, which turned out to be a vast leisure centre, complete with a six-lane bowling alley, a large bar and a dance floor that sported a retro glitter ball in the ceiling above its centre. It felt as though we had stepped into the 1950s, and that at any moment James Dean would walk in and sulkily lean against the bar. The two young men, not quite James Dean, but definitely American, joined us in the bar and started a game of pool.

'Fancy a game of doubles?' called Roland to the lads, who both looked up at us with impassive expressions.

'Sure. Wadaya guys doin' here anyway?' came the response.

Taking a cue down from the rack and chalking it, I stepped up to the pool table and said, 'We're on our way further north into the desert with three dingoes. Making a film with them. Quite a journey I can tell you. This place is amazing! What do you chaps do here?'

Neither one of the young men looked up, but both seemed to tense a little. One leant forward to take a shot and from the corner of his mouth said, 'Stuff.'

Naively I asked what kind of 'stuff' he meant.

'Electrical stuff,' was as much as he was prepared to say. Clearly we were not supposed to discuss what anyone did in Woomera, which made for a pretty strained and one-way conversation. That is, until the subject turned to girls. It was a Saturday night, but besides the four of us and the barman, there was not a soul in sight. The main lights on the dance floor were dimmed and the glitter ball was sending lonely beams across the empty space.

'Don't you chaps get a bit, well, bored out here?' I asked.

'Heck man, this is Saturday, the coach arrives in about half an hour,' beamed the young man. 'Girls from Adelaide. They all club together, hire a coach and come here for a good time. And they ain't comin' here for the scenery!' The American buddies laughed hard, giving each other a high-five.

Adelaide was about 500 kilometres to the south, a very long way to travel for a dance. Clearly the allure of some fit young American men a long way from home was sufficient incentive for some of the girls from the city.

Roland and I finished our game of pool, which we lost thanks to my complete lack of ability in the sport, drained our beers and, as the coach pulled up outside and fifty or more young women – all dressed to kill – poured in the door, we bade our company goodnight and turned in. I have a lasting memory of the look of glee on the two young American men's faces as they greeted their company for the evening.

We completed our long overland journey into the desert

in a little under a week and set up camp at the base of a spectacular mountain range, with immense rounded red boulders littering the lower slopes and providing us with shelter and shade.

The first phase of filming in the Australian desert occurred in the dry season. Actually, it was the dry season for most of the year and, if rain did fall, it tended to be sudden, heavy and very short-lived. As a result, we didn't feel the need for tents during this trip, and our camp was a simple, open-plan affair at the base of a hill, bordered by a beautiful outcrop of rock that offered shelter from the wind, and surrounded by the odd mulga bush which provided natural hooks on which to hang a towel or a Tilley lamp.

Living in the desert was a wonderful experience. At first we spent most nights sleeping under the stars on our swags, where I was often accompanied by the little female dingo, Inura, who snuggled up to me for warmth during the chill of the desert after dark. We cooked over open coals most evenings and lived by the rhythm of the day, searching for the wild dingoes or following the three fully habituated dogs that lived with us from first light to last. Throughout our stay I saw only one aircraft pass over-head, and even that was so high up that I couldn't hear it. Otherwise all sounds came from the natural world: the wind in the bushes, the song of a butcherbird or the screeches of the galahs.

It felt idyllic, and – until the rain fell – it was. It was a very brief shower that broke suddenly one afternoon, barely wetting the earth and evaporating off well before we turned in for the night. In its wake were unbroken clear skies, so I thought nothing of it.

As we prepared supper over the fire in the evening, I noticed a few ants running around the soil in the glow of the flames, but again I didn't pay any attention. Well fed and tired from a long day in the field, Roland and I bid each other goodnight and headed to our swags, each rolled out under the stars about twenty metres apart. I brushed one or two more ants from my sleeping bag, registering that I didn't remember seeing any around camp before then but, after a visit from Inura who was determined to lick my face goodnight, I was soon fast asleep.

I felt the tickling of the ants on my face at first and, through the fug of semi-consciousness, brushed them away. A few more tickled my chest and I pulled the sleeping bag down to remove these too. I drifted back off to sleep, but next woke with the most intense pain in the end of my, well, my urethra. It felt as though acid was being injected into the tip, which is precisely what it was. I yanked back the sleeping bag and shone my torch down below. A large ant had locked its jaws onto the end of my manhood and it felt as though it was trying to slice it off. I yelped with pain and hopped naked in the moonlight, drawing the attention of the three dingoes, which all came over to investigate. The ant must have become startled by my rolling over onto it in my sleep and quite reasonably had defended itself with a squirt of formic acid directly into my most sensitive of spots.

But just what had it been doing down there in the first place? Gradually, it all started to make sense. The rain shower had awoken hordes of ants that must have been in a state of low activity during the driest period of the year. When the rains had failed to bring any real sustenance, and now cheated of a substantial water source, the ants had started searching far and wide for any moisture, and this guy had latched onto what it must have considered to be a potentially life-giving opportunity. I'm sorry to say that he was very much mistaken, for in my attempt to remove him I separated his body from his head. Unfortunately for me, though, his head and jaws remained firmly stitched to me, mandibles locked onto my flesh in his final act of defiance.

'Ow, ow ow, bloody *ow!*' I hissed as I struggled to remove the last tenacious remains. I heard chuckling coming from the direction of Roland's swag and, embarrassed but still stinging, I dashed back to my sleeping bag and dived in.

'Bloody ants! They're everywhere,' I grumbled.

'Yeah mate,' came Roland's reply, 'absolutely everywhere!' And he broke into a full-blooded belly laugh.

As that night wore on, both Roland and I came under relentless attack from the insects. Neither of us had much sleep. The following day I pitched two emergency tents I had in the kit, both of which had netting doors that would exclude even the tiniest insect, but even these defences were breached over the next week or so by an increasingly desperate army of ants in search of moisture, and we had to be enormously careful with our supplies. I made the mistake one early morning of boiling a kettle of water that I had left on a table overnight and then, in the darkness, pouring it into cups to make a brew. When

I took a sip of my tea I nearly retched. It tasted strongly of formic acid, and when I looked inside the kettle I found out why: hundreds of ants had found the water source but had died falling in through the spout. If any one ever offers you ant tea, decline.

We had been living in the desert for about three weeks when we were paid a visit by the chief of the local community, an area that went by the catchy name of Anangu Pitjantjatjara Yankunytjatjara. He was a wonderful, softly spoken man who had gradually come to trust us and allow us to camp in the beautiful back-country that was under his jurisdiction. As well as stopping to see how we were, he also came with an invitation to something called a cross-cultural exchange that was to take place back at the community headquarters later that same evening.

I didn't really know what to expect from a cross-cultural exchange, but having been working long days for almost a month, I thought that a bit of R and R might be just the ticket for Roland and me. So at the end of the filming day, we packed the Land Rover with our swags and some food, and made the forty-kilometre drive to 'the Centre'. This is actually a rather grand term for what was a collection of prefabricated buildings that none of the community lived in – preferring instead to sleep under the stars for most of the year – and some boreholes where fresh water was available. When we arrived there was not a soul to be found at the buildings, but I noticed light in the bush about a kilometre away. We drove on, and as we neared the light source were greeted with a truly awesome and incongruous spectacle.

About twenty four-by-four vehicles were parked in a semicircle, all with their headlights on full beam and pointing towards the centre. In the glare of the illumination were some thirty or so people, men and woman, who most certainly were not Australian Aboriginal in origin. Stopping the car about 100 metres away, we covered the last of the distance on foot, gravitating towards the exquisite sound of a young New Zealand Maori woman singing a traditional tribal song, accompanied by the bass tones of a large male choir. Many of the guys sported dramatic swirling tattoos across their faces, bare torsos and arms, and conducted a swaying, hand-waving dance in time to their chorus. In the shadows beyond the makeshift stage sat perhaps twenty-five men and women from the local community, their numbers doubled by what I took to be Native Americans sitting amongst them.

Roland and I paid our respects to the chief, and quietly introduced ourselves to a very distinguished-looking man sitting next to him, who turned out to be the chief of the Native American contingent. Quite how this eclectic mix of people, some from halfway round the world, had found themselves under the stars in this remote desert outpost, I couldn't quite fathom, but I was so delighted they had and that I – by chance – was privy to it.

When the New Zealand Maori group finished their performance, there was no master of ceremonies to introduce the next. In fact, there seemed to be no formalities whatsoever; instead everyone was just enjoying each other's company and the songs and dances of their different cultures. After a pause during which everyone chatted and sipped nonalcoholic drinks (alcohol is strictly banned in the Aboriginal community lands, so all euphoria came from the natural high of sharing music), a young Native American girl walked confidently into the glare of the headlights. The crowd fell silent and, in her native language, she delivered an incredibly haunting melody into the night air. Every hair on the back of my neck stood on end, the juxtaposition of major to minor notes bringing me close to tears. Her offering over, she confidently walked back to her friends in the crowd. There was no applause – this was not a show for a passive audience – but equally no standing ovation could give as much recognition or appreciation as the smiles and nods of the people gathered there in the dark.

Roland came over to where I was sitting on the red earth and whispered to me. 'Hey, mate, they want us to join in one of their dances. They reckon we've been here long enough to muck in. You up for it?'

I was hugely flattered and more than a little daunted. I was to take part in the Emu Dance, not something I was very familiar with, but I was assured by a couple of the guys that I'd get the hang of it soon enough. One of the young men from the Aboriginal community took me to one side.

'You know how an emu moves, don't you mate? Well, that's all you have to do. Be an emu. When the women sing and beat their sticks, you walk towards them, but when they stop, you stop. That's it, really. Right then, get that shirt off.'

Together with about ten other men, who were all from the local community, Roland and I made our way through the dark to a makeshift changing room constructed from brushwood and branches to prepare ourselves for the dance. Shirts were piled in a heap and I was given a smudge or two of white paint across my face.

Back in the crowd, the women of the community had gathered around a fire and started a falsetto chanting, tapping hardwood sticks together in the rhythm of a heartbeat.

'OK, fellas, let's go!' said one of our company, and with that he burst out of the shelter and into the light, stamping the ground and strutting like a cockerel, arms held at an awkward angle with hands hanging towards the earth in a fair impression of an emu with its wings akimbo.

I threw myself into the spirit of the dance with everything I had, trying to recall the curious head and neck movement of a walking emu and doing my best not to laugh. From time to time the women stopped chanting and all the 'emu men' froze, then we resumed our display when the ladies started singing again. The pauses were accompanied by gales of laughter from the singers, who were obviously delighting in the fact that we were all making absolute idiots of ourselves.

Our progress across the sand was towards the crowd of women; we drew closer to them with every fresh stanza of the chant. Before long, I was standing right next to some elderly ladies, who were laughing so hard they were crying. I kept up the act, pretending to inspect them and peck at their shoulders and arms, which drew squeals and more hysterics.

Then it was over, with again no ceremony to signify the end, just a few of the guys standing normally and talking, signifying that the act was over. Though I couldn't help feeling a little embarrassed, I knew I was overwhelmingly lucky to have been involved, however marginally, in such a heady mix of artistic and cultural offerings. From that day on, for the rest of my time spent in the central desert of Australia, I was referred to as the Emu Man by the whole community.

Chapter 14

Blue Planet

After Australia, I concentrated my professional efforts in the UK for a while, with films on barn owls in Somerset and red deer in Scotland. In 1996 I spent an eleven-week period in Kenya, co-presenting a series of programmes that would, in their way, affect my life quite profoundly over the years to come. *Big Cat Diary* was the brainchild of Keith Scholey, then a producer with the BBC's Natural History Unit and later its head, along with his colleague Robin Hellier. They had the bravery and foresight to suggest that a soap-opera-style natural history series centring around the lives of Africa's big cats would please the usual audience of wildlife devotees but also reach a whole new section of the television viewing public. With the backing of the then head of the unit, Alastair Fothergill, with whom I had made some of my earliest films, the series was produced – and proved to be very successful indeed. So much so, that a programme charting what was originally planned as a one-off experiment led to over twelve years of continuity, following the dynasties of cats in the Masai Mara.

As ever, being away from home brought with it the contradictory mix of emotions: I missed my family badly, but was also fuelled by the majesty and magic of the wild world around me. A few months after we finished the series, I returned to Kenya to follow a cheetah family; this was to be the last of my films that my father would narrate. He had been diagnosed with terminal cancer in the autumn of 1997.

I was in Kenya when my father's illness was discovered. When I learned that he would die within months, a year at best, I was quietly but profoundly affected. My beautiful third child, Greer, had been born in 1995, and I struggled to reconcile the joy and fulfilment of having a new life and love come into my world in the form of my wonderful baby daughter, while so soon afterwards having one of my emotional and practical foundation stones pulled from under me. Throughout my childhood and adolescence, my father had remained a constant and hugely important part of my life, and it was in large part his guidance, support and generosity that had enabled my career in film-making. He was always prepared to move mountains if he thought it would help me, in work or in life generally.

He was not without flaws; who amongst us is? There was some of his advice that, especially as a grown man, I did not choose to follow, or particularly respect. But he was fundamentally a good and loving man and I could not imagine a world without him.

In his last year, we went fishing together from time to time, sharing the air, the birdsong, the hypnotic ripples on the surface of the lake. We didn't discuss much on these trips, but I watched him across the water as he studied his float for signs of a touch from the huge carp that he always dreamed of catching but never did, and I knew I would miss him more than I could ever express. I miss him still.

His illness gave me cause to reflect on my own life, to challenge some unquestionable things and to face some truths that had terrified me for years. It was not because of my father's illness that my personal life became tortured – to suggest that it was would be a disservice to him and a misapprehension of my own will. But over the years I had grown, changed the way I saw myself and those close to me and, despite the cliché, it took the catalyst of the process of someone so dear to me slipping away to turn the spotlight on how ephemeral our time as sensory creatures is. It came sharply home to me that this really was the one chance I had. However logically I might have understood the nature of life and death, watching lions and wildebeest, peregrines and pigeons, I had never before felt it so very personally.

In the winter of 1998, shortly before Christmas, my relationship with Kim came to an end.

On 4 January 1999, my father died.

In the months that followed, I believe I came close to a nervous breakdown, vacillating between feeling utterly wretched and experiencing a curious sense of calm at having tackled terrifying truths. I had challenged the things that I thought made me the man I was, and found that they were wanting. And, once challenged, I could find no way to repair the rift I had created. The most shattering and savage pain throughout it all, which I bear to this day, was no longer being able to watch the minute detail of my children growing. But to have lived a lie and have them never know me, truly know me as the man I am, would – I felt – have been an even greater tragedy.

In the early part of 1998, I had moved out of the family home and into a caravan that I sited in a wild corner of the Somerset Levels. I was making a film about the nocturnal wildlife of the area at the time and so was able to put my insomnia and reluctance to travel far to good use. Throughout this difficult time I had an enormous amount of help from family and friends, and when it came to work I had the good fortune to be assisted by a charming and very able colleague, who had joined the BBC Natural History Unit as its bursary wildlife cameraman, and had plucked the short straw of working alongside me. Paul Stewart was an unflinching and dedicated support to me, and the film we were making, and I owe him a great debt of gratitude for being such a fine professional and good friend in these turbulent times.

As well as the film on nocturnal British wildlife, I had been working as a cameraman on other projects, and, truthfully, travelling to remote corners of the earth gave me time and space to think and solidify ideas. One such assignment that led to some marvellous adventures was an ambitious series about life in the world's oceans, *The Blue Planet*. Over a couple of years I travelled extensively, filming for the series, visiting Russia, the Azores, Scotland, the Falkland Islands and Argentina. In each of these wilderness areas I encountered some of the planet's most spectacular wildlife and met some wonderful and extraordinary people.

I arrived in Russia, with assistant Ben Osborne, and producer Alastair Fothergill, who had ended his term as unit head to get back into the field and steer this landmark series. We were heading for Talan Island, a tiny rock outcrop in the Sea of Okhotsk, where the cliffs were solid sea bird and held the eyries of at least two pairs of one of the largest eagles on the planet.

Steller's sea eagles are immense – females can weigh nine kilos or more – and they have the weapons to back up their body weight. Powerful talons and a huge yellow hooked beak are put to good use in catching fish or tearing into scavenged carcasses. But on Talan they were different in that they fed almost exclusively on sea birds. There was no shortage of those; almost two million sea birds representing twelve species crammed onto the cliffs of an island measuring two kilometres across.

I was thrilled to be visiting such a remote, wild place, and keen to start filming, but when we arrived in Magadan, the mainland port where we were due to take a boat to the island, there was a problem. There was no sea. Actually, there was a sea, but it was frozen solid and so there was no way we could reach the island by boat. Alastair put Plan B into action. We would use a helicopter to get onto the location.

Fab, I thought, much quicker than the boat option, allowing us to get filming sooner. But I did have some sneaking concerns about getting airborne in a machine that doesn't so much fly as beat the air into submission, in a country that did not have the best air-safety record on earth. The commercial airline, Aeroflot, had in previous years earned a somewhat dubious reputation for safety and, though that could well have been based on nothing more than rumours, it certainly coloured my attitude to getting into a privately chartered chopper.

We arrived at the airfield on the morning of departure and were faced with a veritable graveyard of aircraft. Hundreds of helicopters in various states of disrepair littered a vast area alongside some rather worn-looking runways. This sight did nothing to instil greater confidence in me regarding the flight we were about to take. After winding our way through these mechanical carcasses, we eventually came to an area of tarmac in the centre of which stood what looked to be a more-or-less intact version of the hulks we'd seen so far. It also appeared to be a composite of several different choppers, with mismatching paint on panels, like a teenager's do-it-yourself-bolt-it-together-from-a-scrapyard first car.

I turned to Al with what must have looked like a worried face.

'I'm sure it'll be fine, Si,' he reassured me. 'The pilots are ex-military, apparently, and I doubt they'd want to take any risks.'

I couldn't quite follow the logic, but nodded anyway.

The back end of the helicopter seemed to have fallen off, but in fact it was only that the cargo doors had been swung wide open to receive our many cases of camera kit. I was concerned that our gear might weigh too much for the aircraft, but I was dumbfounded when I looked into the back of the load space. There were wooden crates,

furniture, fuel cans and other paraphernalia, filling virtually every cubic metre available.

'Blimey. That's a lot of stuff,' I said to no one in particular.

A voice with a very thick Russian accent came from
what sounded like one of the wooden crates.

'No problem with boxes. Thees hyelicopter very strong.'

Out of a box, well, from behind one anyway, popped
a head. This was Sacha, a scientist of zoology who had
spent many summer seasons on Talan studying the sea
birds, and it was he who would be our guide and support
during our stay. His wife, Louba, was with us too, as were
two young research students. Between them, the three of
us, and our combined kit, I was certain we were well over
our luggage allowance of twenty kilos per person. By
about three tonnes.

Somehow, all of our kit was squeezed onto what little
space was left on board the chopper, and, negotiating a
teetering a pile of cases, we clambered in to what was
nominally called the passenger space.

'Where's the pilot?' I asked Sacha as casually as I was
able.

'Right there.' Sacha pointed to a chap I had taken to
be a casual bystander, who was wearing a leather jacket
and jeans and watching the final stages of the fuelling
process whilst smoking a cigarette. Clearly safety regulations were somewhat relaxed here.

The pilot extinguished his smoke with his heel, climbed
on board and greeted us with a stern-faced nod. Another
man dressed in civvies scrambled into the co-pilot seat

and the door to the chopper was pulled closed. Well, as closed as it was going to get. I could see daylight around most of its margin but decided to put it down to air conditioning.

Once the engines were started, but before they had reached a screaming pitch, the pilot turned to the cabin and shouted, 'Big load today. We use runway. Don't worry, everything OK.'

That made me worry.

I had a rudimentary knowledge of the principles of flight, and assumed that, by using the runway, the helicopter would gain speed on the ground like a conventional fixed-wing aircraft and that its blades would do the job of the wing. I told myself that the pilots must have done this hundreds of times with far bigger loads of troops and their kit (though I don't think you could have squeezed a single extra case on board with us) and waited for the metal beast to growl into action.

My concerns evaporated the moment we were under way. It was very clear that we were indeed in the hands of skilled and confident pilots and that the helicopter was more than a match for the heavy load. After a very short run, we were airborne and heading to the island.

We spent the next few weeks based in some rudimentary huts on the beach on the northwest point of the island. For much of the first seven days or so, the sea remained frozen, a shattered causeway linking us to the mainland several miles away. I discovered that, from time to time, brown bears crossed the ice to Talan searching for a meal, and had sometimes become stranded when the ice broke up. I saw only one, a long way off, pacing across the shimmering white flats, and though I would have loved to have had a closer encounter, thought it best that we did not have to share the little island with a large, hungry predator.

When the thaw came, its effect was sudden and profound. After a night of groaning, sighing and creaking, the ice finally relented and broke into a myriad floes and sheets that, within a few days, had almost entirely drifted away or melted. This was the starting pistol for the breeding sea birds that crowded to the island in their millions. Horned and crested puffins, auklets, kittiwakes and auks all thronged to the cliffs. And with them came the hunters: peregrines, ravens, and the Steller's sea eagles.

I saw my first eagles one dawn against a saffron-coloured sky: two great hulks of birds circling high on a thermal created by the island. As I studied them through binoculars, I realised I was looking at white-tailed eagles, the same species that lives over much of northern Europe, and was enjoying the spectacle when they were joined by the Steller's. If a white-tailed eagle makes a golden eagle look like a pipsqueak, then the Steller's had the same effect on the white-tails. They were simply huge, imposing and very beautiful. Working with them was going to be a joy.

I spent every hour of daylight searching for the best vantage point from which to observe the eagles hunting. Even though the island was small, the cliffs were irregular and very high, so getting a view that encompassed enough cliff face to give me a good chance of witnessing the eagles chasing nesting birds was a challenge. Having investigated the majority of the cliff tops, I identified a couple of spots on the rocks below that might fit the bill, but which would require some pretty serious rope-access work – or else a boat – to reach. I discussed my hopes with Sacha that evening over a supper of tinned fish stew.

'I'd love to reach the rocky outcrop on the eastern shore, Sacha. Any advice on how I can get to it?'

'We use rubby boot,' came his reply.

'Ah, right then. Any chance you could help show me the way down tomorrow? It looked pretty steep to me.'

'No problem. You come here to beach in morning. I bring rubby boot.'

'Oh don't worry, I have my own,' I said.

At this Sacha looked a bit confused, but went back to eating his stew.

I was on the beach at first light the next morning armed with a day's rations, camera kit and wearing my wellies, or 'rubby boots'. After a short wait, I heard the growl of an outboard motor and around the headland came Sacha in a small inflatable boat.

'Here, Simon, get in rubby boot, we go round to rocks.'

Ah. Now I understood. I felt like a complete idiot, but fortunately my colleague seemed oblivious to the misunderstanding.

In the event, the rocks offered some great views of the sea-bird colonies from below, but were not really the best spot for trying to watch the eagles, which drifted in and out of view within thirty seconds or so each time they patrolled the area above me. If I were to stand any chance of filming them hunting, I would have to organise much more protracted views and be able to access my vantage point autonomously.

I eventually found a narrow spit of land on the south-west side of the island that offered a view down a large stretch of cliff which was colonised by thousands of guille-mots and kittiwakes, both favourite targets for the eagles. Most of the snow and ice had melted by now, and Ben Osborne and I established camp on the high ground to make for easier access to this vantage point. Alastair had left to help set up other shoots on the series about a week earlier, leaving Ben and me alone on the island with the Russian researchers.

The days were getting long now, stretching the light into ever more remote corners of the day, giving me more hours to try and witness the hunting behaviour I was looking for, but in turn making for very protracted days in the field.

I discovered that if I remained reasonably well hidden, one pair of eagles would use the headland I was filming from as a cover, cruising tight along the cliffs behind me, then popping over the peninsula to bolt into the cliffs ahead, trying to surprise a kittiwake or an auk before it had time to get off its nest and into the relative safety of open airspace. I managed to film the gargantuan raptors from time to time, and even witnessed one outflying a peregrine falcon that had recently caught an auklet, causing the falcon to drop its hard-won meal and snatching it from the air before it could reach the sea below. Knowing how agile and fast a peregrine was, this display gave me an even greater respect for the aerial prowess of the eagles.

Over the weeks I managed to film one or two distant kills involving the Steller's, but the date of our departure caught up with us, and before we knew it, it was time to leave.

We relocated back to the huts on the beach for the last day or so, to pack the kit and prepare the film for transportation to the laboratory the moment we got back to the UK. Our departure had been organised aboard a large fishing vessel, a crab boat that had been helpful to the research team in the past, and we had to ensure the gear was packed in waterproof cases in case we dropped one as we passed them up to the ship from the tender.

In the early morning on the day we were due to leave, the wind began to pick up. With all the gear packed and sitting on a heap on the beach, I waited for a sign of the ship; tired, but happy that within a few days I would be seeing my kids again. I was joined by Louba, Sacha's wife, who had been enormously helpful throughout our stay.

'The wind's picking up,' I offered.

Louba's soft voice was adorned with her caramel-rich Russian accent. 'You know, Simon,' she told me, 'this island has a soul. There are people it likes, and people it doesn't like. It doesn't like the crab boats – it has sunk three already over the years.'

A sobering revelation, given our proposed mode of transport, but Louba went on. 'Some people it loves. It hasn't had time to get to know you properly yet, so it doesn't love you. But it likes you a lot. That is why it wants you to stay. That is why the wind is here, to make you stay.'

I was deeply moved by this profound and generous thought, and felt suddenly very sad to be leaving. I hadn't allowed myself to become attached to Talan, but this charming concept made me realise that I had come to care about it too. Perhaps Louba's sensitivity to this, and to people who cared about the wilderness as she and her husband so clearly did, enabled her to reveal what I had kept hidden even from myself.

We watched the waves in silence for a while after that, enjoying a shared love of the energy and pace of the wind, the birds and the sky.

Our reverie was broken as the crab ship, an immense hulk that seemed to be made from pure rust, rounded the headland from the west.

Within an hour, we and our gear had been ferried over to the ship by the captain himself, who rowed a sturdy tender to and from shore through the increasingly angry sea. In the event, the island failed in its mission to prevent us from leaving, but I promised myself, and it, that I would return some day. Having arrived with all the clatter and aggression that comes with a helicopter, we left Talan as I believe one should leave all places that have touched your heart: slowly and with a lingering view. I gazed from the stern of the ship as the cliffs were gently swallowed by distance and mist, then turned to make the remainder of the seven-hour journey to Magadan in the bubble of my cabin.

✻

Another shoot for *The Blue Planet* took me back to the Falkland Islands, but where in the past I had only spent the briefest time in Port Stanley before sailing to South Georgia, this time I was based on the islands for their own magnificent mix of wildlife. Vast colonies of black-browed albatrosses, sea lions and rock-hopper penguins all featured on our wish list and demanded an island-hopping itinerary.

In addition to the more remote corners of the islands, we were also based in the British armed forces complex at Mount Pleasant for a while, filming Commerson's dolphins from a sandy beach on the south of the mainland. During this time we were kindly hosted by the air force and army, and chatted with many of the troops who were posted there. Lots of these young men and women thought they had been dumped in hell, and could see no redeeming feature in the treeless, bleak landscape. They had a knack of creating their own fun, though, and in downtime would organise fancy-dress parties or themed evenings to keep spirits high. I joined them for a drink on one such evening, and asked a young soldier how relations were between the native Falklanders and the members of the forces, which outnumbered the indigenous residents by a considerable ratio.

'Oh, you mean the Essbees? Not bad,' I was told.

'I'm sorry, what's an Essbee?' I asked.

The story was that when British forces first established a major presence here in the wake of the 1982 Falklands War, the popular British TV soap opera, *Crossroads*, was still on air. One of the best-known characters in it was

Benny Hawkins, a harmless but rather dimwitted chap, sporting a woolly hat in all weathers and remaining somewhat naive to the ways of the world.

The British troops adopted the moniker 'Benny' to describe any indigenous Falklander; it wasn't intended to be especially malicious and, by and large, it wasn't taken to be. In my first brief visit there I had heard exchanges along the lines of a soldier saying, 'All right Benny?' to a chap working in a field, which was met with a laugh and a wave. Apparently, though, military top brass had got a whiff of the nickname and insisted that it be dropped, believing (quite reasonably) that it could be construed as an insult. With typical forces humour, the squaddies never again used the name Benny to describe a Falklander, but instead came up with the name 'Essbee', which was written 'SB' and stands for 'Still Benny.'

One of the locations we wanted to feature whilst in the Falklands was Steeple Jason Island, in the far northwest of the archipelago and the nesting place of the most important colony of black-browed albatrosses in the world. It was also uninhabited and very exposed to the elements, both features that were very much a part of its spectacular charm. I was once again with Alastair Fothergill and Ben Osborne for much of this shoot, and together we camped at the base of the sheer hills in the island's centre that give it its name. In addition to the birds, I also wanted to film the extreme weather that the islands are sometimes subject to, and my chance came with a savage gale that blew in from the north. The seas lifted into mountains, dwarfing the largest of the sea birds that rode through their crests and troughs, the gales battering the camera kit as I tried to film.

I did the best I could in such blustery conditions, then we all retired to the camp to take a break from the beating. As we made a brew in the largest of our tents, Ben thought it would be fun to discover each of our top camping tips. After discussing the merits of denture tablets for cleaning vacuum flasks, and always carrying dry socks, we turned to Alastair who was looking a little dejected and cold. As he was a veteran producer of wildlife documentaries with around fifteen years' experience of fieldwork under his belt, I was curious to hear his thoughts.

'What's your top tip, Al?' I asked him.

'Stay in a nice hotel,' was his rather forlorn response.

Chapter 15

Killers Up Close

It has been my good fortune to be offered some truly extraordinary filming assignments over the years, but I almost refused one that was to prove to be among the most fulfilling and memorable.

During the production of *The Blue Planet*, Alastair called to ask if I would be prepared to film a sequence of killer whales, or orcas, taking sea-lion pups from the shallow waters of the Patagonian coastline.

The same behaviour had been filmed once or twice before, most memorably by Mike deGruy and Paul Atkins for the *Trials of Life* series. Their astonishing sequence revealed to a global audience the might and majesty of these glorious creatures in a dynamic and breathtaking way. So much so, that when asked to film the behaviour again I was worried that any footage I might be able to get would be seen as a shadow of their work. It was because of this concern that I very nearly said no when asked to return to the spot where Mike and Paul had filmed some years before. Fortunately, I managed to check myself mid-sentence and accept the project, feeling that at the very least I would be adding an amazing life experience to my catalogue of animal encounters, and that perhaps I might be able to do something a little different with the sequence. With this in mind, I suggested we use a very high-speed film camera, one that would record the event up to twenty times slower than life. That, at least, had not been done before.

Equipped with conventional and high-speed film kit, I arrived at Peninsula Valdés in Argentina in March 1998 and settled in to a rhythm of looking out for orcas along the sea-lion breeding beaches in the north.

The interest generated in the event by the *Trials* sequence had placed an added pressure on the area in the form of film crews, photographers and naturalists all wanting to witness it first hand. As a consequence the strictures placed on visitors were significantly greater than those in place during Mike and Paul's visit. I had a 'minder' with me, appointed by the state wildlife department, and we were also guided by the reserve warden, Roberto Bubas.

I instantly hit it off with Roberto, or Beto, as he preferred to be known. He was a man driven by a passion for the wild and for the orcas in particular, and came to each day with a ready smile and a bag full of hope. In his down-time he rode his white Arab stallion bareback across the sand dunes and, when there was no one else around, he sometimes waded chest deep into the sea to commune with the orcas. This extraordinary display of trust from both the man and the whales was made all the more astonishing because Beto would also play his harmonica to the orcas, and they in turn seemed to appreciate the offering – or at least be all the more inquisitive as a result. Beto showed me treasured photographs of him with his hand reaching out to touch the nose of an adult female orca that was lifting her head clear of the water to get a good look at him no more than a metre away from his half-submerged body.

These stories and images were a powerful inspiration for me and what I hoped to achieve. But there was a problem. No orcas.

We had targeted a period in March when, historically, the orca families had arrived to capitalize on a new crop of young sea lions learning to swim for the first time. The sea lions were there in abundance but – so far – their nemesis was elusive. Each day I would arrive at dawn at the lookout point on Punta Norte and scan the ocean for the telltale black dorsal fin of a whale. Every day, as the evening shortened my vision and chilled the air, I reluctantly packed away my binoculars and telescope and went back to the little farmhouse where I was staying with my assistant Richard Wollocombe. This pattern continued well past the latest date so far recorded for the orcas' arrival, and I started to get worried calls on the satellite telephone from Alastair, the series producer.

'Hi, Si, any luck yet?'

'No sign yet, Al, but Beto thinks it could be any day now.'

'That's what you said last week, Si. Don't you think we should pull the plug on this one?'

It was a tricky question to answer. I was well aware that every day we spent with no results in Argentina, money was effectively being wasted that might be better spent on other shoots elsewhere on the planet. But I just couldn't bring myself to give up hope.

'Al, I think we should give it another week. There were reports that orcas were seen about ninety kilometres from here yesterday, so they could be on their way. What do you say we give it another seven days and then see where we are?'

'OK, Si, you're right. Let's give it a bit more time. Good luck, matey, speak soon.'

As Al hung up the phone back in Bristol, I was left with the sound of the waves and the wind and an anxiety that perhaps we were making a big mistake.

After five more days with no sign of the orcas, that sense of self-doubt was all the more acute. Then came the morning we had hoped for. I was on the beach by first light as usual. Beto joined me and quietly scanned the horizon.

'There, Simon. There they are. They are coming!'

His excitement and joy were infectious and, as I strained to pick up the sign he was talking about, I found my pulse start to race and my breath quicken. And there they were indeed. Distant at first, but the distinctive, sickle-shaped dorsal fins were breaking the surface and cutting a line towards the beaches. I readied the camera, and together we made our way to the low hide that had been given us for our shoot. It was the practice now to assign a film crew one of three low blinds from which to watch the hunting activity of the orcas, and ours was in pole position, looking straight at an area of beach that was flanked by a deep channel in the sea, a known favourite spot for the hunting killers.

Once installed, we settled and scoured the waves for

signs of the approaching hunters, but after an hour or so had to accept that they had gone elsewhere. It was a great disappointment to us all, and when that evening I spoke once again with Alastair, on the phone, it must have been clear to him that I'd suffered a blow to my confidence and hopes. We were already overrunning the allocated number of days for the shoot, and we had absolutely nothing to show for it. With characteristic bravery and support, Al told me exactly what I had needed to hear.

'Give it another week, Si. You've seen the orcas, so they are definitely in the area. One more week, and see what develops.'

It was precisely the kind of support that you hope for when you've been in the field for weeks on end with no success. And, as it turned out, it was the right decision. Two days after the brief and frustrating distant encounter with the orcas, they returned, and this time with a vengeance. Day after day they visited the beaches, searching for a meal. They timed their visits to coincide with the high tide, which enabled them to charge towards the sloping shingle and snatch young seals in the surf line. The strategy was a dangerous one for the orcas, since they risked beaching themselves and becoming stranded, but these killers were practised at the art, one that had been uniquely handed down by generations of killer whales in this region before them.

We worked flat out for seven days, filming strike after strike as the adult females in the group feasted on the pups. From time to time they took a seal just offshore and played with it, tossing it in the air with their jaws or, on one memorable occasion, knocking the now-dead seal so far out of the water with their tail flukes that it sailed over the heads of gathering gulls and petrels.

Filming the orcas hunting was thrilling and fascinating, but I was left with a sense that there was something missing from the experience. Whenever an orca arrived on the scene, I was studying it through the camera and trying to film its actions. That, after all, was what I was there to do. But I didn't have a personal sense of the animal's character as Beto so clearly did. During his studies he had come to be able to identify each of the members of the group individually, and had given them names. Angie, Tania and Exequiel all made an appearance whilst I was filming, but it was one female especially that stole the show. Jazmin was a relatively petite orca, but a mercurial and opportunistic hunter. It was her curved fin I had watched time and again cut the surface of the shallows before disappearing below the surface, only to reappear at blistering speed, surging towards the beach in a headlong charge to grab a sea lion. And it was Jazmin that was to give me one of the most memorable of all my close encounters with a wild animal.

After a week of manic activity I had managed to film the orcas at Peninsula Valdés catching many sea-lion pups, including recording a couple of takes using the high-speed camera, and was feeling reasonably confident that the main body of the sequence had been achieved. With the professional pressure off a little, I was able to cherry-pick shots from the orcas' hunting forays, all the time looking to improve on close-ups or more slow-motion material.

My friendship with Beto the warden had built up over the weeks of waiting and during this last week of full-on filming, and he and his colleague Hector had come to trust me around the sea-lion colonies. One of the reasons filming on the peninsula was so tightly controlled was to prevent disturbance to these sensitive creatures, and I had shown that their welfare was more important to me than trying to get a shot. As a result I had been given more and more freedom to work around the colonies, and even to follow the hunting orcas away from the hides as they patrolled along the beach to the west. This freedom had resulted in some extraordinary views of the orcas playing with their quarry, and allowed me a little more freedom to compose images based on what I thought was most attractive rather than simply staying with the one view afforded by the hide position.

After a particularly tiring day, which we had spent running up and down the landward side of the high shingle banks unsuccessfully trying to keep up with the killer whales, I rested the camera kit, and sat on the crest of the beach with Beto, overlooking the sea. The filming trip was coming to an end, and with the light fading, I wanted simply to soak up the atmosphere of the place. Beto prepared a small campfire; he had brought with him his maté and a flask of hot water for a drink of the bitter brew.

As we gazed at the waves, I turned to Beto. 'Do you think it would be OK if I went down to the surf for a little while?' I said to him. 'I can't see any seals or orcas around, and I just want to touch the sea before I go.'

Beto instantly understood my need to connect with the elemental side of this wild place, and granted me permission to walk alone down to the water's edge.

There was very little light left in the sky as I bent to touch the cold waves, lapping onto the shingle bar. As I did so, I noticed a movement in the surf about eighty metres to my right and instinctively dropped to my knees to reduce the amount of human profile I was presenting against the sky.

It was a well-grown sea-lion pup, perfectly relaxed and cruising towards me in the water no more than a couple of metres from the shore. As it came closer, I lay down lower still, concerned that I might spook it. The incoming tide pushed the surge up to where I lay, soaking my legs and the left-hand side of my body. As I watched the rolling form of the seal, another shape – the unmistakable scythe-shaped fin of the orca Jazmin – cut the surface of the waves behind it.

My pulse quickened instantly. It was too late for me to get up and walk back up the beach: doing so would almost certainly have resulted in the seal pup spotting me and heading out to sea, and I didn't want to be responsible for pushing it towards its demise. Instead, I lay as low as I was able and waited. My point of view was on the same level as the water's surface as the sea lion made its way purposefully towards me. There was no sign of Jazmin's fin, which I knew meant she was beneath the surface and listening for the movements of the seal; only this time those sounds would be mingling with the crunches and scrapes I was making in the shingle with my feet and body.

The pup was no more than four metres to my right when the orca made her move. I first saw the water lifting in a great bubble of a bow wave as she powered towards the shore, then her fin cut the surface, spewing water from its tip with the speed of her approach. The pup didn't stand a chance. The orca broke through the waves and snatched the sea lion in her mouth, throwing a sheet of water over me and pushing a third of her four-ton body onto the beach.

The moment stood still for me. I can vividly recall being able to see Jazmin's eye staring into mine – an orca has a dark eye which is very hard to see against the black of its skin unless you are exceptionally close – and she seemed to be lifting her head the better to see me. The pup was struggling, firmly gripped in her mouth, when she started to shift her head and body around to wiggle her way back into the water. The tide had lifted further still by now, and I was lying in a few centimetres of water when the orca finally managed to wrench her great bulk from the shackles of dry land and into the freedom of the sea.

But her game was not over yet. She surfaced once or twice, very close to shore, and swam with her prize until she was directly in front of me. There, no more than five metres offshore, she rolled once more, and again I was able to see her eye staring directly at me before she released the sea-lion pup from her jaws. It naturally bolted for the only safety it knew, the shore, and straight in my direction.

I could see the pup, very close now, paddling for all it was worth along the surface, and behind it, dark and immense, the great head and jaws of the orca. Jazmin surged once more, only this time straight at me, and as she caught the pup in her jaws she pulled up sharply, once again throwing a wave over where I lay and soaking me to the skin. No more than three metres away, her head and back well clear of the water, she turned and eyed me, then pulled herself back in the waves and brought the seal pup into deeper water. With the last of the light, she played with her meal for another ten minutes or so, just offshore, regularly lifting her head well above the surface and looking towards where I was still lying.

The thrill of being so close to such a powerful and sentient killer had taken me to a euphoric plane; the sequence of events will forever remain as a slowed-down version in my memory. I knew I had been exposed to a once-in-a-lifetime encounter and wanted to savour every last minute of this intense and personal experience.

When it really was too dark to see what was going on, I slowly rose to my feet and, with the sound of an orca's breath blowing just offshore, I walked back up the sloping beach to where Beto was sitting in the glow of the fire.

He looked up at me with the smile of a man who knew precisely what I was feeling at the time and said simply:

'*Sin palabras.*' There are no words.

Chapter 16

Living Desert

Working alongside the goliaths of the sea will remain one of the most moving experiences I shall ever undergo, but it was with a much smaller creature that I now wanted to forge a relationship.

Meerkats were famously brought to our televisions in a wonderful film made by Richard Goss and David MacDonald called *Meerkats United*. The little mongooses' sociability and humanoid postures and features made them an instant hit in the hearts of millions. Ten years on, I wanted to work with these charming animals and thought that illustrating the methods a film-maker used to get inside their world would give the project a fresh approach.

Together with my colleague and partner, Marguerite, we planned a year-long project for the *Natural World* series in which I would be filmed trying to habituate a wild troop of meerkats – that is, to break down the instinctive barrier of fear they had for humans – and, once their trust was won, follow them through the trials and challenges of their daily life.

We started work early in the year, enlisting the help of research scientists who had worked with meerkats before in a protracted study for Cambridge University and who had refined methods of habituation. These approaches were perhaps counterintuitive because, far from trying to be inconspicuous and quiet, they involved adopting a unique and very obvious behaviour that the creatures would come to recognise over time; if it was done sensitively, they would recognise the people producing the actions as benign. Our chosen repertoire of unique sounds and movements included making a gargling sound, clicking our fingers regularly and waving our hands in a fluttering motion. Each call and hand movement served a different purpose. The gargling sound was soft but far-carrying and, though not mimicry, it was not unlike a meerkat's comfort call. The finger-clicking caught their attention at a distance, and the hand wave, which always immediately followed the clicking, was a clear visual signal. The idea was that once a meerkat family was used to these curious behaviour traits in a human, it would accept us at close range. But, if a human approached them and did not display the same odd behaviour, then it would be treated with suspicion.

That was the theory, anyway. And, after about three months of very gradual, painstaking work, it proved to be very effective indeed. I was soon able to head out at dawn and sit alongside a burrow where the meerkat family we were following had spent the night. As they emerged to warm up in the morning sun, they ignored me completely, affording me a very intimate view of their lives. Before long, I was able to follow them on foot as they foraged by digging into the sand for beetles, grubs and scorpions, and I could film every detail of their day using a tiny camera mounted on a stick to get down on their level.

The location we had chosen to shoot the film was a huge, privately run reserve called Tswalu. I had mentioned to the managers of the reserve that – once our filming project was over – they would have a unique resource for showing tourists the meerkats at very close quarters, so long as they stuck to our behavioural guidelines, and their guides told visitors to do the same. It did strike me that if we had decided to habituate the troop to an even sillier set of sounds and movements, we could have left a very amusing legacy.

The advantages the meerkats gained from living in an extended family were never better illustrated than when the whole troop was foraging. The vast majority of their food was discovered by digging, but with their heads and shoulders buried in the sand, the foraging members of the troop were vulnerable to attack from birds of prey or jackals. To counter this, one of the troop members would stand on sentry duty, keeping an eye out for trouble and so allowing the rest of the family to relax and dig for food. This sentry duty was shared by a number of animals in the troop, ensuring that there was never a moment that their guard was down.

The main trouble while filming was that what the meerkats saw as a threat and what I might consider a bit dodgy were two completely different things. For example, they would alert other meerkats if they saw chanting goshawks, which were not likely to trouble me. Conversely, white rhinos were ignored by the family, whilst I had to be very much on my guard if the big guys were in the neighbourhood. When it came to snakes, however, we shared a common concern. Over the months, we saw surprisingly few of them, and I only witnessed the meerkat family tackle a serpent on two occasions – once a mole snake, and once a puff adder. Sightings of snakes may have been rare, but there was one evening when I had more than my full quota of close encounters of the serpent kind.

After a particularly long, hot day, I had followed the troop back to their sleeping burrow with the mini-camera, recording their final foraging attempts right up to dusk. Then I watched them disappear into the safety of the burrow to spend the night. With a fix on where I would find them the following dawn, I returned to where I had left my film camera earlier in the day; I had lodged it in the shade of a large tree that supported a vast colony of sociable weavers. Their immense thatch of nesting mate-rial filled half the tree, providing a wonderful, deep shade under which my camera kit had been protected from the searing sun.

I was tired, and keen to get the camera gear back in the car and make my way to our rented farmhouse where I could have a shower, supper and sleep. With the light turning blue-grey and the shadows deepening, I broke into a jogging run to cover the distance more swiftly. I had about half a mile to cover, and was happy to be stretching my limbs properly at last after spending twelve hours moving very slowly around the meerkats.

I heard the hiss first – an astonishingly loud expulsion, like a burst tyre – explode from the vegetation at the point my right foot was about to hit the ground. I was midway through a stride, and about to stamp on the biggest puff adder I had ever seen. Its girth was thicker than my upper arm and its broad head – the size of my hand – had drawn back prepared to defend itself with a strike.

I had no idea, before that moment, that a human being has the capacity to change direction through about forty-five degrees in midair. Don't ask me how I did it – I'm guessing it would take the threat of standing on a deadly venomous snake to repeat the feat – but I somehow shifted direction and landed heavily a metre to the side of the angry serpent. Fortunately, puff adders are peace-loving critters at heart (unless you are a mouse) and they certainly don't tend to hold a grudge. This gargantuan creature simply settled back into her coiled slump and her cryptic patterning melted into the vegetation once more.

I continued my journey back to where I had left the camera at a more sober pace, careful to avoid any clumps of thorn or other vegetation as the light faded further still. When I reached the tree, night already had a grip and I was barely able to make out the silhouette of the tripod and camera still nestled beneath the huge weaver nest that had given it shade through the heat of the day. I walked beneath the canopy and leant the tripod against my shoulder, preparing to lift it, when I heard another, very loud hiss close to my right ear. Without moving my head, I turned my eyes as far as I was able in the direction of the sound and could barely believe what I saw. An adult Cape cobra was hanging from the weavers' nests, staring into my face with its hood fully extended in alarm.

Snakes, per se, do not scare me. But looking into the

face and flicking tongue of one of South Africa's most deadly serpents did make my heart race a bit. My arrival had obviously startled this reptile and I thought that if I made any other move it might be tempted to strike in its own defence. The few other cobras I had seen before had been very shy and slithered away into cover the moment they had seen me coming. I had no doubt this fellow wanted to do the same, but I had compromised him in the middle of his hunting foray and he had nowhere to go. We were in a stalemate, neither one of us wanting to budge for fear that the other would make an aggressive move.

I decided to avert my eyes, figuring that if the cobra felt it could slip away without being watched, it would take the opportunity. A full five minutes passed with us both playing statues, before I heard the grasses in the nest above me rustling, and I looked up to see the end of the cobra's tail slipping into the darkness of the nest chambers.

That evening, when I got back to the farmhouse, I had a beer. Two actually.

I continued work in the Kalahari desert region on another project at about the same time, only on this occasion it was going to be people rather than wildlife that were to be our focus. The team working on the David Attenborough series, *The Life of Mammals*, wanted to include some scenes shot in Botswana, with Sir David delivering pieces to camera next to elephants and antelopes. They also wanted to feature an event about which I had read, but which I had difficulty believing really took place: the endurance hunt of the San Bushmen.

Before concentrating on the Bushmen's hunt, we travelled to the Chobe River, where I was to film David talking to camera with herds of elephants nearby. He and I had met on many occasions since my first star-struck encounter with him on the steps of the Natural History Museum in London, and, if I'm honest, I'd remained star-struck. This man had been and remains an inspiration to millions, myself included, and he had always been enormously kind and civil during our brief encounters. This – oddly, perhaps – was the first time we had ever worked together, and I was very nervous. My duties as a cameraman were modest, but when you are in the presence of an erudite, amusing man, who also happens to be a legend and your hero, it's very difficult to remain normal. I worked hard not to appear too fawning, or, worse still, indifferent to his company, and hoped that I had managed to strike a balance between the two. But I could not help catching him alone a few days into the shoot, and telling him what an honour it was to work with him. I'm glad I did. David was a joy to be with in the field; always prepared to muck in and help carry camera kit, despite his advancing years, and always ready with a witty anecdote over supper. I was, and will always remain, in awe of him.

Whilst in the Chobe National Park, we hired a helicopter to film aerials of the great herds of elephants and some bird's-eye views of David too. We also wanted some air-to-ground tracking shots of the San Bushmen we were to work with later in the shoot and, for logistical and budgetary reasons, we asked the guys if they could join us at Chobe for a few days to make the most of having the helicopter in one place.

The men of the desert travelled by road from their home further north with a friend, Louis Liebenberg, who was working with them, trying to put their astonishing tracking skills into a modern context. He had equipped them with small, handheld computers linked to satellite navigation GPS; thereafter the San Bushmen, experts in deciphering animal tracks, could record information about animals – their movements, food sources and so on – as they moved through their traditional hunting grounds. The data could later be analysed and used to inform conservation projects.

I was immediately struck by the Sans' sunny disposition, diminutive stature – and their capacity to smoke. It was impossible to be sure how old each of them was, but the chap who looked to be the youngest of them, Karoha, was the man who had the reputation for being able to run a healthy antelope off its feet. Watching him chain-smoke huge roll-ups, often using torn newspaper as skins, I couldn't imagine him being able to run 100 metres without coughing up his lungs.

All that we wanted to achieve whilst in Chobe was a few aerial shots of them running that we hoped would cut in to the main body of the sequence yet to be shot. The guys had been on the road for some hours and so we invited everyone to stop for a spot of lunch before we headed out into the field. The lodge where we were staying had prepared a large buffet and I suggested to

Karoha, !Nqate and Xlhoase that they help themselves. (The !Xo San use many clicks in their language and the written version incorporates exclamation marks and 'Xs' to denote these.)

Each of the small men filed past the mountains of fruit and vegetables in turn, ignoring them completely, but when it came to the selection of meats on offer, each paused to load their plate. And when I say load, I *mean* load. You could not have balanced a single morsel more onto any one of their plates without bringing the whole lot collapsing over the edges. I patronisingly assumed that they were unused to seeing such a laden table, and that their eyes would be bigger than their diminutive stomachs. How wrong I was. I watched, astonished, as each of the men silently worked his way through his meat mountain, and then, after a small drink of water, went back to the buffet for a refill of equally immense proportions and devoured that too. By the end of the meal their naked stomachs were distended to what looked like bursting point, as though they had each eaten the equivalent of half a horse, which they very nearly had. I realised that the cultural prerequisite for making the most of times of plenty was deep-set in these extraordinary people, and that I would have to shift all of my preconceptions about what a human being was or was not capable of.

The filming in Chobe went well, and all too soon we said our farewells to David, who was due to meet another crew, elsewhere in Africa, to shoot more pieces to camera for the series. With my assistant Ted Giffords, and the programme producer, Vanessa Berlowitz, we travelled north with the San to their ancestral hunting grounds, where we were to attempt to film the near mythical endurance hunt.

It was reputed that, over the millennia, the San had developed a method of securing a meal that involved two superhuman abilities. The first was the capacity to track an individual antelope over many miles of open desert, without having to see the creature in question, and never waiver from the course. The second – and this was the bit that I found very hard to believe – was that the same trackers would do so at a run, and that their quarry would, over time, become so exhausted that it would literally drop from its feet. In preparation for the shoot, I had taken to jogging a few miles every morning, and felt that I should be able to keep up with the runners for at least a part of their course. As it turned out, I was deluded.

At dawn on the day of the run, the men sat beneath a small desert tree, talking quietly to each other, smoking and drinking water. I wondered why they did not make a start, capitalising on the cool air of first light, but it was pointed out to me that they wanted the heat of the day to exhaust their quarry; they were strong enough to endure the furnace.

By ten in the morning, with the sun high and the sand already too hot for my soft Western feet to stand on, the Bushmen gathered their spears, bows and arrows and set off at a brisk walk. I followed with Ted and Vanessa in a four-by-four vehicle, driving ahead of the men and hopping out from time to time to walk with them and film their progress. The whole time they walked they studied the ground and the vegetation all around them, holding their hands in curious positions, a sign language that told of the tracks they were seeing.

When !Nqate held his hand high in the symbol that signified that he had found the track of a kudu, the atmosphere changed. The men came closer to each other, and picked up the pace. Their excitement was tangible; their focus on the spoor they followed undivided. Then there they were, four kudu bulls standing alert in the shade of a small tree some 500 metres away. I expected the men to stalk close to the herd, but they did quite the opposite, walking as tall as their frames would allow and shouting at the huge antelope to startle them. The kudu ran off into the blistering sun and the men trotted to the shade where they had been resting. Their faces a study of concentration, they allowed their fingers to hover over the hoof-pummelled sand, identifying which of the bulls they would follow in the group. This astounded me. I could see that there were kudu tracks there, but separating one individual from the rest seemed an impossibility. These men were doing just that.

Having chosen their intended quarry from its tracks alone, the men conducted a brief ceremony, burying the animal's droppings in the sand around its spoor and mumbling a mantra to the sky.

Whilst filming this ritual, I suddenly felt very self-conscious and embarrassed, like a peeping tom spying on something very private and sacred. But in me too was the desire to see this through, to witness just what these men were capable of and to record it for others to see in all its raw honesty. I am not a hunting man (though my love of fishing is something of a contradiction), and I have always found it difficult to reconcile the taking of a life with pleasure, but what these men were doing was something different; a legacy of survival handed down over hundreds of generations. Despite my intrusion, they were very much in the moment; their focus on the subtle marks in the sand and on the effort that they were about to expend was absolute and undivided. They were living the hunt that was to come, seeing its outcome before it had happened, understanding the creature that was their target and thinking as it might think. The only parallel from my world that I could think came close was the preparation a top sportsman might undergo before a game; but the bushmen added a layer of spirituality that I had never witnessed before.

The moment of reverence over, the men set off at a fast trot, all the time staring at the ground and using their sign language in an expression of what they were seeing. Twice more, they caught up with the kudu, whose numbers dwindled to three, then two, and on each occasion the men charged at the animals to scare them out of the shade they craved and into the sunlight. We had been travelling at a fair pace for the best part of two hours, and neither the men nor the kudu were showing any sign of flagging. As for my doubting the guys' ability to run with their smokers' lungs, I had to admit I was very wrong. I, on the other hand, was exhausted, despite only having run a tiny fraction of the distance the San had covered so far. I wondered how they could keep up this pace, particularly now that the sun was reaching its zenith and the heat was intense. In the event, they did not: they got even faster. Specifically, it was Karoha, the youngest of them and the man they all referred to as 'the runner', who took the chase to the next level. When the men next encountered the kudu bull, which was now alone, the others having peeled away one by one, Karoha stepped the pace up a gear and left the rest of his colleagues behind. They would continue to follow his tracks at a slower pace, but before long we were driving the camera vehicle a few hundred metres to the side of a lone figure running through the blistering white light of noon.

I marvelled again at the flowing, instinctive way Karoha read the signs in the sand, with a focus and purpose that took him into a sort of trance. Once or twice he faltered, going back on his own tracks and with his hands telling the story of an unseen animal running through the scrub, he moved through the bushes as his quarry might. He was soon literally back on track and running again at an astonishingly brisk pace. We continued like this for hours, covering kilometre after kilometre, with me jumping out of the car to run with Karoha from time to time, then getting back in to drive ahead and try to spot the kudu he was following. His quarry became a ghost, an invisible spirit that ran its trail through deep thorn scrub and rocky ground, and we never did see it again until the end, which came abruptly and – for me – unexpectedly.

Some seven hours and over thirty kilometres had passed when Karoha suddenly stopped and crouched. In a clearing ahead of him, and staring back, stood the kudu bull,

mouth slightly agape, eyes glazed with exhaustion. Karoha
stood slowly now, wracked by his own physical pain,
sharing with the kudu a racing heart and the agony of
acid in his muscles. He walked forward and, for a moment,
no more than two metres apart, man and antelope were
fixed in each other's gaze. I was out of the vehicle and
filming this extraordinary, intensely moving moment as
the kudu seemed to crumple, going down on its front
hocks into the sand. Karoha did not look at me, but said
quietly 'we end this now', and with that he threw his
spear into the heart of the dying creature. Strangely, there
seemed to be nothing violent about the act: it was pure
and without malice.

I retreated to give Karoha the space he needed to pay
his respects to the animal whose life he had shared for
seven hours and now had taken. He lifted sand from the
desert floor in one hand and sprinkled it over the body,
quietly muttering words, the meaning and significance of
which I shall never fully understand, but which felt
complete, a recognition that from the desert had come
this creature that now would sustain Karoha and the rest
of the community, and the sands of the desert would take
it back once more. He gently put his fingers into the still
warm mouth of the bull, and spread the saliva over his
aching limbs, sharing the strength of his quarry. I could
feel that through his own pain this man was as much a
part of the rhythm of the earth as the rise and fall of the
sun and the wind that brushed across us all.

I was emotionally and physically exhausted, at once
disturbed by witnessing the death of a beautiful creature,

and at the same time seeing the beauty in its demise. As a final shot, I felt compelled to tilt the view away from the scene before me, man bent over bull, and lift the camera up to the clear blue sky. And once I had done it, I slumped behind the vehicle and cried.

Chapter 17

Wild Live

Africa was where I came into this world, and the great continent continued to enrich my life through contact with its extraordinary people and wildlife. The *Big Cat Diary* series became an established brand and I revisited the Mara in Kenya many times to follow the feline families I had come to know so well. My on-screen presence in the UK developed too, with new live programme strands like *Britain Goes Wild*, which went on to become *Springwatch* and *Autumnwatch*, all affording me wonderful travels and adventures in wild corners of the country.

Presenting live shows on telly was not new to me. I had cut my broadcasting teeth as a kid in programmes that were transmitted to the public raw and uncut, and had found my way back into the genre when the BBC Natural History Unit decided to resurrect live wildlife content with a programme following the tide cycle on the Norfolk coast called *Beachwatch*.

In its wake came *Heading South*, a live event that followed bird migration, and *Flamingowatch*, a series that did what it said on the box, transmitting live to the UK and the USA from Lake Nakuru and Lake Bagoria in Kenya.

But the real precursor to *Springwatch* and *Autumnwatch*

was a series called *Bird in the Nest* hosted by Bill Oddie and Peter Holden. My part in this production was largely as a specialist cameraman, concentrating on a kingfisher's nest burrow I had painstakingly prepared for filming. I popped up on camera from time to time to give reports of the day's events with the birds, but it was an unfortunate twist of fate that brought me a more central role in the series. The kingfisher nest was dug into a steep river bank, not far from my home on the Somerset Levels. The single-track road that ran alongside the river bore very little traffic, and the birds had nested successfully in the spot the previous year. Like my work with the bee-eaters in Africa, filming the kingfishers in their nest burrow took many days of careful digging and the gradual introduction of artificial light to reveal the intimate details of their family life. Everything had gone well during the lead-up to transmission and the first of the shows revealed – for the first time on live television – a view of the newly hatched kingfisher chicks being fed and brooded by their parents. But on the second day of live transmission I received a call from my assistant saying that we had a problem.

I sped to the location to find hordes of people scrambling over the river bank and wading up and down the stream in front of the nest. My mind scrambled for an explanation. We had been enormously careful to keep the location of the nest a secret and I couldn't imagine how, or why, so many people would suddenly flock to the spot and behave in such an inconsiderate way. I ran up to a chap who was inspecting the bank directly below the nest.

'Excuse me, could I ask you to move away as quickly as possible, please? You're disturbing the birds,' I panted.

'What birds?' he answered with a look of suspicion in his eye. 'I'm on the treasure hunt, and one of the clues is around here somewhere. Are you trying to throw me off the trail?'

The awful truth dawned on me. This gathering had nothing whatever to do with the kingfishers; instead it was just sheer bad luck that one of the clues for a treasure hunt involving more than thirty people just happened to lie very close to the vicinity of the nest. Most of the folk I implored to move away were very considerate and concerned that they might have been disturbing the birds, but one or two insisted on continuing their search along the river, assuming we had been instructed by the treasure hunt organisers to provide some sort of red herring.

By the time the last of them had left the area, well over two hours had passed. I had seen the parent birds dashing past their nest from time to time, calling in alarm, but once the coast was clear the damage was done. At least one of the newly hatched chicks had died of hypothermia, and the others were weak and sickly. The female bird visited with a fish the moment the coast was clear, but her frail youngsters were too weak to take it from her, and by evening all were dead.

I was distraught. I played the events over and over in my head, wondering if there had been anything I could have done to prevent the chicks dying; but the harsh truth was that had we not been filming the nest, precisely the same thing would have happened. The only difference would have been that not a soul would have known about it.

That evening, I joined Bill and Peter during the live show to recount the events of the day. I was pretty upset by the whole thing, and Bill was wonderfully understanding, trying to assure me that I had done everything in my power to prevent the loss. It was the start of a mutual trust and friendship that remains to this day.

Bill and I combined forces once again on an ill-fated live series that rather ineffectually tried to dig up dinosaurs on the Isle of Wight, before working on *Wild in Your Garden*, where we were joined for the first time by Kate Humble.

This rather provincial series that celebrated the flora and fauna that was beneath, over the top of, or in your garden shed was based around the gardens of Bristol. It spanned a week, and after only a couple of days it was clear we were going to be a bit hard up for things to talk about. Despite showcasing badgers, foxes and a host of birds, it wasn't long before Bill, Kate and I were starting to pass the buck whilst on air. A typical exchange might go something like this.

Bill: Well, Kate, it doesn't look like the blackbird family is getting up to much at the moment. How are your blue tits?

Kate: All quiet here too, Bill. It must be siesta time for our wildlife stars. What's happening with the fox family, Simon?

Me (doing my best impression of a rabbit caught

in headlights): Well, ummmm, not much here
either, guys. I did see a cub stick his nose out
from beneath the shed about half an hour ago,
but nothing since [long pause]. So, Bill, any more
news on the blackbirds?

You get the picture. It was excruciating at times, and I
could almost hear the producers' knuckles splintering as
they chewed them to the bone.

Amazingly, though, the series proved to be a hit with
the viewers. The charming, sometimes edgy banter
between Bill and Kate, and my occasional reports from
the wilder end of the garden, struck a chord with viewers.
There was a distinct paucity of wildlife, but those creatures that were featured, though familiar, were show-
cased in an unfamiliar way, lending a soap-opera flavour
to their life stories. The combination of compelling animal
tales and the team's interpretation of their lives led to
the commissioning of a more ambitious series for the
following spring. *Britain Goes Wild* was to look at wildlife
from around the UK, and my role was to provide on-the-
spot reports from the field.

My first location was the Bass Rock off the Scottish east
coast, home to over 40,000 breeding pairs of gannets and
thousands of other seabirds from puffins to guillemots.

The programmes ran for an hour and appeared live on
air every night, Monday to Friday. Gannets are truly
magnificent birds, and the spectacle of the immense colony
on the Bass rivals any natural wonder on earth. But I have
to say that, having chatted about gannets for hours on

end, for five days straight, even I was beginning to wonder what was on the other channel! I needn't have been concerned, though. The mix of my somewhat repetitive reports with the lively elements from Bill and Kate won the hearts of the viewers, and the series was watched by over three million people each night.

During one of my live inserts to the show from the Bass Rock, I was revealing the intricate details of the non-breeding club of gannets that hung out on the north-east of the island. The cameras were trained on me for the beginning of the piece, but the director soon cut to the view of the birds offered up by one of three cameras equipped with telephoto lenses. My attention was drawn to the small TV monitor that lay at my feet, from which I could see the output of the cameras, and so deliver live commentary on whatever behaviour was being picked up. By then, I was used to the odd fleck of guano hitting my hat or jacket from the many hundreds of birds that constantly passed overhead in squadrons going to or coming back from the sea. What I was less used to was eating the stuff. Mid-sentence, a small but significant blob of bird poo was blown into my open mouth. Since the camera was not trained on me at the time, I had no way of referring to my predicament that would make any sense whatsoever to the viewer, and so instead coughed and choked my way to the end of the piece, discussing the age of the non-breeding birds and how long it would be before they settled down to raise a family. When the cameras did finally cut back to me before I handed back to Bill and Kate, they found me looking like a strawberry swirl; red-faced with a splash of white running from my right temple, across my mouth and onto my chin.

Gannet guano was as nothing compared to the layers of Arctic tern droppings that coated me on a later series of what was now under its new and current moniker of *Springwatch*. I was showcasing the birdlife of the Farne Islands and was based on Inner Farne, along with its substantial tern colonies, for the week. Every day I walked up the public gangway to the top of the isle and came under attack from hundreds of terns that chose to nest close to the path. The attacks were largely bluff, with lots of chipping and screeching calls, but from time to time a dagger-like bill was brought down hard onto the top of my head. With no hair to cushion the blow, I was glad of my hat for protection, but even this needed reinforcing with a bit of cardboard to prevent the most enthusiastic of the birds from drawing blood. Their beaks were a powerful deterrent to any would-be predators, but they backed up their assault with well-aimed dollops of guano. On the occasions we went on air to talk about the terns, I was repeatedly pecked and pooed on. It added an interesting layer of challenge to keeping my train of thought whilst warm droppings ran down the back of my neck.

Springwatch proved to be so popular that its autumnal cousin was created to satisfy a demand to follow British wild creatures through the seasons. My role was once again to report from the field, kicking off by charting the fortunes of a group of red deer on the Isle of Rum. The animals in question had been the subject of a study spanning over thirty years and consequently we had access to an astounding font of knowledge. Being able to confidently give a potted history of a stag's life, from birth to present day, added texture and sometimes pathos to what might otherwise have just been shots of a bunch of big goaty things bashing their heads together. Telling these animals' life stories in an accessible and contemporary way helped to bring their wild world a little closer for millions of people who might otherwise have felt removed from such tales.

After following the stags on Rum, we chose to take on a sort of wildlife road trip around Britain, to get a broader flavour of the changes in the nation's flora and fauna over the autumn months. I tracked down wild boar in the Forest of Dean, spawning salmon in the rivers of Scotland, and grey seal pups in the Farne Islands. But it was when looking for hibernating bats that I found myself somewhat compromised when we went on air.

The location for the transmission was a cave system in northern England, which could only be accessed by dropping about twenty metres through a very narrow passageway into the chamber below. The technical team did an amazing job of preparing the shoot in record time, having travelled from a remote location the day before and laying out over a kilometre of cable to get the pictures back to the trucks and transmit them live on the same evening. My task was simple by comparison: I had to abseil down a rope system into the cave chamber, chat about bats with a local expert, and climb back out at the end of the show. I had done quite a bit of rope-work previously, but was by no means an expert. Fortunately, experts were on hand to make sure I didn't muddle my lines (the physical ones rather than the spoken word; the latter was entirely my responsibility) and to help with preparation of my descent.

The plan was for me to deliver my opening comments as I dropped into the cave, and to pick up the story of the bats once I'd entered the chamber. I dressed in my climbing harness and – to be certain of the routine – did one trial descent before we went on air. Access to the cave was through a very narrow fault in the rocks, known to cavers as a 'squeeze'. These gaps are so narrow, in fact, that at its tightest point the rock walls crush your chest, making it impossible to manipulate the descending gear in the usual fashion; instead you must hold it out to one side. I quite literally had to exhale to make my chest sufficiently narrow to get through the gap, but the rehearsal descent went without a glitch and we all felt prepared for the transmission.

An hour later I was being given the cue in my earpiece to start my piece and to make the drop into the cave. But an hour later, there had been one or two subtle changes. Specifically, the climbing harness I was wearing had shifted a little. The moment I allowed the rope to take my body weight I knew I was in for a very uncomfortable experience. The lower crutch straps of my harness had shifted ever so slightly to one side, trapping some very delicate body parts. I found my whole body weight crushing down on my modest jewels; stuck in the squeeze, I was powerless to shift my weight and do anything about it. Reaching the bottom of the ropes and having the pressure taken off this sensitive spot was an enormous relief, which apparently showed in my face. It might well have showed in my voice, too; I think it went up by an octave for a while.

It is the unpredictable nature of live television, and the inevitability that once it has been transmitted there's absolutely nothing one can do to tweak or change it, that make it such a fun – and challenging – arena for a presenter. Where a great many presenters of live television use an autocue, an invisible screen in front of the camera lens that has a scrolling word script from which the presenter reads, in *Springwatch* and *Autumnwatch* we use no such technology, largely because we have little or no idea just what might happen from one moment to the next, and we have to respond to events in a spontaneous manner. This also means that we can be a little more flexible about what it is we are saying than an autocue would allow.

One expression of this flexibility comes in the form of the 'famous phrase' challenge, first started by a particularly mischievous vision mixer who asked if I could shoehorn 'you have no future, bitch' into one of my pieces to camera. The prize for fulfilling the mission was a beer, more than enough incentive. In truth, I only half managed to squeeze the line in to a narrative I was delivering about a peregrine nest in middle England. Whilst discussing the future of a family of jackdaws that were nesting within a few metres of the peregrine eyrie, I came up with the line '. . . but quite frankly, if you're a jackdaw chick nesting here, you might think you have no future between the peregrines and all the other hazards facing a young bird.'

I slurred the 't' in 'between' to sound more like a 'ch', but had to confess to only partially completing the set task. I settled for half a pint as a reward.

I was rather more successful on the Farne Islands when asked to include the line 'nobody leaves Baby in the corner', delivered by Patrick Swayze to Jennifer Grey in the film *Dirty Dancing*. I spotted my opportunity whilst recounting the tale of an eider duck female that had chosen to nest in the walled garden of the chapel on Inner Farne. Whilst the adult bird could easily flap her way out of the metre-deep pit where she had incubated her brood, her flightless chicks were powerless to follow in her wake. If they didn't manage to make it down to the sea to feed alongside their mother, they would perish, and so it was that I came to help them over the steep walls of their natal home and into the big wide world. You can imagine how I managed to sneak the requisite line into the show.

Flushed with success, I was brought firmly back to earth when the next line challenge was presented to me over supper that same evening.

'Simon,' called the vision mixer from the far side of the table, 'I'll bet you can't get "Scaramouche, scaramouche, will you do the fandango?" from 'Bohemian Rhapsody' into tomorrow's show.'

I know when I'm beaten.

Still, you never know, I might manage to sneak it in to a live broadcast one of these days, and I shall most certainly be claiming my pint if I do.

As well as being tremendously good fun to work on, the live shows have afforded me some wonderfully rich wildlife watching experiences. From orcas and otters in Shetland, to encounters with wild boar, red squirrels, pine martens and ospreys, I have been enormously fortunate to have been able to travel over much of Britain in search of its natural jewels. Typically, when one begins to unpeel a fine fruit one is left with a hankering for more, and the time I have spent visiting new parts of the British Isles has served to confirm that I shall never be able to see it all, or to do it justice in the programmes I am involved in. It is a bitter-sweet truth that the more I know about a place or its wildlife, the more I have to concede I shall never know. But how lovely it is to be able to say with absolute confidence that I cannot imagine a day when I will have nothing to do, or nowhere left that I aspire to visit.

Perhaps one of the greatest privileges afforded by working on the live programmes has been to have entered the lives of the nation's wild inhabitants and to have shared their highs and lows over many weeks and – in some cases – years. From frail families of ducklings waddling through countless dangers to the twilight years of mighty red deer stags, I have been given the opportunity to see these already compelling creatures as individuals and to share some of their anxieties and joys. Every year, advances in technology have given us ever-greater opportunities to spy on the secret lives of wild animals. With cameras now no bigger than the nail of your little finger and thermal-imaging systems that can reveal a multicoloured view of life after dark, there are few places we cannot penetrate to unfold a world of intrigue and wonder. But in essence the ingredients that make compelling tales of the lives of these creatures remain the same. In their fortunes we see a reflection of our own and, hopefully, by engaging with them, we each of us begin to care more about their future and to make positive moves to ensure we all lead a harmonious co-existence.

If programmes like *Springwatch* and *Autumnwatch* have any real value, it is actually to encourage people to switch off the TV, and to get outside to see these natural wonders for themselves. I hope that we have been able to show that you don't have to live in a remote area to benefit from engaging with the wild world. Every city has its forgotten corner, every garden is a wilderness of mini-beasts. It has been my great good fortune to have been born with a passion that has remained with me to this day. If any of that passion can rub off onto others and encourage them to look beyond our human construct and into the colossal treasures of the natural systems all around us, then I am luckier still, for we all of us benefit from a collective will to make the world a better place.

Chapter 18

Toki and Sambu

It was in Africa that an opportunity arose that changed the way I would perceive the wild world forever. Whilst working with the lions of the Mara I heard a report that some friends of a friend were raising two orphaned cheetah cubs. Marguerite and I had recently finished the meerkat film in the Kalahari, and had been discussing the possibility that we might be able to help with the rehabilitation of orphaned predators as our next project. It seemed like fate.

I contacted Jane and Ian Craig of Lewa Wildlife Conservancy immediately, and asked if we might be able to visit with a view to helping with the care of the young cheetahs and, in time, their release back to the wild. I couldn't have met with a more enthusiastic response and – after a whirlwind return to the UK to discuss the potential for filming our progress with the cats for the *Natural World* series – we were soon back in Kenya and driving north to Lewa. We had a basic camera kit and a couple of weeks to discover what, if anything, we could do to help.

We were greeted on arrival by a very welcome cup of tea and the story of how the cheetah cubs had come to be in the Craigs' care. About a month before, the cubs

289

had been found by a couple of Samburu boys in the harsh country of the Northern Rangelands. The cheetahs' mother had been killed by a lion and the boys knew that without help the tiny cats would certainly die. They brought the cubs to a remote tourist lodge in the area and news swiftly reached Ian Craig, the then director of Lewa Wildlife Conservancy. Ian immediately mobilised a light aircraft and brought them back to his home in the shadow of Mount Kenya. His wife, Jane, was very experienced when it came to helping orphaned wild animals, having helped raise everything from warthogs to giraffes in the past, and even having worked with cheetahs some years earlier. It was Jane who brought the emaciated scraps of life back from the brink, feeding them a magic mix of milk formula with added extras and watching them round the clock to ensure they were well. At a little over three weeks old, the brothers, for they were both males, were still entirely dependent on a mother figure for food, warmth and protection and, with Jane providing all of these in spades, the cubs flourished.

When we met the cheetahs first they were about twelve weeks old, still feeding on milk and entirely dependent on their human guardians for protection from all the dangers that the African bush posed for them.

We discussed with Ian and Jane the possibility of Marguerite and I taking on the responsibility of the day-to-day management of the orphans, and the idea was met with enthusiasm. I had no previous experience of raising cheetahs, but had worked with other orphaned predators, like otters, badgers and foxes, and had a basic idea of how we might go about introducing the cats to the wild over time. I don't think either of us appreciated just how much our lives would be touched by these extraordinary creatures the more we became enmeshed in their battle for survival. With the assistance of some of the Lewa ranger staff, most notably Stephen Yiasoiole, a young Masai man whose dedication and commitment to the young cats was astonishing and very touching, the best part of two years was spent helping the brothers reach the point of independence.

The story of their development and adventures was chronicled in the *Natural World* film *Cheetahs – Fast Track to Freedom* and versioned for American viewers as *The Cheetah Orphans*. I hoped that the films portrayed something of the remarkable experiences we had the privilege to live through, but in truth the responsibility of helping these beautiful cats lead as near natural an existence as possible was very hard to portray in all its emotional detail. Every day, from the moment we took on the challenge, we worried about their welfare. Were we kidding ourselves that they could ever live again in the wild? There were some people, more learned than I, who had suggested so. Would they ever learn to hunt effectively for themselves? Could they learn to discern between creatures that were benign and those that presented a mortal threat?

Our constant comfort came from the thought that at least we were doing our best, and that they would most certainly be dead already were it not for the intervention of human beings. I personally wrestled with the fact that their mother had died a violent but natural death, and that if I were true to my moral code, the cubs should have died too. But I convinced myself that the moment the Samburu boys altered the course of the cheetahs' fate by picking them up and bringing them to the lodge, it became reasonable that we humans should do our best to give them a fighting chance.

Over the months, despite trying hard to remain detached, I became very fond of the cubs, which we had named Toki and Sambu, and their demonstrations of affection towards us, with head-rubbing, licking and purr-filled cuddles, only bolstered the bond.

It soon became clear that they would not have to be taught to hunt, which at least was innate in their character, but they would have to be given the opportunity to perfect their skills. Time and again, I watched with my heart in my mouth their adolescent and misguided attempts to tackle prey far too big for them. I lost count of the number of times they came to within a whisker of having their skulls crushed by the flailing hoof of a zebra or waterbuck. As they became more confident of their speed they tested their mettle against some of the real heavy-weights of the bush too. My incompetence as a surrogate mother was never better illustrated than when Toki and Sambu decided to tease an adult bull white rhino, and looked back at me with incredulity when I did not opt to share their dangerous game of tag.

After almost two years the brothers were living wild and free, hunting for themselves and growing in strength and confidence with every passing day. Marguerite and I were preparing to leave Lewa, satisfied that the boys had a bright future ahead of them, when the unthinkable happened.

We arrived at the spot we had left them the evening before, and almost immediately sensed that something was wrong. We quickly found Toki, but he was alone and calling constantly for his brother.

I had a dreadful sinking feeling, but wanted to believe that Sambu was just stuck up a tree or else had gone hunting alone, and had become momentarily separated. Both cheetahs were wearing radio collars, and I picked up a strong signal from Sambu's transmitter just north of where we stood. The closer I got to the source of the transmission with no sign of Sambu, the more I felt certain that something dreadful had happened. As I rounded some large rocks at the base of a hill, I spotted lion footprints in the sand. They were huge, certainly from an adult male, and had been made very recently. Spurred on by the rhythmic bleeping from Sambu's collar, I rounded the rocks, fully expecting to surprise a lion from its sleep. I still had a glimmer of hope that the cheetah was safely stuck up a tree with the lion pacing beneath, and that once I had scared the great cat away, we would all be reunited. But there in the grass lay the awful truth. Sambu had died in the jaws of a lion in the small hours of the morning. He was virtually untouched but for the marks where the massive teeth had gripped him around his back and shaken the life from him.

I knew that both he and Toki had already encountered lions on many occasions in the past and learned to be very wary of them. Sambu must have been surprised by an ambush and, replete from his big meal that evening, not reacted quickly enough to escape.

I was devastated, wracked with doubt and guilt that perhaps the brothers were not and never would be ready for life in the wild, and that hoping that they might be was naive and stupid. The only comforting thought I could cling to was the fact that they had been thriving independently for months, living wild and free as their birthright intended. I had to remind myself too that the most experienced wild cheetahs sometimes die in the claws and jaws of lions; their mother was an example of just this.

We did not have time to indulge our grief. There was the far more urgent question over the future of Toki, the surviving brother. In the end we spent another two years working with Lewa Wildlife Conservancy, their neighbours, and eventually another privately owned reserve in Northern Kenya, Ol Pejeta, to ensure Toki's quality of life was undimmed. We faced countless hurdles, from him being savaged to within an inch of his life by a coalition of wild male cheetahs, to losing him for days in community farmlands adjacent to the reserve. Once we made the decision to move him to Ol Pejeta for his own safety, the ultimate question of what constituted a reasonable existence for a lone male cheetah had to be addressed. He was well able to hunt for himself, and was now wise to natural aggressors like lions and territorial cheetahs. But he was – and would always be – different when it came to reacting to human beings. Despite our taking great pains to ensure he would remain wary of strangers, there was no getting away from the fact that he showed less fear of people than his wild neighbours did. Even the most timid free-ranging cheetah came to a sticky end at the tip of an arrow or spear from time to time, and I couldn't live with the possibility that Toki might suffer the indignity and pay the terrible price of trusting a human being that might not be benign.

With Ol Pejeta's support, we introduced Toki to a vast enclosure, over 4,000 acres of bush and grassland that hosted a good population of zebra, impala and other animals he could hunt. The fence prevented him wandering onto neighbouring community farmlands, and so protected him from potential conflict with goat and cattle farmers, but it also stopped other creatures wandering in. We had to accept the sad truth that he was alone, and unlikely ever to meet a female cheetah to sire his own cubs, unless a hand-reared female cheetah could be found to join him. We cast our net wide in search of any cats that might fit the bill, but no suitable candidates appeared.

I was out early one morning, researching the wild population of cheetahs in Ol Pejeta to see if releasing Toki into the main reserve might be viable one day, when I received a radio call that he had escaped the confines of the enclosure. I sped back to the south of the reserve, and when I reached the gate to Toki's domain was greeted by Stephen, who had continued to work with the cheetah throughout the four years since he'd been brought into care. I learned that Stephen had seen a cheetah pacing outside the enclosure, but he was certain it was not Toki.

'It is not him, Simon. But I do not know where it came from. I think it is tame.'

I was very confused, but thought perhaps that our dreams had come true. Maybe this was a hand-reared cat that someone could no longer manage, and, knowing that we had the facilities to look after Toki, they had anonymously dropped their pet at our door, hoping we would give it a good home. This would be a real problem if it was another male, since the two of them would almost certainly fight, but if it were a female, then we could be looking at Toki's future mate.

I left the vehicle and walked around the back of the gatekeeper's house, close to the fence where the strange cat had last been seen. I spotted it resting in the shade of some thick prickly-pear bushes, and at first it didn't give me a second glance. I felt confident that this was no wild cheetah; if it were, it should have been running fast in the opposite direction by now, so I took a pace or two towards it and spoke in soft, comforting tones. The cat lifted its head and stared at me, then slowly rose to its feet and stepped out of the shade in my direction.

'Hi there, how are you doing?' I continued to mutter gentle sweet-nothings to try and ensure the cat remained calm.

I took another step towards it; the cheetah responded by walking more boldly towards me. I could see now that it was indeed a female, and looked to be in very good condition, with a shining coat and powerful chest and rump muscles. She would be a perfect companion for Toki, and her offspring would help bolster the foundering cheetah population of the area. She took another pace and I thought I heard her starting to purr, further reinforcing my belief that she was hand-reared and happy to have a bit of company at last, but the purr turned into a deep growl just before all hell was let loose.

The cheetah charged at me, and when a metre or so away leapt up to attack my face. I instinctively planted a boot in her chest to repel her, and received a bite that pierced the tough Cordura fabric of the shoe and entered the flesh of my foot. I also got scratches on my shin and calf through my trousers.

I was astonished by the behaviour. In the four years of raising the cheetah brothers, never once had they displayed anything like this level of aggression. I assumed that this was why the cat's previous owners wanted rid of it and why they had been reluctant to come to us directly with the proposal. Still, there was something very odd about this cat. I could see no sign that she might ever have worn a collar, which was strange if she had indeed been in captivity. She had the look of a cat who had to run for a living too, her slim waist and powerful hind quarters suggesting a life of constant exercise.

The cheetah stared at me for a while, growling in defiance, then turned to amble down the hill towards the wilds of the main reserve. Still shocked, but determined to find out more about this cat, I asked Stephen to follow her at a distance on foot to keep an eye on her progress, whilst I drove down the slope to head her off before she could make it to thick cover. By the time I reached her she had attacked again, this time turning on Stephen and biting his hand. I did not stop to think but leapt from the car and ran to Stephen, who had lost his balance and was sitting on the ground, the cheetah holding his hand in her jaws with her claws digging into his thighs.

I grabbed the cheetah by the scruff of the neck and the base of the tail and heaved. She did her best to turn on me, reaching round behind her head with her forepaws and scratching my forearms, but I managed to hold tight and pull her away from Stephen, telling him to get to the car. At this point my overriding emotion was anger that this cat had launched an unprovoked attack on us both, and had badly hurt my friend. Fuelled by fury, I hurled her away from me. She landed squarely on all four feet and immediately turned to face me, head low and growling before she started to pace back in my direction. I had had enough, and thinking I might not be so lucky if she attacked again, I joined Stephen in the car and drove away.

As I did so a niggling and terrifying thought came to me. What if this was not a hand-reared cheetah? What if, in fact, her bold and aggressive behaviour had been provoked by a much more sinister agent? The only first-hand experience I had of the killer disease rabies had been years before, with the hunting dogs in the Masai Mara. They had displayed very different signs of their illness. But I knew that the final stages of the disease spurred normally timid wild animals to lose their fear of man, and that they became unpredictable and very aggressive. I already had a degree of immunity from rabies from routine vaccinations I'd had in the past, but Stephen had no such protection. However remote the chances of us encountering a rabid cheetah, I could not take the risk; I immediately put out a distress call on the reserve radio asking that Stephen be taken for post-exposure treatment in the Nanyuki Hospital, an hour and a half's drive away. I thoroughly cleaned and treated his wounds before he was picked up by one of the rangers and whisked away for the first of a course of injections.

Meanwhile, another ranger car and I kept tabs on the cat whilst we sent for more help – specifically someone who could immobilise her with a tranquillising dart so that we could get her into an enclosure. I was now very concerned that she might be ill and wanted to be sure that we could keep an eye on her over the next few days. Keeping her in quarantine was the only guaranteed solution to this. If she was healthy, and just a cat in a very bad mood, all well and good, and in time we could still introduce her to Toki. If she was indeed sick, we would know soon enough.

After a couple of hours of keeping tabs on her from the safety of the vehicles, we were joined by Richard Moller, who had flown in from Lewa with the necessary equipment to dart the cat. He was very experienced in the art of tranquillising wild animals, and before long we had the cheetah, now asleep, in a small holding cage, ready for close observation whilst we prepared a much larger secure enclosure in which she could safely be kept for the three or four weeks we would need to be sure of her health. She was very soon back on her feet and, though not looking particularly happy – perfectly understandable given the extraordinary events that she had experienced over the past few hours – she otherwise looked healthy and normal. We left her in shade close to our camp and gave her plenty of peace and quiet. By midday the following day she would have the run of the new enclosure and the freedom to stretch her legs.

During the course of the night, I heard her getting more and more agitated, so I went out and checked her once or twice under torchlight. What I saw was increasingly disturbing. Her pupils remained dilated even when I shone light in them and looked sunken and, more worryingly still, she seemed to be losing her coordination. I wondered if this was an aftereffect of the tranquillising drug and decided she was best left alone. At dawn the situation had worsened further still. When I checked her at first light I found that she was lying in one corner of her cage with sunken eyes and froth was coming from her mouth. I still could not be absolutely sure of the cause, but thought it judicious to go into hospital too for a top-up course of post-exposure rabies vaccine.

By the time I returned to camp in the late morning she was dead.

I felt dreadful. If her demise had been caused by the effects of the tranquilliser, then I had been responsible for her death. If it was a disease that had killed her, then should I have suggested she be put out of her misery sooner? The only way to be sure of what had killed her was to send tissue samples to a laboratory in Nairobi immediately and await the results.

The analysis was conducted within a couple of days

and the tests on her brain tissue showed unequivocally that she had died of rabies.

The moment I knew that both Stephen and I had been exposed to the saliva of a rabid animal I had a cold, sinking feeling in my gut. I knew that – once infected with the disease – there was almost no chance of survival, and could only hope that the modern vaccines we had both been injected with had the capacity to keep the disease at bay.

Now, three years on, I can safely, and thankfully, say that both Stephen and I are clear of any risk the disease might pose. Toki the cheetah continues to thrive in Ol Pejeta, though to date is still within the secure enclosure and does not have a mate. We have spoken with the reserve managers about a scheme to introduce an even larger enclosure that can offer sanctuary to other needy cats and we remain hopeful that one day, before it is too late, a female cheetah will need a home and ensure Toki's legacy lives on. I have not been able to visit him for several months, but I keep in touch with Stephen, who assures me they are both well.

Epilogue

The first swallows of the summer arrived three days ago to inspect their traditional nesting places in the outbuildings of my home in Somerset. As I write, one of the males sits on a wire that runs from the gable roof and sings his silver refrain to charm his mate. Chaffinches, siskins, a great spotted woodpecker and, most excitingly, a male brambling in full summer plumage have been feeding on the bird table ten metres from my window. Moments ago, they all dashed for cover as a sparrowhawk belted over the hedge in a failed attempt to snatch one of them for a meal.

My lovely daughter, Savannah, born to Marguerite and me in the autumn of 2006, is playing next door and is off soon to spend the day with her grandma, my mother, who lives nearby. I travelled last weekend with my eldest daughter, Romy, to Dublin, and Greer has been to stay with me for the past few days. My son, Alexander, is in Wales, busy writing his dissertation for his degree in religious studies. All very different from travelling to the far corners of the earth in search of exotic wild creatures, and perhaps not what you would describe as a particularly wild life, but it is a happy one.

So, have I hung up my walking boots and packed away

the camera? Not quite yet. In a week or so, Marguerite, Savannah and I will be travelling back north to Shetland, the land of otters, orcas and puffins, to continue with a television series we have been involved with since last July. We have recently returned from a five-month stint in the Masai Mara in Kenya, where we were working on a feature film about big cats, and within a month I shall be in North Wales presenting *Springwatch*, the live wildlife series that has become a well-established part of the British television schedule. The more I see and do, the more I realise I shall never see and do. The more I travel, the bigger the planet gets. Even on a walk over the fields behind my house, I know I shall never get to explore them fully, to know them as intimately and thoroughly as I should like.

These are not the thoughts of a pessimist, gloomy about the future of our planet. We all by now have reason to question the effect of our massive consumption on a natural system that is unable to sustain our greed; but I hope, and believe, that we will make the changes necessary to ensure the sustainable future of this rich earth and that our species, alongside all others, will have a place in it for many thousands of years to come. No, my fear of time running out is from a selfish and personal point of view. I would need a hundred lifetimes or more to see the things I wish to see, to travel to the places I want to visit, and to witness the natural dramas I want to share.

Life is still so busy that I have little opportunity to properly reflect upon my astonishing good fortune. Luck is an elusive treasure; perhaps my most precious stroke of good luck was coming into this world with a passion, a certainty about what it was that made me smile. Even on days when I am feeling a little blue, whether I sit gazing out of my window here in the West Country, or huddled against the freezing winds of the high Arctic, my life is always enriched by the lives of others: the people I love; the creatures I share time with; the trees, the hills, the wind.

Acknowledgements

By its very nature, this entire book pays homage to a great many of the people whose influence, patience, care and love have been instrumental in its creation.

My eternal gratitude goes to my mother Eve, and sister Debbie for checking over every word and for offering me quiet sanctuary and sustenance whenever I needed it.

To my late father John, I owe a debt of thanks that I shall never have the chance to articulate as fully as I wish.

Huge thanks too to Jenny King for checking the early manuscript and pointing out my lapses of childhood memory, in addition to being one of my very best friends.

It was Rupert Lancaster from Hodder & Stoughton who first approached me with the idea that I might write a memoir, and who persuaded me that I had already lived enough to justify such a venture. My thanks to him, my editor Penny Isaac, my agent Marcella Edwards from PFD and all who have worked tirelessly to knock my tangential ramblings into a more accessible read.

My entire professional life has been enabled and ably supported by a legion of people within the industries I have worked, without whose practical support none of my adventures would have taken place. From booking flights and hotels to fire-fighting practical crises in the field, these unsung heroes of television and film are the backbone that supports us dilettante travellers. They are too numerous to mention by name, but each of them has in his or her way contributed to making my life such a wonderful adventure. Thank you.

And to my wife Marguerite who has had to suffer my absence, if not physically then of mind, whilst I took this journey into my past, I thank you from the bottom of my heart.

Picture Acknowledgements

Author's collection: 1 top, 2. © BBC: 1 bottom. © Simon King: 3 top left and right, 3 bottom (photo Matthew Wilson), 4, 6 (photos Roland Breckwoldt), 8, 11 top, 13 top, 14 bottom left. © Naturepl.com: 5 top (photo Martha Holmes), 5 bottom (photo Nigel Marven), 7 top (photo Angela Scott), 9 bottom (photo Ben Osborne), 10 top (photo Roberto Bubas), 10 bottom (photo Mike Salisbury), 14 top and bottom right (photos Marguerite Smits Van Oyen). © Ben Osborne: 9 top, 11 bottom, 12, 13 bottom. Radio Times Magazine: 16. © Angela Scott: 7 bottom. © Marguerite Smits Van Oyen: 15.

Index